"It took abou
memory ban
Bronx. . . . Thi
many young
learn . . . This
—Luis

"Ivan Sanchez
time period, h
know one of th
—Ap

"*Next Stop* is so
buggin' out or
just plain grow

"Reading Ivan
the Bronx. His

"*Next Stop* captu
is a must read!"

"This is a truly
like to grow up
wonderful trans

(*Just

"I was raised in the shadow of the number 2 train, and *Next Stop* took me back in the day, when a slice of pizza was a buck and a quarter, video games were still in an arcade, and a train ride from the Bronx to Brooklyn was not undertaken at night! If you've ever slept with one eye open on the subway or barreled across potholes on the Grand Concourse, you will love this book. Simply put, it is poetry. *Next Stop* is the reason Ivan Sanchez made it out!"

—Lee Davis, writer and director (*3 A.M., Hoop Realities*)

"*Next Stop* is a nonstop, no-holds-barred trip into a time and place that only a chosen few can truly relate to. It's a story of Latino survival in the belly of the beast that we call the Mecca, the Boogie-Down Bronx, the birthplace of hip-hop."

—DJ Disco Wiz, historian, poet, and activist

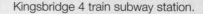

Kingsbridge 4 train subway station.

Ivan Sanchez

A Touchstone Book

Published by Simon & Schuster

New York   London   Toronto   Sydney

NEXT STOP

Growing Up

in the

Touchstone
A Division of Simon & Schuster, Inc.
1230 Avenue of the Americas
New York, NY 10020

First Touchstone trade paperback edition October 2008

TOUCHSTONE and colophon are registered trademarks of Simon & Schuster, Inc.

For information about special discounts for bulk purchases, please contact Simon & Schuster Special Sales at 1-800-456-6798 or business@simonandschuster.com.

Designed by Joy O'Meara

Manufactured in the United States of America

10   9   8   7   6   5   4   3   2   1

Library of Congress Cataloging-in-Publication Data

Sanchez, Ivan
Next stop : growing up wild-style in the Bronx / by Ivan Sanchez.
  p. cm.
"A Touchstone Book."
1. Sanchez, Ivan, 1972—Childhood and youth. 2. Bronx (New York, N.Y.)—Biography. 3. Puerto Ricans—New York (State)–New York—Biography. 4. Bronx (New York, N.Y.)—Social life and customs—20th century. 5. Bronx (New York, N.Y.)–Social conditions—20th century. 6. Street life—New York (State)–New York—History—20th century. 7. New York (N.Y.)—Biography. 8. New York (N.Y.)—Social life and customs—20th century. 9. New York (N.Y.)—Social conditions—20th century. I. Title.
F128.68.B8S265   2008
974.7'270046872950092—dc22 [B]   2008007826

ISBN-13: 978-1-4165-6267-2
ISBN-10:   1-4165-6267-2

I DEDICATE this book to those
whose souls touched me and whose souls I touched in return.

To those who lost in this game called life and paid the ultimate price
of lost years in the penitentiary, or the loss of their lives,
this book was written to share their stories with the world.
They will remain in my memory and in my heart forever.

RIP tag on Webb Avenue in remembrance of Porky and Mazo.

EXT STOP NEXT STOP NEXT STOP NEXT STOP NEXT STOP N
TOP NEXT STOP NEXT STOP NEXT STOP NEXT STOP NEXT S
EXT STOP NEXT STOP NEXT STOP NEXT STOP NEXT STOP N
TOP NEXT STOP NEXT STOP NEXT STOP NEXT STOP NEXT S
EXT STOP NEXT STOP NEXT STOP NEXT STOP NEXT STOP N
TOP NEXT STOP NEXT STOP NEXT STOP NEXT STOP NEXT S
EXT STOP NEXT STOP NEXT STOP NEXT STOP NEXT STOP N
TOP NEXT STOP NEXT STOP NEXT STOP NEXT STOP NEXT S

NEXT STOP

OGUE PROLOGUE PROLOGUE PROLOGUE PROLOGUE PRO
PROLOGUE PROLOGUE PROLOGUE PROLOGUE PROLOGU
OGUE PROLOGUE PROLOGUE PROLOGUE PROLOGUE PRO
ROLOGUE PROLOGUE PROLOGUE PROLOGUE PROLOGU
OGUE PROLOGUE PROLOGUE PROLOGUE PROLOGUE PRO
ROLOGUE PROLOGUE PROLOGUE PROLOGUE PROLOGU
OGUE PROLOGUE PROLOGUE PROLOGUE PROLOGUE PRO
ROLOGUE PROLOGUE PROLOGUE PROLOGUE PROLOGU
OGUE PROLOGUE PROLOGUE PROLOGUE PROLOGUE PRO
ROLOGUE PROLOGUE PROLOGUE PROLOGUE PROLOGU
OGUE PROLOGUE PROLOGUE PROLOGUE PROLOGUE PRO
ROLOGUE PROLOGUE PROLOGUE PROLOGUE PROLOGU
OGUE F   UE PRO
ROLOG   OLOGU
OGUE F   UE PRO

Prologue

When I close my eyes, I can still see them.

Acquaintances, friends, and cousins—I'd seen them all laugh. Chill. Run. Party. And eventually stretched out in a strange, unnatural-looking sleep, planted inside dull-colored coffins. Sometimes, as I lie silent in bed, I still hear the gunshots going off in my head, the terrifying screams of young men being stabbed or beaten with baseball bats, their heads being smashed into concrete sidewalks or metal light posts. I can still smell the gunpowder and the abandoned cars burning, still feel the blood dripping from my nose and the zoom of cocaine as it went up my nostrils. I can smell the fumes of crack and marijuana being smoked in the hallways, and the spray paint we used to write graffiti on the walls of the projects. I can feel the paranoia of waiting for a bullet to hit me, whether it was a stray shot from a car or coming from a gun aiming right at me. The pain of losing each friend, whether fallen to the streets or to a cell block for the next twenty, thirty, or fifty years, fades but never goes away. The memories haunt me.

I grew up on the corner of 196th Street and Creston Avenue in the Kingsbridge section of the Bronx, New York City. I was named after my uncle Ivan, who died in the Vietnam War a few years before I was born.

I always felt like he was my guardian angel. After all, I couldn't have possibly survived all those years in the Bronx on my own. I wasn't the toughest kid on the block, but my street sense was keen and my wisdom for avoiding trouble seemed to be second nature. It was the little voice in my head that always told me what direction to go in. It was the same voice that saved my life too many times to count. In this book, I write about those times when the voice in my head told me to go left and the man who went right was murdered or jailed. The times when the voice told me *not* to go somewhere, to avoid a party or a situation, only to find out the next day that a friend had been jailed or murdered at the party or because of the situation. You can call it intuition. You can call it dumb luck or even an active imagination. But without that voice, I wouldn't be here to share these short stories that, when put together, made up the scariest, roughest, and most difficult days of my early life.

They say there are eight million stories in New York City. I would have to disagree. I know that I have hundreds of stories to tell myself, and I'm only one man. I'm a man who barely escaped destruction while growing up in the perilous streets of New York during the most violent times in the city's history. I'm the statistic you hardly ever read about, the positive statistic that never gets any press, the statistic that actually made it out of the street life I was so deeply immersed in. Most of the time you read about the nineteen out of twenty who ended up dead or in jail, or about those who are still on the corner selling drugs to the next generation of the hopeless.

It is rare that you hear about the ones who made it out. But I made it out, and it wasn't because I was tougher or smarter than the next guy. Truth be told, I really don't know how I broke those chains that locked us all into a world of poverty, violence, and despair. Why was I the lucky one? I may never have the answer to that question, but in search of the answer, I will share all the stories that made me the man I am today. I will share the friendships that I built on the streets and the harrowing effects I endured due to losing those friends overnight. Some may choose not to understand why we did the things we did, and my purpose isn't to justify or condone our actions. I simply want to share our experiences as young products of our environment, trying to find our way in this world.

These stories are all I've got left of what seems like a Hollywood movie echoing through my mind. Sometimes it is difficult for me to believe that some of these things really happened, but there is no need for exaggeration when the streets of the Bronx are dictating the stories. It is always hard for me to understand how I walked away unscathed from many of these occurrences of violence, but although I walked away physically I left a bit of my psyche behind. A small price.

I am uncertain of so many things, but I'm just as certain that it is my responsibility to share these stories—stories of the people, places, and situations that no longer exist today, the stories of those who never made it out. We were a family, and we always had each other's backs no matter what the cost. Just like in the movies, some paid for their loyalty to their street families with their lives; others paid with their freedom; and some, like me, paid with their sanity. I'm the only voice they have left. Their stories have to be told.

In search of the answers to why we did what we did, we will journey through the streets of the Bronx and a train of connected circumstances. I will take you all for a ride through what was once my reality. Pay attention, you might just learn something at the *Next Stop.*

APARTMENT 5F APARTMENT 5F APARTMENT 5F APARTMENT 5F
ENT 5F APARTMENT 5F APARTMENT 5F APARTMENT 5F APAI
APARTMENT 5F APARTMENT 5F APARTMENT 5F APARTN
PARTMENT 5F APARTMENT 5F APARTMENT 5F APARTMENT 5I
ENT 5F APARTMENT 5F APARTMENT 5F APARTMENT 5F APA
APARTMENT 5F APARTMENT 5F APARTMENT 5F APARTN
PARTMENT 5F APARTMENT 5F APARTMENT 5F APARTMENT 5I
ENT 5F APARTMENT 5F APARTMENT 5F APARTMENT 5F APA
APARTMENT 5F APARTMENT 5F APARTMENT 5F APARTN
PARTMENT 5F APARTMENT 5F APARTMENT 5F APARTMENT 5I
ENT 5F APARTMENT 5F APARTMENT 5F APARTMENT 5F APA
APARTMENT 5F APARTMENT 5F APARTMENT 5F APARTN
PARTM   MENT 5
ENT 5F   5F APA
APAF   APARTN

Apartment 5F

At a time when money-hungry slumlords were burning down apartment buildings with the tenants still inside to collect insurance, my family was moving into a spacious three-bedroom apartment at 60 East 196th Street, apartment 5F, at the corner of Creston Avenue. None of us had any idea that apartment 5F would eventually become a kind of headquarters. If the graffiti that plastered my bedroom walls at the time could talk, it might just say we were destined for a life of lunacy the likes of which most don't live to tell about.

The year was 1978. There were few Puerto Rican families in the neighborhood, and none in our building. At the time, 60 East was predominantly Italian and Irish. My family had the privilege of being the first Hispanic tenants. Although racial tensions existed at the time, we managed to be welcomed into the neighborhood, despite the "spic" comments. Growing up in the Bronx, my mother had seen her brothers get chased down the block and beaten because they were Puerto Rican. To protect us, she "Italianized" us. She did a good job. My mother very rarely spoke Spanish at home. If she did, it was because she was hiding something from us or she was very upset about something and most likely cursing up a Spanish storm. If you ask her today, she'll tell you she can't even speak "real" Spanish. She speaks more of a Spanglish—a dialect that mixes Spanish slang with English slang and melts them together with a New Yawk accent.

Since we weren't taught how to speak Spanish, we didn't have the *ju* accent you heard from the other Spanish kids who would eventually move into the neighborhood. The best example of the *ju* accent was in the *I Love Lucy* show, when Desi Arnaz would come home and say, "Lucy, ju got sung splaining tu do."

We were second-generation New Yorkers and we dressed, walked, and talked like any other Italian or Irish kids walking the streets of New York with Catholic school uniforms and attitude to match. It would be years before the movie *Donnie Brasco* would make the catch phrase *fuggedaboutit* popular, but I'm telling you if you messed with my family . . . *fuggedaboutit.* It's a lucky thing for me I wasn't really born Italian, because from the time I turned fifteen to the time I turned twenty, my biggest dream was to be in the Mafia.

When we moved into apartment 5F, my mother, Patricia, was twenty-four years old. She was a beautiful single mother of three children: my brother, William, was eight; my sister, Tanya, was four; and I was six. We were a young family on welfare, but my mother very rarely allowed us to see what we didn't have. My mother always wanted to provide a better life for us. It was her reason for living, and she always said, "If I can raise you guys in a nice place and make sure you get a good Catholic school education, then I have no doubt you'll all make it to college." The word *college* was equated with success for my mother, and although my father's side of the family wasn't educated, my mother came from a family of doctors and lawyers in Puerto Rico. It was only natural that she have those same hopes for her children.

Before apartment 5F we had lived with my *abuela* Francesca and my uncle Georgie for a while. Moving to Creston Avenue marked a new beginning for my family, but especially for my mother, who was escaping from an abusive relationship with a man named Mike, whom we knew as our stepfather at the time. Mike drove for Pepsi and eventually went on to become the first Puerto Rican to have his own million-dollar Pepsi route.

Years later my mother would say she regretted leaving Mike because, in her words, "He was wonderful to you kids." Financially he could have given us a very different life, but it wouldn't have been worth seeing my mother be tortured, so I'm grateful she found the strength to leave an abusive relationship.

The neighborhood was rough, but the apartment felt more privileged than our surroundings. All of the rooms were huge and we always had more space than we really needed, even if my brother and I had to share a bedroom. My mother's bedroom door had glass on it, giving it an elegant feel, and the living room was big enough for Tanya and me to dance around in it while imitating the moves on *Disco Fever*. There was no elevator, so we had to carry our bikes down five flights of stairs when we wanted to ride, but if nothing else we stayed in shape the entire time we lived there.

My mother might have been single and raising us on welfare, but she knew how to make things look good, and the apartment was a perfect example of just how far my mother could stretch a few dollars. She took pride in her home. I wish I could've said the same thing for her kids.

After having lived there for a while, Willie and I discovered that by opening the window in the hallway between the fourth and fifth floor landings we could throw the garbage out, instead of carrying it down five flights of stairs and around the corner to the alley. The bags never landed in garbage cans, though. They usually exploded on the sidewalk, splattering anything nearby. No one actually saw us do it, but when the superintendent accused us of it, our poor mother always defended us and couldn't believe the man's audacity in accusing her Catholic schoolboys of such a thing.

Sorry, Mom, it was true. Your sons did it. We were lazy.

When we first moved in, the building was completely surrounded by lush gardens. In the late '70s, it was rare to see a building in the Bronx with flowers all around it and a large fountain in the center of the courtyard, complete with water running out of the mouth of a lion. It stayed beautiful for a few years, but by the early '80s the building was made up of more minorities than Irish and Italians and the gardens had been stomped into submission. The neighborhood kids would run relay races right through them, over one staircase and down the other side and right back through the other gardens.

The Puerto Ricans, including me, who now occupied the building seemed to care more about beautifying the building with their own brand of artwork—graffiti art. I remember my mother finding out my graffiti tag was STUD, which was written all over the building. She gave me the beating of my life and told me it was because she didn't want me calling myself a stud. I was only about nine years old, ten tops. I wasn't getting it for defacing the building but because I was calling myself a man-whore.

Eventually, all the gardens turned to concrete and instead we had a milk crate hung off the fire escape, which served as our private basketball court for hours on end. This was our hood, and I was comfortable even if we were destroying its natural beauty.

One day I heard what sounded like a big explosion. Turns out someone had thrown a dresser off the roof. The crash woke the whole building, and I laughed once I realized the building wasn't collapsing. The culprit was a kid named Ray. His family was the second Puerto Rican family to move in. Eventually we became best friends. Growing up, Ray and I spent most of our time playing on the rooftops and generally getting ourselves in trouble.

Ray and I had a lot of fun, and even today we haven't settled the egg argument. One winter night a few days after it had snowed, Ray and I stole eggs out of our refrigerators and peered over the edge of the roof in search of victims to pelt. I tapped Ray on the shoulder and pointed down Creston Avenue at a young man walking up the block carrying a Christmas tree. Ray gave me the nod. As the man walked below us, we each dropped our eggs at the same time.

We ducked beneath the ledge of the roof and began to quietly laugh as hard as we could. Something was different about this time, though. Usually when we pelted someone with eggs they stood on the street below, wildly waving their fists and cursing. This man wasn't yelling anything.

"Yo, Ray, what's going on? Poke your head out there and see what's up," I said.

Ray looked over ever so slowly and then dropped back down and said, "Oh shit, I think we killed him, man."

"What do you mean we killed him?" I asked.

"He's dead, man. He's lying on the ground. The tree is lying right next to him, and he isn't moving," said Ray.

I was scared and wondered how things would be in juvenile hall for a ten-year-old. I was never a good fighter. My brother had only taught me how to take a punch after several years of beatings. I collected so many black eyes from Willie that my mother must have thought I was the clumsiest little bastard she had ever met. Although my brother tortured me for many years in that apartment, I never saw reason to rat him out. I figured that eventually I would get the best of him in one of our fights. One day I finally did.

I don't remember what the hell we were fighting about, but I remember running through the long hallway trying to get away from him, and he was coming at me with everything he had. I reached my mother's room and Willie was trying to throw a punch just as I slammed the door. His hand went right through the glass, and he began to bleed profusely. Tanya witnessed the whole thing and she was screaming bloody murder.

My heart just about beat right the fuck out of my T-shirt. I didn't want my brother to bleed to death, but I also didn't want to be on the receiving end of another vicious Ill Bill beating.

As my brother went into the bathroom and wrapped his arm in a towel to stop the bleeding, I went close to cop a plea. "Bill, can we call a fucking truce, man? I didn't mean for this to happen. Are you okay, bro?"

"If you don't get the fuck away from me I am going to pound your face into the fucking windowsill and throw you *off* the fire escape to the street below."

"Come on, man. We're both going down for this shit if we don't make something up. Let's just tell Mom we were playing tag and you ran into the door, man. Puhlease, bro, I'm begging you."

My brother, being my brother, had to get the final word in. "Just know this, you little faggot. One day when you least expect it, I'm going to fuck your shit up."

"Yeah, Bill, so what else is new?"

By the time Mom got home, we all had the story rehearsed and ready for prime time. Even Tanya was coached to perfection. As always it worked like a champ, and Mom was none the wiser that her little Bill was the bastard terrorizer of the house.

We always covered for one another. I loved my brother to death and hated his ass at the same time. But the last thing I wanted to witness was him getting his ass tore up by my mother and her *chancleta*. As we got older we came to realize that if we ran around the dining room table long enough, Moms would get tired of chasing us and eventually just throw her slipper at us.

At the end of the day we were brothers, so I silently endured his torture for years, much as my poor little sister, Tanya, endured mine.

On the rooftop that night with Ray and the eggs, I was still operating on the rule of "no snitching."

"We have to try to cover these footprints. If the cops come up to the roof to find out who killed this man, they're going to trace the footsteps in the snow back to us and we're going to jail," I said.

Ray agreed, and we carefully tried to kick the snow around and smooth it over. When we got to the rooftop door, we glanced back to make sure there were no more footprints. When we felt safe about covering our tracks, we ran down to Ray's place—apartment 5H.

After spending half an hour talking about what the likelihood was of the cops figuring out who killed a man with an egg, we started to argue about whose egg had hit him.

"It was your egg, man," I said. "My egg was off by a mile."

"Fuck you, man! It wasn't my egg. I dropped my egg closer to the building and you threw your egg right at the guy," Ray reasoned.

Either way, we knew we would both go down for murder-by-egg, so we decided to go outside and investigate and see if the cops had any leads on the killers.

We walked very cautiously out of the building and as we turned the corner onto Creston Avenue, we were both a little amazed to see there were no cops, no crime scene tape, no dead person, and no Christmas tree. Ray and I just looked at each other, shrugged our shoulders, and decided to go back up to the roof and wait for another victim.

Eventually we graduated to throwing D batteries. We'd call four or five different cab companies and ask them to send a cab to 60 East 196th Street. Once the cabs lined up on the street below to pick up their fares, we launched as many batteries as possible. I can still hear the thuds on the hoods, trunks, and roofs, along with startled shouts and profanity. I wouldn't be surprised if we gave one of the cabdrivers a stroke, since it must have seemed as if they were under guerrilla attack. The cabdrivers would sit there for hours waiting for the cops to come investigate. They never caught us. We'd sit in the house laughing hysterically about all the commotion we had caused. For better or worse, Ray and I remained best friends for years after that.

Contrary to what my mother believed, I was a bad little motherfucker, always trying to get away with something, no matter how small. I guess I enjoyed the adrenaline rush I got from getting away

with things. Being mischievous was a rite of passage in my neighborhood, and each successful criminal act I committed made me realize
that I could do worse and get away with more. There were no rules
when it came to living in the hood, with the exception of one: Don't
get caught.

In New York City, it's a tradition on hot days to turn streets into swim-
ming pools. We couldn't actually swim in the water rushing out of an
illegally opened fire hydrant, but it still provided a wonderful way to
cool off on those ninety-degree days. The FDNY would show up and
close the hydrants, and we'd reopen them seconds after the truck
pulled off. We had a lot of fun playing in the water, but those hot summer days were dangerous, and one day things got out of hand and led
up to a mini neighborhood war.

When I was about eleven years old, Willie, Ray, and I had just finished playing Wiffle ball and were walking to the bodega to buy some
Popsicles. Depending on how hot it was, cooling off in the fire hydrants
came second to Wiffle ball, which was our favorite pastime. We would
paint a strike zone on a garage door and pitch the plastic baseball what
felt like 100 mph. If you were small like me and you got nailed by a
pitch from one of the older guys, you'd be left with a huge red welt,
which would eventually turn blue and burgundy.

If we weren't collecting the baseball cards of our favorite players,
we were imitating them in the streets. Our casualties were the plastic
balls, which would often be run over by passing cars, or hit into the
sewer systems or behind barbed-wire fences, where we had no chance
of retrieving them. In order to hit the ball farther, some of the guys
wrapped the plastic bat in black electrical tape. Later on, the bat would
come in handy as a weapon when fights broke out in the neighborhood.

On this day, as we got closer to the bodega, we noticed a Dominican
kid named F-CE and his cousin using a gutted Goya bean can to aim

the water from a hydrant wherever they wanted it to go. They were shooting water at anyone who tried to pass on the sidewalk, soaking the shit out of them. Willie told F-CE that if he wet us he was going to have a problem. F-CE put the can down and motioned for us to pass. The second we got to the front of the store, F-CE picked up the hollowed-out can and used it to shoot water at us.

Willie ran across the street to F-CE, who was twice his size.

"Why the fuck did you wet me, man?" my brother asked.

"I know you are not talking to me, little man. You should take your ass back across the street before I stomp the shit out of you," said F-CE.

My brother took a swing at F-CE and they started to throw each other around like rag dolls, bouncing from parked car to parked car. F-CE was getting the best of Willie, and he cut my brother's face using that bean can as a weapon. I tried to jump in, only to meet with a vicious beating from F-CE's cousin. While my brother and I exchanged blows with F-CE and his cousin, Ray was nowhere to be found. Once the older people in the neighborhood broke up the fight, my brother and I walked back to our building, defeated but with our pride in place. Unfortunately, my brother hadn't thought to use his Wiffle ball bat when he was fighting F-CE.

When we reached the stoop, Ray ran up to us.

"Yo, what happened to you guys? I was looking for you," he said.

During the fight I hadn't realized that Ray was gone, but we could have used the additional manpower. Ray told us he was looking for the Wiffle ball, but later we heard from people who were there that Ray actually threw the ball down the block when the fight started and then chased after it. I have to admit, it was a clever plan. Why help your friends in a fight when you can chase a Wiffle ball? This was the first time Ray left us stuck, and it wouldn't be the last.

We retaliated against F-CE by sending our cousins Herman and Johnny over—along with the rest of Bailey Avenue, where they lived— to even the score with baseball bats and brass knuckles. The mothers

of these kids didn't take kindly to their sons being beaten to the point
of Elephant Man—ugly, so eight Puerto Rican and Dominican women
came to Creston Avenue and waited for my mom in front of our building and jumped her.

I didn't see the fight happen, but my mom was barely bruised when
I saw her. Word on the street was that she'd held her own against all of
them. Soon after, she'd squared off with some thugs from Morris Avenue as they tried to stab my cousin Johnny one afternoon. She took a
bat to one of their heads and saved Johnny's life. She was tough.

And Ray would be paid back for abandoning us on at least two separate occasions. The first time was when my cousins Lulu and Fufi were
babysitting Ray. They lived on 196th and Grand Concourse, just up the
block from Creston Avenue. Lulu put a spoon in a pot of boiling water
and let it heat up for a while. She then asked Ray to grab it for her. Ray
wasn't the sharpest kid on the block, and my cousins used to laugh
every time they told the story of Ray burning his hand on the obviously hot spoon. It wasn't exactly payback for leaving my brother and
me out there to get our asses kicked by bigger guys, but it was a start. It
was wrong, but my cousin only did it so she could laugh.

Years later, when I was about fifteen and living on my own in apartment 5F, I almost shot Ray by accident. My cousin Richie had lent me
his 9 mm pistol, and I was lying down on the sofa with the gun on
my chest. When Ray walked in, I removed the clip from the gun and
pointed it at Ray as I talked shit. I told Ray I should blast him and that
he was a punk. Of course I was only joking, and he knew it. Still, I was
pointing the gun at him. I loved him like a brother and would never
have intentionally shot him. As I waved the gun and prepared to pull
the trigger, something told me to move the gun a little to the left.
Something didn't feel right about pulling the trigger with Ray staring
right down the barrel.

POP!

Ray was screaming. My cousin Richie ran out of the bedroom asking what the fuck was going on. I froze and couldn't hear jack shit because my ears were ringing. When things settled down, my cousin grabbed the gun off my chest and began to call me all sorts of names. I had the hot shell casing lying right on my chest, and I was still somewhat confused by what had just happened.

"What the fuck, Rich?" I shouted. "I took the clip out of the gun!"

Richie told me that there was still a bullet in the chamber. That day I learned a few things about guns. Thank God I didn't have to learn them at the expense of my friend's life. The wall in apartment 5F had just taken its first bullet.

As time went by, things got worse in the neighborhood. My mother had a reputation as a tough woman, but even she had a breaking point. I don't believe she could have possibly done a better job raising us in that environment, but she eventually left for a better life in Virginia. My brother and I decided to stay behind, in our home, in our neighborhood.

At the time, Willie was seventeen, I was fifteen, and Tanya was thirteen. My mother was hurt when my brother and I refused to leave, but she had had enough of the Bronx and she was determined to save at least one of us, that one of us being my sister.

The turning point came when from the window of our apartment my mother witnessed some gunrunners shooting at me.

It was early one summer evening and I looked up from the stoop of my building to see Tanya talking to two grown Dominican men in a nice sports car.

When I reached the car in the middle of the street I said, "Tanya, what you doing talking to these guys?"

Tanya, as feisty as ever, shot back, "Mind your business and leave me alone."

The man standing in front of the passenger-side door said, "Yo, my man, you heard her right, get the fuck out of here."

I looked to the corner, where all the fellas were hanging out, and when I saw we had a full crew, I turned back to the guy and smacked the shit out of him with everything I had.

The guy fell backward into the car, the car door shut, and they took off, headed toward the Grand Concourse.

I told Tanya to get the fuck upstairs while she cursed me out for messing up her game.

About ten minutes later, I was standing in the exact same spot when I heard someone yell, "Yo, Ive, get the fuck down! Get the fuck down *now!*"

Normally I would have looked to see what the commotion was about first, but something in the yelling made me duck down immediately behind the parked car I was standing beside. As soon as I did, I heard shot after shot.

Someone was mad enough to try to end my life. I looked up just in time to see that same sports car peeling off back toward the Grand Concourse.

My mother heard the shots and looked out the window in time to see the attempted assassination of her son in broad daylight.

The car disappeared and I talked to my guys for a few minutes about what had just happened. All of a sudden, I heard what seemed like the entire neighborhood yelling, "Get down! They're coming back!" With that, another barrage of bullets lit up the streets.

This time when I got up and dusted myself off, P-Funk said, "We're gonna get these motherfuckers. Enough is enough already."

P-Funk was one of my closest friends at the time and had been a neighborhood drug dealer from the age of thirteen. We ran up to P-Funk's second-floor apartment and his mother handed us a sawed-off shotgun.

As we were running down the stairs of the building P-Funk said, "You need to take care of this," and handed me the shotgun. My

mother had to watch helplessly out the window as her son went running off with a shotgun, headed for trouble or death.

I remember thinking that I didn't know if I could do it. And I didn't
even know how to use a shotgun. How was I going to find the balls to
pull this off?

I had adrenaline working for me, but I was shaking uncontrollably
while running up Creston toward 198th Street, where we figured they
were headed if they were going to make another pass. It must have been
a sight to see a little dude like me running down the middle of Creston
Avenue holding a sawed-off shotgun like I was out hunting prey. When
we got to 197th Street, Frankie, the neighborhood car thief, grabbed
the shotgun right out of my hand and said, "Give me that. You ain't
gonna do shit with this, little man."

Phew. I was off the fucking hook, and I ran feeling so much better
that Frankie had the shottie.

When we got to the corner of Creston and 198th, we ran smack
right into the car. I couldn't believe it.

Frankie pumped the shotgun to load a round and as soon as the car
got to the middle of the intersection he pulled the trigger—*BOOM!*

It looked like he had hit the driver's-side door, but when he pumped
the shotgun again and again he said, "Oh, fuck . . . no more bullets!"

The passenger and driver of the sports car jumped out and stood
in the middle of the street, T.J. Hooker–style, and just started blasting
from two or three handguns. It sounded like the Fourth of July: *pop, pop,
pop,* and *pop.* . . . I was ducking and diving and running, and when I hit
197th Street I dove into some thick shrubbery behind a house and lay
there until I heard the cops showing up and all their doors slamming.

When it was clear the cops were canvassing the neighborhood, I
cleaned myself off once again and calmly walked back toward 196th
Street. Out of the corner of my eye I saw arms flailing, and when I
looked closer I saw P-Funk in the back of a police car.

I stood there frozen. P was the one who had come to my defense and now he was sitting in the back of a blue-and-white, about to be locked up.

As if by divine fate, a call came on the cops' radios: "We have a Puerto Rican male running down the middle of the street carrying a shotgun."

With that, all the cops took off on foot, running up toward 196th Street. I took a few looks around the neighborhood, inched my way over to the police car, opened the door, and let P-Funk out. Once he was free we both took off running in the opposite direction from the cops, toward the Grand Concourse.

We showed up in the neighborhood about twenty-five minutes later, much to everyone's surprise. My mother was elated; she thought we had been arrested. But it was the final straw. She no longer had the heart to see her children like this.

When she decided to move to Virginia Beach, my brother and I never even entertained the idea of leaving with her. Why would we? The streets around Kingsbridge Road were all we knew. This was our life. My girl was there, my crew was there, and my heart was there.

"Sorry, Mom, I hope you enjoy living in the boonies, but I'm staying here with Bill," was all I could say as the door on the back of the U-Haul truck came crashing down. This marked the beginning of the toughest lessons I would have to learn on the streets. And it was the end of an era for my neighborhood.

The day my mother left the Bronx, the borough lost one of its strongest and toughest. Things would only go from bad to worse once Mom was gone.

I lived with my brother and my cousin Richie in apartment 5F for a little while and things were good. But not long after my mother left, my brother decided to move down to Heath Avenue to live full-time with his girlfriend, Tina, and their newborn daughter, Meghan. At the time I felt as though my brother was abandoning me, but once I had a daughter of my own I understood. Since we grew up without a father, it was important to my brother and me that we be good fathers.

Tina was a cute girl with the reputation of being a big-time gold digger. I don't believe there was a day that passed when someone didn't warn my brother about falling in love with her. But after the baby was born, my brother would go to extremes to keep his family together. He walked the same fine line I walked for many years, between having a job and robbing anything not nailed down at night to give Tina the extras.

It was just my cousin and me left in apartment 5F. But that didn't last. The end came when my biological father knocked on our door and asked if he could stay for a few days. I barely knew him, but I wasn't the type of person who carried grudges, so I let him crash. I was fifteen and had no steady job, so Richie now had two freeloaders to take care of. I came home one day and saw Dad wearing my clothes—even the new sneakers I'd bought after robbing an audio place. It was a good thing he'd showered and found something to wear. That alcoholic stench always brought back bad memories for me, so I was happy anytime he washed it off.

One night my dad let my friend Ray and me drive a hooptie he had borrowed from a friend while he sat in the back and got drunk off a bottle of some shit and a few tall cans of Budweiser. When we got back to the neighborhood, I couldn't park the fucking boat to save my life.

Back and forth, forth and back, tap, tap, bump, bump . . . I was hitting the two parked cars, trying to make it fit into the space. Finally my father, whom my older brother Willie had been named after, told me to get the fuck out of the driver's seat and, as drunk as his ass was, perfectly parallel-parked the boat like it was nothing.

I didn't really think twice about the fact that I couldn't park a car. Who gave a fuck? I had gotten to drive that night and I was feeling good.

"Yo, Pops, thanks for letting me and Ray take your car for a spin," I said as we walked up the stairs to the apartment.

"You drive like a little bitch. You can't be my son," Willie slurred.

Ray laughed hysterically and repeated my father's words.

I could feel emotions bubbling deep inside me. The same emotions I felt every now and then just before I blanked out and did something stupid.

"Yo, Ray, chill the fuck out, kid. That shit ain't funny," I said as we walked up to my apartment door.

My father laughed and slapped Ray on the back.

"Ray, you might be my son because you drive better than that little bitch right there."

When we walked into the dining room I turned to him and said, "You need to shut the fuck up and stop dissing me in front of my boy."

"What the fuck you gonna do about it, little bitch?" shouted my drunken father.

"I'm gonna kill you, motherfucker," I said, and picked up one of the dining-room chairs Richie had bought and threw it across the room, hitting Willie with it.

He started to charge toward me and I picked up the glass dining-room table and threw it on top of him. When he tried to get up, I took another chair and broke it over the table and started to scream, "You're not my father, you fucking faggot! You were never there for me or Bill or Tanya. I'm not the bitch, you're the little fucking bitch!"

Hearing all the glass breaking, Richie came running out of his bedroom and tried to calm me down. Ray was standing half in the living room and half in the dining room, probably feeling bad about how things had escalated and how he had laughed when my dad insulted me. Richie just wanted to know what the fuck was going on and why I had broken his table.

It was a table he bought with his own money and I had had no regard for that, as I had no regard for anything. I was a selfish motherfucker and my biological father had just pushed me to the brink of a nervous breakdown.

"You are not spending another night in *my house*, motherfucker," I screamed. "Get the little bit of shit you brought in here, get in your fucking boat car, and get the fuck out of here before I kill you."

Willie tried to apologize, gave me the same sad look he probably gave my mother a million times after beating her, and walked out of the apartment and my life forever.

He was never really there anyway, but hearing him speak to me the way he did broke my heart even more than not having him around all those years. He was supposed to be my father and all he thought of me was that I was a little bitch.

Richie calmly swept up the glass, with Ray helping, as I just stood there in a state of nothingness.

"Yo, Ive, I can't do this shit no more, man. I'm gonna be moving out in a few weeks. I'm sorry," said my cousin. Fuck, I couldn't blame him. He took care of me long enough and it was about time I found out what being on my own and being a man was all about. It was what I'd asked for when Mom left. Now it was going to be time to prove to myself I had what it took to survive. I was the king of my own castle, with no fucking idea how I was going to pay the rent. That's when things got interesting.

Shortly after everyone left, my good friend P-Funk asked if I was interested in turning the apartment into a stash house. I immediately knew what he was talking about. At first I wasn't sure, but when he said the Jamaican drug dealers would cover all the bills, put food in the refrigerator, and pay me eight hundred dollars a month, I decided to go all in. I knew most of the Jamaicans who were running an extensive marijuana network from the neighborhood. They went by names like Barney, Chippy, Redds, Money Merv, Trees, and Bowlen. I had no problem going into business with them. At the time it seemed like a no-brainer.

I was right. No brains were involved when I decided to go into business with these guys.

Everything was beautiful in the beginning. The Jamaicans were taking care of things just as they said they would. The man running the stash house in apartment 5F was Chippy. Chippy and I hit it off, and I found him to be a very laid-back individual who just wanted to smoke a lot of weed and make a lot of money. While Chippy was in charge, life was good for me. Unfortunately, Chippy didn't last long. One night, while trying to rob the rapper Slick Rick, Chippy was shot with a machine gun and died on the spot. Shortly after that came the end of life as I knew it.

After Chippy's murder, new faces started coming around the drug house.

Barney took over running the drug spot, and he was always showing up with Money Merv. Merv made me very nervous. He was the known enforcer of the crew, the kind who was comfortable with murder as a job description on his résumé. Soon, Barney became more belligerent and disrespectful toward me.

His attitude was, *What the fuck is this little punk going to do to me and my crew of killers?* He was right. I couldn't go to war with the Jamaicans by myself if I wanted to. I had to figure out what I was going to do about making things right. Although I was nervous at times, I was never really scared of these guys. The worst-case scenario was that the Jamaicans killed me, and that wasn't as scary as not having a future.

But the truth of the matter was that I didn't think I had a future at all. By then, I had dropped out of school; I had no education, no hope for a career, no money, no prospects. Losing my life seemed like a good outcome at times.

Shit, if I was dead, I'd be memorialized on the wall and my boys would pour out a little liquor for me when they were getting drunk and high. They'd say, "That little nigga Ive was cool as shit, man. I miss that little motherfucker."

My moms would miss me and my father would regret not being a father to me. My girlfriends would never forget me and my cousin and brother would feel bad that they left me behind in the neighborhood. It was a win-win situation for me, so if the Jamaicans were going to kill me, there were some days when I was okay with that.

When I talked to P-Funk about how bad the situation was getting, he asked if I wanted to sell weed instead of depending on the Jamaicans. I figured I had nothing to lose, so P-Funk had the crew front me half a pound of weed. The truth was that I didn't intend on paying them back. As far as I was concerned, this was money owed to me, since Barney had stopped paying the bills as soon as Chippy was murdered. He didn't give a fuck about any deal previously made. So I was going to sell the weed, make some money, buy some gear, and get back on track. Unfortunately, it didn't go down like that at all. Instead, I smoked a lot of weed with my boys for free, bought some clothes with the very small profits, and smoked more weed with my boys until it was all gone. Soon Barney came looking to collect his money.

Barney caught me in the lobby of the building one afternoon. I mouthed off to him and he tried to choke me. Luckily, two older guys in the neighborhood, Zen and Zef, intervened. I decided it was time to go. A few days after having the shit choked out of me, I packed a few bags of clothes and moved to Bailey Avenue with Titi Vilma and my cousins Herman and Johnny. My cousins ran Bailey Avenue, and I knew if the Rastafarians came down there looking for me they'd have a good gun battle on their hands. I wasn't going to be a sitting duck, even if I didn't care most days if I lived or died. I only lasted in the stashhouse business a year or so, and apparently things weren't going to work out for me in my new career.

After my escape to Bailey Avenue, the Jamaicans took over apartment 5F. Shortly after that it was raided by TNT, the Tactical Narcotics Team, NYPD's equivalent to the Drug Enforcement Agency. The task force was infamous for making raids and closing down drug houses left and right, only to see them continue to pop up right and left. Word finally got back to TNT that 5F was indeed a stash house for large quantities of marijuana. They also knew who ran it. Redds had been one of the first Jamaican drug dealers to move into the neighborhood. He was a very charismatic dude who dressed the part of the flashy drug dealer, complete with nice jewelry and a nice ride. Redds was one of the first guys I ever saw pushing a Nissan Maxima with the ground-effects kit to make it seem like it was sitting on the ground. The burgundy Maxima had nice rims, a sunroof, and a sound system you could hear blaring reggae at all hours of the night.

When TNT executed the warrant, they found Redds's wife, child, mother-in-law, and a room full of marijuana in big shipping barrels. They pressed Redds's wife to play along or catch prison time. She agreed to cooperate.

Apparently the plan was for the wife to set a trap by calling Redds and telling him to come to the apartment because she needed him. As Redds got within a block of the building, P-Funk and my future brother-in-law, Jorge, intercepted him. They told him the task force had raided the spot and the narcos were waiting for him to show up. Redds then called the apartment and told his wife to put the pigs on the phone. When the detective took the phone, Redds told him he had a bomb hidden in the marijuana and that he was going to blow the entire building up. TNT had no choice but to evacuate the building, and because the Jamaicans were known for their extremely violent tactics, the NYPD had to respond by sending in the bomb squad.

According to Jorge, the bomb squad ran into the building to see if Redds was telling the truth. Of course, they never found a bomb. Redds made them work for their money that day. That ended apartment 5F's days as a drug spot for a little while, but it wouldn't end the story.

In 1991, the FBI was following up for the NYPD on an old murder that occurred during the armed robbery of a check-cashing place somewhere in New York City. The murder weapon was found in apartment 5F during the raid. The feds wanted to know what my mother knew about the guns, drugs, and Jamaicans, so they sent field agents out to her office at the Hampton VA Medical Center in Hampton, Virginia. Although the apartment was still leased under her name, she hadn't lived there since 1988. It didn't take her long to drop names, along with my Social Security number, where to find me, and every street alias she knew. The feds probably got family photos if she had them.

I couldn't believe my mother had betrayed me like that. I guess she no longer believed in protecting her little babies. But then again, I wasn't a baby anymore, and my mother had her own new life in Virginia Beach to protect, complete with a nice house, a new car, and a government job. At the time I felt like my mom betrayed me, and I was pissed, but the truth was that I was betraying her and every hard-core sacrifice she ever made for me. I understood it wasn't fair for her and her husband to have to deal with the questioning.

As soon as the feds turned the information over to the NYPD, I was picked up from my aunt's apartment on Bailey Avenue and taken in for questioning.

When the detectives ushered me in, I felt a little twinge of nervousness, but I wasn't part of the Jamaican drug crew any longer and didn't feel like I was in trouble for anything. If in fact I had information that could help the police and it wouldn't put any of my boys out there, the guys I had grown up with and still had love for, I was okay with talking to the cops.

The first thing the police did was mention all my driving offenses, the fact that I'd been arrested for hopping the train, and other small shit. One of them said, "Listen, kid, if you can help us with any of this, we're going to wipe all these offenses out of the database. You're going to have a clean slate."

At the time I didn't realize this was what they offered informants, and I didn't see myself as that. I was there to clear my mother's name and my own name of murder.

They showed me photographs of everyone in my neighborhood: Zef, P-Funk, Ray, Jorge, Eric, Zen, J-Hood, Muhammad, Sal, and

Macho, along with Redds, Trees, Barney, Bowlen, and Money Merv—all the guys I grew up with and anyone who had ever set foot inside 5F or chilled out in front of the building.

Most of the pictures had names on the bottom, and the detectives asked me if I knew any of the guys. I told them I knew all the neighborhood guys, but not all of the Jamaican guys.

When I looked a little closer at Bowlen's picture, I saw that it had VIOLENT written underneath it. I told them I knew that guy—pointing out Bowlen's picture. I wondered if he was actually called Violent and I had been pronouncing it wrong the whole time. I also pointed out Barney's picture and told them I definitely knew him too, and that he was the leader of the Jamaicans.

I was honest and told them I'd gone into business with the drug dealers some years earlier and that Barney forced me out because of an unpaid marijuana debt. I also told them I believed Barney would have killed me if he had had the chance. They told me I was lucky to have gotten out alive, because these were cold-blooded killers. I explained that I'd had no dealings with them for the last eighteen months or so. The cops never said I'd be arrested for admitting to going into business with the Jamaicans and living in a stash house.

As I was walking out of the room, I looked down at the table and saw a picture of my childhood friend Ray. The same Ray I'd thrown eggs off the roof with and the same one who laughed when my father called me a little bitch.

"If you see this guy, you should ask him what he knows. He lives right across the hall from the drug spot in apartment 5H."

It was a statement I would later live to regret. The detectives already knew where Ray lived. They went directly to his house and said, "Ivan said you might be able to help us."

Ray then went straight to P-Funk's house and told him I sent the detectives to his house. I would be known on the streets as a rat. Not a good thing.

A rat means you're the lowest form of dirt. You become an immediate outcast, someone who cannot be trusted. It was never a title I felt I deserved. I had no problem telling the cops about what I knew when it came to the Jamaicans. For me that was a pure form of retribution; the cops had no way of knowing, but they were offering me a way to get back at the people I hated. 196th Street and Creston Avenue was my home; it was my haven and it was the place I felt the safest in this world. When the Jamaicans ran me out of there, they took everything from me.

Even though the cops would tell Ray I was a snitch, I didn't deserve the title. For me, snitching was when a guilty person decided to give up his partner in crime to save his own ass. I wasn't in trouble when the cops questioned me; they had no evidence tying me to any crimes committed in the apartment and it had been about eighteen months since I'd lived there. Yes, I gave them a few names and told them what I had been directly involved in, but I didn't have any info to offer, nor would I have offered any if it involved any of my brothers on Creston Avenue. I never would have said shit about P-Funk working with the Jamaicans for years and setting up stash houses and businesses all over the Bronx.

Regardless of what I believed, though, just the whisper of *snitch* in the streets of the Bronx stays with you for life. I even heard rumors that I'd be shot on sight by the same people I grew up with and fought battles with. It was even rumored that J-Hood—one of the softest guys on the block until he was introduced to a gun—was talking the most shit and that if he ever ran into me he would make sure he set things right, at least in his own mind.

A couple of months before being called in for questioning, I had gone to the old neighborhood. My issue with the Jamaicans had died down some, so I would run up to Creston Avenue every once in a while to see how the old crew was doing. It seemed that every time I went back for a visit, there were more and more BMWs parked on the block.

On this night, while my cousin Johnny and I stood on the stoop talking to P-Funk and J-Hood, a small RX7 drove at a very high speed down

196th Street, barely missing the three BMWs that were double-parked. The RX7 seemed as if it was being chased by a taxicab for some reason, and as the taxicab tried to squeeze through it hit two of the BMWs. The cabdriver never stopped to view the damage done. He just kept driving toward Jerome Avenue. But he was soon trapped by the traffic.

P-Funk and J-Hood ran toward the cab, and Johnny and I followed. I knew we were going to pull the driver out and give him the beating of his life. Johnny and I were five to seven steps behind P-Funk and J-Hood, and just before we reached the cab, J-Hood pulled out a large black handgun and shot right into the driver's-side window. It's not that I had never seen or been involved in a shooting, but it surprised me that J-Hood ran right up to the driver and started pumping bullets. The way he gave chase and shot with no hesitation let me know J-Hood had been busy since I left the block. I never looked into the cab, and the second J-Hood ran by us, Johnny and I took off, too.

The cabdriver lived, but it was a wake-up call for me. The guys I had grown up with on Creston Avenue had become shooters—the type that let bullets fly first and asked questions or questioned their actions later. This was no longer a place for me.

About three or four years after I left New York completely, I missed a lot about the neighborhood, so I drove along Creston Avenue. As I came up 196th Street from Jerome Avenue, I noticed there were about fifteen guys right in front of the bodega I used to stand in front of on so many days and nights so many years before. In the back of my mind, I knew word on the street was that J-Hood would shoot me if he ever saw me. I made the left-hand turn onto the Grand Concourse and wondered if I should come back up Creston and get out of the car to say what's up to the fellas.

I wondered if the kid I grew up with would really shoot me. I needed to know.

I contemplated many things on the slow drive up the Grand Concourse. I was a professional living in Virginia Beach with two daughters.

I was living a good, clean life, and I didn't need to drum up any old memories, especially memories that could get me shot in cold blood staring up at the sky. I never considered myself a punk and I knew for damn sure I was no rat, so why was I hiding like a punk and a rat? I decided to get out of the car and approach the fellas on the corner—some soldiers loyal to J-Hood and some guys who had never seen my face before. I approached with a bit of caution.

"Yo, Ive, is that you?" came a voice in the darkened night.

It was Eric B. As I got within arm's length, Eric B reached out and gave me a big hug. Next was P-Funk, who didn't like me. P-Funk and I had really lost touch since the time he'd help set me up with the Jamaicans. In his business, you couldn't even entertain someone who was thought to be a snitch for any reason whatsoever. It didn't matter that we'd known one another since we were little kids, learned to write graffiti together, and stolen our first bike together—or that I'd never told the cops anything about him. My old friend Ray had made sure the boys on Creston Avenue knew I had mentioned his name to the cops, and that was all they needed to know.

"Yo, Ive, where the fuck you been, kid?" P asked as he gave me a big hug.

I was making small talk with Eric B and P-Funk when I noticed J-Hood walk over to his Cadillac. He opened the door and stood halfway between the door and the sidewalk. I figured he was going to go into his stash box, pull out a gun, and unload a few rounds into my body. He looked at me as if he wanted to kill me right in front of the bodega, but doing so would make his spot hot.

I'm not sure why J-Hood decided not to shoot me that night, but he never said a word. I knew deep down inside he was itching to let a few rounds pop off, but he held back. Most likely because he didn't know how the neighborhood guys would react. After all, I did grow up there. I can only assume the real beef J-Hood had with me was that my brother-in-law, Jorge, slapped the shit out of him on several occasions due to the

schoolboy crush he had on my sister, Tanya. We all knew in his heart that
J-Hood was the softest guy on the block, but once he discovered a gun
and figured out how to pull the trigger he became the enforcer. All of a
sudden the neighborhood was supposed to fear and respect a guy who
used to run from every fight, just as Ray had done so many times.

Where I came from, it took heart to stand there and fight with your
fists, especially when you were outnumbered or knew you had a beating coming your way. Before the guns, you had to be tough and have a
heart. I preferred to take a beating any day and keep my dignity rather
than be a scared punk with a gun. Yes, it's true I carried a gun at times,
but really I was just looking to stay alive one more day or night; my
gun was for protection, so I never felt bad about carrying it. It doesn't
take a man to pull a trigger, and J-Hood would never have my respect.

Guns always had their place. The first time I got one was after I
moved to Bailey Avenue from Creston. I was about seventeen years old
and I used to trade stuff all the time with a neighborhood hustler who
called himself Smurf. He was around my age and he was always into
some shit, whether it was moving small amounts of drugs, selling a few
guns here and there, and even dabbling in the sale of steroids.

He always kept a few guns around the crib, and one day he told me
he was looking to trade guns for jewelry. I had a large diamond ring
that spelled out HITMAN. When I bought the ring, some of the fellas in
the neighborhood had thought a shooter who called himself Hitman
was going to fuck me up. But he understood that the ring represented
my MC name, which was MC Hitz the Hitman when I used to dabble
in hip-hop, and he was cool with it. He saw me as a little brother, so it
wasn't an issue.

Smurf traded me a .380-caliber pistol with no clip. I could shoot off
only one round at a time by placing a bullet directly into the chamber
of the gun. It would have made for a problem if I had ever gotten into
a gun battle. A few years later I would upgrade with my cousin Freddie
and carry around a 9 mm and sometimes even a TEC-9 submachine-

gun in a book bag. I wasn't a shooter, but in the Bronx you never knew when you'd need a gat for protection.

Apartment 5F saw me grow from Catholic school boy to lost teenager to lost soul. I had to completely leave the environment before I could discover the truest definition of being a man. I learned many life lessons in that apartment, from the love and strength of a single mother raising three kids to the life and death decisions we contemplated sitting on our beds at night. I'll never forget the night some rivals shot up our neighborhood. My brother and I hit the deck, looking at each other as if the bullets could somehow reach us on the fifth floor of the building.

However, that was just it—we never knew where life on the streets would take us next. We always hoped like hell we'd end up right back there at the end of the night. Right back in apartment 5F and not in jail or the morgue. Man, if those walls could talk.

Alleyway where Bill and I used to throw trash out the window.

WHITE LINES BIOLOGICAL WHITE LINES BIOLOGICAL WH
NES BIOLOGICAL WHITE LINES BIOLOGICAL WHITE LINES E
OGICAL WHITE LINES BIOLOGICAL WHITE LINES BIOLOGIC
HITE LINES BIOLOGICAL WHITE LINES BIOLOGICAL WH
NES BIOLOGICAL WHITE LINES BIOLOGICAL WHITE LINES E
OGICAL WHITE LINES BIOLOGICAL WHITE LINES BIOLOGIC
HITE LINES BIOLOGICAL WHITE LINES BIOLOGICAL WH
NES BIOLOGICAL WHITE LINES BIOLOGICAL WHITE LINES E
OGICAL WHITE LINES BIOLOGICAL WHITE LINES BIOLOGIC
HITE LINES BIOLOGICAL WHITE LINES BIOLOGICAL WH
NES BIOLOGICAL WHITE LINES BIOLOGICAL WHITE LINES E
OGICAL WHITE LINES BIOLOGICAL WHITE LINES BIOLOGIC
HITE L   CAL WH
NES BI   LINES E
OGICAL   IOLOGIC

Biological White Lines

There is a rap song called "White Lines" by Grandmaster Flash and the Furious Five, an old-school hip-hop group from New York City. "White Lines" was one of the first rap songs I could recite word for word; the funny thing is, the song was about cocaine and I never knew it at the time. At the height of the song's popularity, I was probably around ten years old, and I had no idea that I was rapping about the cocaine epidemic in New York City. At ten years old, I don't think I even knew what cocaine was, but it wasn't going to take much longer for me to find out. Family members eventually introduced me to cocaine, and like the rest of my family tree, I became another infected branch.

My father's name is Willie Sanchez. He was the man generous enough to donate his sperm to my mother and give me life, but not generous enough to share much else. The definition of a deadbeat dad, my father left the survival of his three children to a single mother and society's contribution of welfare funds. My mother did the best she could to keep a firm hold on us as we slipped deeper and deeper into the streets, but a mother isn't always strong enough to instill the kind of fear a child needs to have to walk the straight and narrow. Although the word *father* in my dictionary couldn't be more meaningless, I do want to thank him for contributing to my dashing good looks.

My father didn't teach me much growing up, but I do want to share the three lessons he did find it in his heart to "teach" me as a youngster. The first was how to pick my battles. He asked me one day if, going into a fight with a group of guys, I knew I was going to get my ass kicked; would I stay and take the beating or would I run? Being the macho tough kid that I thought I was, I told him I would take my ass-whipping like a man. I puffed up my chest and expected to be rewarded for my male bravado and for not being a punk. My father didn't reward me. Instead, he told me to run away and live to fight another day. As I grew up in the Bronx, this was a message I had to fall back on quite a few times, and thanks to this and my quickness, I avoided many an ass-whipping growing up.

The second life lesson my father passed along was that I should always tip people who provided a service for me. Although the man never tipped his kids with any money, for some reason the message stuck with me.

The last lesson my father taught me was that drug use was not only acceptable but pleasurable. Although he didn't stick the cocaine in front of me and tell me to take a hit (at least not until I was older), he stripped me of the fear I might have had had I not seen him abuse the drug at a very young age.

I was first introduced to cocaine when I was about nine or ten years old. Although I can't time-stamp the exact date, the memory of the day is as clear as if it had happened yesterday. My father had picked me up to go bowling with his friend and the friend's younger son. This wasn't a common occurrence. There were only a handful of times when I went anywhere with him. As this was one of the very few times he actually showed up to take me out on a father-son date, it might explain why I remember the night in such vivid detail.

We were sitting in a van on Bailey Avenue in front of a bodega. My father's friend had gone into the store to get a couple of sodas for us kids and some beer for himself and my father. I noticed the man didn't give us the straws for the sodas. (I was one of those kids who liked to chew on the straw after I used it.) As we were sitting in the back of the van, I saw him put the straw on the dashboard and cut it in half with a razor blade. I thought this was a little funny, but I had no idea what he was doing. My father then said he was going to close the curtain between the front and back of the van so he could talk "man stuff" with his friend. I heard a lot of sniffling up front, like someone had a bad cold, and I assume the men forgot about us, because we sat back there for quite a while with the curtain shut.

I finally walked up and pulled the curtain open. I remember the look my father gave me when he turned around to look at me. I had just witnessed him stick the straw up his nose and sniff white powder off the dashboard of the van. He yelled at me and told me to get to the back of the van.

A little while later, he calmly explained that "Papi was using medicine."

It took me a few years to realize what that "medicine" was, but when I became a teenager, I remember thinking how wrong it was for him to expose me to his drug habit that way. It also made me a firm believer in the fact that kids never forget seeing certain things in their life.

By the time we were fourteen years old, my best friend Ray and I were using marijuana. Ray's cousin, Eric, was a small-time drug dealer in the South Bronx, and after we visited his house one Thanksgiving, he gave us a joint. When we got back to Ray's house that night, we lit it and smoked a very small amount. Eric B. and Rakim's "I Ain't No Joke" was blaring from Ray's boom box, and within minutes we were laughing and giggling. It was like a Cheech and Chong movie. We just couldn't control the hysteria.

After smoking weed together for a year or so, Ray and I were standing on the roof talking about the newest plague to hit our neighbor-hoods—crack. We were afraid of becoming crackheads one day, so we made a pact never to use any other types of drugs. In our eyes, people who used cocaine were no different from crackheads. To this day, Ray has never used cocaine. I guess he lived up to his part of the pact.

I was sixteen the first time I used cocaine. I was driving around with two family members and a friend from the same Bailey Avenue neigh-borhood where I had first witnessed my father using cocaine. I won't mention the names of my family members, because they may not want anybody to know they used. I watched them in the front of the car sniffing and I was curious, so I asked what the drug did for them. They never asked me to try it. They probably never wanted me to use it. But I was watching them having fun and I didn't feel like I was on their level of conversation. To put it bluntly, I felt left out. I wanted to feel what they felt.

I asked one of my relatives to let me get a blast. One of my cousins looked at me like I was crazy. The other one asked me if I really wanted to try it. They finally agreed and one of them poured a small amount of cocaine out of the dollar bill and onto my thumb. I sniffed it up my nose. It would be the beginning of an addiction I would have until I was twenty years old.

Getting cocaine was never a problem. Cocaine was everywhere. We had so many friends selling it that the price was always next to nothing, and at times it was nothing at all. We also had so many friends using co-caine that when we all chipped in, we usually bought enough to get the whole block high for two days. There were days when we did get high for two days straight. It was a fun drug for me for the simple reason that it made me feel very powerful and erased my normally suspicious state of mind. Growing up in the Bronx left me with a very paranoid mentality. I always felt like at any time I could be robbed, shot, jumped, killed, or jailed for some of the stupid shit I was doing. When I was high on cocaine I didn't care about any of that stuff, and it caused my addiction to the drug to become stronger. As long as I was high, my worries no longer existed.

My cocaine habit got so out of control that I began to miss work regularly. Since quitting school I'd been working in the financial district printing stock exchange reports. Although the job gave me an opportunity at a real career, I was still walking a fine line between being a professional and being a hoodlum. I'd run out of sick days in the first few months of the year, so I made up stories about family tragedies almost once a week. I must have buried four grandfathers and four grandmothers. I had critically ill aunts and uncles. A car hit my poor sister right after she moved to Virginia. The list of excuses I would give my boss went on forever. The only time I wasn't making up stories was when my friends really were murdered. These were the times I'd take a whole week off from work just to get high with the crew and mourn the loss. Tommy Finelli was my boss at the time and he cared a great deal about me. He treated me like a son and tried his best to deal with my ridiculous absentee rate. But even he couldn't protect me forever, and sixty sick days a year just didn't fly. There were bigger bosses to deal with, and finally Tom had to break the news to me: I'd be fired if I missed one more day of work.

And this was when I found out just how bad my habit was.

One night, I hit the block dressed and ready to hop on the number 1 train for the one-hour ride to my job in lower Manhattan. My route went from the 225th Street station to the World Trade Center exit, basically the entire run of the 1 line. It was a Thursday night, and my boys were out in full force. They were making plans to go score a large amount of coke, preparing for a night of getting high and playing spades. They sat there trying to convince me that I needed to chill with them and forget about going to work that night. They didn't want to hear that I'd be fired from a great job if I missed one more day. They didn't much care that I wouldn't be able to feed my newborn daughter or support myself. The only thing that mattered was another night of partying with the boys. We made our way up to my boy Fat David's house, mistake number one on my part that night. I told myself that I could chill for an hour and then make my way to work. Being late was better than not showing up at all, I reasoned.

After about an hour of getting high, I knew I wasn't going to work that night, and I knew I had just thrown away a great job. At this time, my daughter, Heaven, was around four months old, and I wondered how I would provide for my baby girl. Somehow, a conversation started about all of us becoming partners in the drug business. Turned out some kids from up the block had started making a lot of money selling crack, and my friends, Will and Manny, decided that if we teamed up we could take over the Marble Hill housing projects and become the next big thing in the Bronx. Someone suggested we swear an oath to each other in blood. Since I was already high from the cocaine and feeling no fear, I stepped up and took my shirt off. I told them they were my brothers and I would walk through any situation with them, even if it meant giving my life. Thinking back now—that must have been some good cocaine. Fat David got a knife out of his mother's kitchen. He came back and asked if I was ready and where I wanted to be cut. I told him I was ready and that he could cut my chest. Fat David handed the knife to Rico first, but when Rico tried to cut me, he barely made a scratch. Fat David grabbed the knife out of his hand and ripped my chest wide open.

When the other guys in the room witnessed the blood squirting from my chest, they had two things to say: "You are fucking down for life," and "You are fucking crazy."

Needless to say, no one else volunteered to stand in front of Fat David's vicious blade. I had sworn an oath of loyalty to myself.

We didn't exactly build a fellowship based on spilled blood that night. However, I did end up keeping my job. I called my boss and told him I had been robbed near the train station on way to work and been knifed in the attack. I had the scar to prove it. I not only kept my job for a little while longer, I also had that Friday off, so I hung out and got high with my crew. I had Rico call my wife, Stormy, and tell her the same story I'd told my boss. To this day, she doesn't know the truth. Once she reads this, she will probably be upset with me for a couple of days. The only people who knew the truth about that night were the people at Fat David's house. I knew I was in too deep with my cocaine habit and if I didn't find a way to pull myself out of the situation, it would only be a matter of time before I hurt somebody or got hurt myself while under the influence.

I remember that my own father offered me cocaine when I was six-teen years old. I don't know if he was testing me or if he really wanted to get high with his son. I'll never know, because I turned him down. "I don't do that shit," I told him. Although I was getting high at the time, I didn't feel comfortable doing so with him.

It seemed like I was destined to do it. I was surrounded by the drug and continued to use cocaine more and more with family and friends. Eventually, Tommy couldn't cover for me any longer and I ended up losing my job in the financial district.

Once I lost my job, I started to work with Manny and Will in the drug trade. Years before, I had sold marijuana on Creston Avenue, so I had some familiarity with the drug business. The problem came when I actually went to Queens, where my friends were selling crack. It only took me a few days to realize I wasn't cut out for it. When a mother comes to purchase crack with her food stamps, child's diapers, or baby formula, there is a special kind of coldness you need to possess to make that transaction. I'm not saying Will and Manny were evil. They are some of the best friends I've ever had. I simply couldn't do it. I was stu-pid, but I was not heartless. I loved hanging out with Will and Manny while making quick and easy money, but I didn't have the heart to get paid in that scene for long. My man Teddy Ted made sure to call me out one night and let me know just that.

Ted was a young buck on the block, an upstart who had just recently earned his stripes by way of hand-to-hand combat. Prior to Ted's induction as an official member of the crew, he was just another young cat trying to be hard but looking awfully soft as the older neighborhood guys slapped him around.

Growing up in our neighborhoods, one thing we learned was how to take a punch, because we were sure to be everyone's punching bag. Whenever I saw Ted around the way I saw a new jack, a young kid trying to prove he was tough enough to handle the shit that happened on a daily basis. The streets didn't tolerate soft crews walking on them. When it came time for battle, everyone in a crew had to stay and fight. Running was seen as an intolerable sign of weakness.

The fellas on Bailey Avenue had spent years spilling blood in some of the meanest neighborhoods, ensuring that their reputation of being the toughest crew in the area was secure for years to come. We would never have allowed Teddy Ted to roll with us if he proved to be soft for even a second.

One afternoon I was on my way to visit my daughter, Heaven. Stormy had kicked me out because I hung out on Bailey Avenue and told me to go back to my aunt's house, since I was always there anyway. The walk took me through the middle of Born Crazy territory, which normally wasn't a problem, because I knew a few of the guys in that crew and could walk through their neighborhood without being fucked with. Born Crazy was respected in the area as the only crew of white boys crazy enough to beef with the blacks and Latinos in the area. This particular afternoon, though, four white boys decided to start some shit as I approached 232nd Street. They were actually sitting on the steps of a church and decided to call me from across the street.

One of the guys said, "Look at this nerdy motherfucker walking through our neighborhood."

I assume the "nerdy" reference was an ode to the glasses I had just started wearing. I stopped and looked at the guy talking all the shit.

When I did, he and the three guys he was with jumped up and came across the street to confront me.

When they got close I said, "You motherfuckers don't want no problems with me!"

"Who the fuck are you?"

I realized they were trying to surround me, so I shifted position—just as one guy threw a punch. I turned and ran back toward the Marble Hill projects, where my people were playing handball. It was the "run to live and fight another day" lesson that made me do it.

Out of breath and mad as hell, I got to the handball courts and watched as the white boys turned in the other direction, not daring to follow me into the projects. I told my boys I'd just been chased out of Born Crazy territory and that we needed to go get those four motherfuckers. A few cats I'd just met from Heath Avenue were ready to roll, and a few guys from Bailey Avenue, including my cousin Herman and my boys Rico and Ted, were the first ones to get up and start heading back toward 232nd Street. This would be Teddy's first chance to really prove himself. Although I was hesitant about him coming, he was already a block ahead of me, running full speed ahead. I could barely keep up, as I was still recuperating from being chased a few moments earlier. All I had told the fellas was that it was four guys sitting on the steps of the church, and they took off running. By the time I reached the corner, I could hear screaming, as well as a loud noise that sounded like a bell ringing. When I turned the corner I was shocked to see Teddy Ted banging one of the guys' heads against the bottom of the metal light post.

BOOONG, BOOONG, BOOONG.

It seemed that Ted had caught up with the guy who had instigated the whole shit—the one who first confronted the "nerd" walking through Born Crazy territory. Now the poor bastard was helping Ted earn his stripes. Ted continued to beat the guy's head into the light post until a much older Born Crazy member came out of his house.

Just as I went to grab the guy Teddy was mercilessly beating, I turned to see the new guy raise his hand and start firing a small handgun in our direction. It couldn't have been more than a .22- or .25-caliber pistol.

The shit sounded like a small firecracker going off—little more than a muted *pop, pop, pop*.

The bullets didn't put the fear of God in any of us, because it was a small gun, but they did send us running in all directions.

As Herman and I ran for cover, we could see the guy trying to shoot over the parked cars. We decided to cut through the back of the church, and when we got there we discovered that we were trapped.

"What the hell are you doing out there? Get the hell out of here!" shouted the priest who had come outside to see what all the commotion was about.

"Father, we're being shot at!" I boldly told the priest.

"You better get the fuck out of here before the police come," he shouted back.

Herman and I were shocked to hear a priest talk like that. "Fuck you, Father," we yelled, and took off, looking for a way out of the back of the church garden.

By the time we reached the street, we could see cop cars coming. The 52nd Precinct was only a few blocks away. Herman and I walked calmly past the approaching police cars and back to the safety of the projects. I gave Teddy Ted a big hug when I got back to the neighborhood. I knew that the soft little kid had just earned himself a place in the crew. It was the first time I saw Teddy beat someone's head into a light post, but it wouldn't be the last.

Even though I didn't sell crack with Will and Manny in Queens for more than a day, I did start to hang out with them a lot more after losing my job. One night we went up to a bowling alley to settle a beef Will had with some black kids from the neighborhood. Apparently the black kids didn't like a bunch of Puerto Ricans trying to move in on their drug trade, and there had been a few fights between their crew and Will and Manny's crew. Will, Manny, Johnny, Teddy, and I walked into the bowling alley, which was predominantly black.

Everyone froze when we walked in. The funny thing is, we were outnumbered and we didn't have any guns. It was just four crazy Puerto Ricans and my scared ass about to start some shit. Will asked the leader of the other drug crew to step outside. When the guy refused, Will and Teddy snatched him up and dragged his ass outside. Being the ever-observant one in the crew, I noticed one of his partners get on a cell phone. Although I couldn't hear what he was saying, I could see the fear in his eyes. I could tell it was a desperate call for backup. They must have thought we were strapped; that's the only reason they wouldn't have come out to help their boy. I was the last one of my crew to get outside. I had stayed with Johnny to see who was going to make a move for the exit where Will, Teddy, and Manny had taken the leader of the Queens drug gang.

BOOONG, BOOONG, BOOONG . . .

What the fuck was the deal with Teddy and these damn light posts? Will was kicking the shit out of the guy while Teddy beat his head into the light post—over and over and over again. I ran to get the car, because I knew their backup was coming. When I pulled up, I talked Johnny and Manny into getting in quickly, but I literally had to drag Will to the car, and almost fist-fight Teddy to get him off the guy and into the car.

As I turned the corner of the bowling alley I saw three cars filled with guys racing up the block, headed right toward the spot we'd just left. If we had still been there when those guys showed up, our crew probably would have been lit up like the Christmas tree in Rockefeller Center.

When we got back to our neighborhood's pizza shop, Teddy screamed, "You're a fucking pussy" from across the table.

With my adrenaline still pumping a million miles a minute, I jumped up and grabbed him by the throat. Will and Johnny broke us up pretty quickly, but I tried to get at Teddy again. And he was trying equally hard to get at me.

"If you ever talk to me like that again I will fucking kill you, Teddy, do you hear me? I swear to God I will fucking kill you!"

Being called a pussy was reason enough to kill someone. If I had not reacted like that, I would have surely been seen as weak, and I couldn't have that after all the shit I had been through with them. When things calmed down, I told Teddy I was trying to save his life. Will was the only other person who had noticed all the cars racing up the street as we fled the bowling alley and he spoke up for me. Teddy and I lost a lot of respect for each other that night. He was a tough kid and he'd do well in the neighborhood, but I was getting tired of the bullshit and my heart wasn't going to be in it for the long haul.

It was around this time that I began to get very depressed. I'd lost a decent, well-paying job. With a ninth-grade education and no refer-ences, I knew the chances of me landing another opportunity like that were slim to none. So I drowned my depression with heavy cocaine use. I was losing control so fast, I didn't think I'd ever be able to make it out. Soon after, I sat Stormy down one night and told her that if we didn't leave the Bronx, I would be dead or in jail. I asked her to move to Virginia Beach with me, where my mother was living at the time. She agreed to leave everything behind. It was probably the second or third time Stormy saved my life.

I still have family members and friends who are hooked on cocaine. I can see it in their eyes and I can feel their obsession. I'm just grateful I could let it go and not depend on the drug to get me through life's obstacles and ease my paranoia.

   The blood of my father continues to run through my veins, but the biological white lines have ceased to travel up my nostrils. While no families are immune to the effects of drugs, I want to make sure that my own children never lay eyes on them—especially not at the hands of their own father. I want my children to know what a father should be, so that they, in turn, can show their own children.

Lighting a blunt filled with weed for my eighteenth birthday.

JWS VVAI\S ALL I IALLUVVS VVAI\S ALL I IALLUVVS VVAI\S
JARS ALL HALLOWS' WARS ALL HALLOWS' WARS ALL H/
LL HALLOWS' WARS ALL HALLOWS' WARS ALL HALLOWS'
OWS' WARS ALL HALLOWS' WARS ALL HALLOWS' WARS
JARS ALL HALLOWS' WARS ALL HALLOWS' WARS ALL H/
LL HALLOWS' WARS ALL HALLOWS' WARS ALL HALLOWS'
OWS' WARS ALL HALLOWS' WARS ALL HALLOWS' WARS
JARS ALL HALLOWS' WARS ALL HALLOWS' WARS ALL H/
LL HALLOWS' WARS ALL HALLOWS' WARS ALL HALLOWS'
OWS' WARS ALL HALLOWS' WARS ALL HALLOWS' WARS
JARS ALL HALLOWS' WARS ALL HALLOWS' WARS ALL H/
LL HALLOWS' WARS ALL HALLOWS' WARS ALL HALLOWS'
OWS' V   WARS
JARS A   ALL H/
LL HAL   LOWS'

All Hallows' Wars

Celebrating Halloween in New York City in the late eighties and early nineties was not about running around and collecting candy.

Once the youths of the city became too old to get tricks or treats, we decided instead to hand out terror and destruction in the neighborhoods we called home. We didn't live by the "Don't shit where you eat" rule and terrorized everything that moved on Halloween night. It was an opportunity the delinquents in the inner city waited for all year long, an opportunity to wreak havoc and run amok in the streets without ever being held liable for our behavior. It took years for the NYPD to bring these situations under control. By the time I moved out of the Bronx in 1993, there was a special task force assigned to arrest any suspicious-looking characters out looking for trouble on Halloween night. This task force was created too late to stop my friends and me from creating scarring memories for too many unlucky New Yorkers caught in the path of our destruction.

As Halloween approached, we'd make sure to stock up on supplies for the wars that took place once the sun went down. On the checklist would be eggs, as many as you could possibly afford. In this war, eggs were like bullets: The more you had, the likelier you were to outlast the enemy. Eggs made you very powerful on Halloween night. An egg could be launched from an entire city block away, knocking an unsuspecting victim in the head or face. We also had shaving cream and chalk-filled socks. The socks were reserved for the tougher kids on the block, because you had to get up close and personal to use these weapons. If you were hit in the face and head with a chalk-filled sock you would be left dazed, confused, and covered in white powder. There would be red welts on the body, bruises on the face and head, and burning eyes. I remember being hit a couple of times with one of these, and it was painful. The most important item on the list was a mask. We didn't want to be recognized by the cops or become targets for retaliation for the beat-downs we handed out to other crews.

These wars started out small, usually twenty to fifty kids running the streets with their weapons of choice. They were mainly egging wars, where guys from different neighborhoods stood on opposite ends of a city block and launched eggs back and forth. You could always find shelter behind parked cars or buildings. The problems came about when one neighborhood was heavily outnumbered by another neighborhood. When the larger crews realized they had a clear advantage, they would usually commence handing out ass-whippings and stealing the other crew's supplies. They would usually beat the other crew with chalk-filled socks and cover them in shaving cream. Sometimes the two crews would fight with fists until the smaller crew could safely retreat. When the wars were small, our neighborhood usually went against the guys from Morris Avenue, and sometimes we'd face off against guys from 198th and Creston and other crews coming from the Grand Concourse and other surrounding areas. Once in a while, a crew would walk right through our neighborhood; if we saw them coming or had advance warning they were headed our way, we would try to run them off. If their numbers were far greater than ours, we would run our crew of twenty or thirty guys up to the rooftops and prepare our attack.

The crews would proudly stomp through our neighborhood, making all kinds of noise. The Creston Posse was famous for never backing down from any challenge from a rival neighborhood. But they thought we would run scared, because it seemed like there were hundreds of them. They'd get a rude awakening as soon as they were squarely positioned in the middle of the block—like sitting ducks. Once we had them in our sights, someone in the crew would yell: "Get those motherfuckers!"

And we would rain hundreds of eggs down on their heads.

I was lucky enough to never be hit with an egg dropped from six or seven stories, but I'm sure it didn't feel good. The eggs weren't just dropped, they were launched. This was a battle, and we wanted to see every last one of them scream, drop, or run off our block. The Halloween battles would get worse, as the weapons eventually turned from eggs to apples, oranges, and even watermelons. Can you imagine looking up and seeing a watermelon coming at your head from six stories up? The morning after, the streets would look like a giant fruit stand had exploded. Everywhere you looked there was produce. We never paid for it. We'd walk down Kingsbridge Road and hit every fruit stand we could find—stealing as much as we could carry back to the neighborhood. The fruit stands were owned by immigrants. We had them outnumbered fifty to one, and we all wore masks, so who was going to stop us?

As the wars began to grow, we joined forces with other neighborhood crews who had ties to us in some form or fashion. I knew a lot of guys from different neighborhoods, acquaintances I had met writing graffiti or in school. We would come together with other crews to number a hundred or more guys with one objective in mind: Destroy everything in our path.

With numbers like these, the wars would soon grow way out of control. Eventually there were a few kids who started bringing knives along, and there'd be that one kid who'd bring a gun. It wasn't about who had the most eggs anymore, it was about who could destroy the most. If people were outside they were usually egged and beaten; sometimes they were robbed. Cars were destroyed and buildings and storefronts were vandalized in the process. We'd bring spray paint and mark the territories as we marched through. If the crews weren't writing on a building or storefront, they'd be writing on some poor fool who was the last one to run when his crew took off. You never wanted to be the one caught all alone. The beatings were brutal for a rival taken hostage. He would usually be stripped to his underwear and beaten until he was crying and running.

I remember spending Halloween one year with my cousin's crew, the Crazy Young Criminals, down on Bailey Avenue. Up on Creston we usually managed to assemble crews that numbered close to one hundred. But in my cousins' neighborhood, Herman and Johnny assembled a crew straight out of the damn movies. There were easily two hundred guys ready to attack the Born Crazy crew (this would be before they tried to attack me one afternoon). My cousins had brought together guys from Creston, Morris, University, Webb, Heath, Sedgwick, and Bailey avenues. This was basically the entire Kingsbridge section of the Bronx, from the number 4 train to the number 1 train and everywhere in between.

Born Crazy also had a crew of younger guys who ran with them called Crunch Bunch. They all wore logos that read either BC or CB, along with red or blue ski coats in the winter. Ninety percent of the crew was white, but they had some Hispanic and black members. There were more than a hundred of them, and they were the ones destroying shit on that side of the Bronx. The time had come for us to dole out some punishment to Born Crazy and Crunch Bunch, and judging by the numbers, this night was going to get very crazy. To make matters more interesting, BC and CB lived just a few blocks away from the 50th Police Precinct in the Bronx. We called them the Five-O. The cops from the 50th were crazy; they would talk like they were from the streets themselves, and most of them knew most of us by name. The women in the Five-O were the worst. They kicked the most ass, so if we saw a female cop we'd run first, no questions asked. The cops knew both the Crazy Young Criminals (CYC) and Born Crazy very well. So on this Halloween, we not only had to worry about what Born Crazy had in store, we also had to avoid being caught by the cops, who wouldn't take kindly to a bunch of minorities from the projects coming into the nicer areas surrounding 231st Street and Broadway to stir up trouble.

We set off toward Born Crazy territory. It was about six blocks away, but if you cut right through the middle of the Marble Hill projects, it seemed like it was across the street. I felt so powerful walking with close to two hundred soldiers to wage war against one common enemy. But I knew these guys were worthy adversaries and should not be taken lightly. I also knew that my own crew from Creston Avenue had taken on larger crews, using the rooftops as our forts and launching massive attacks without ever being in harm's way. If I had been smarter at the time, I would have realized that we were about to walk into the same thing: a well-planned roof attack that would forever etch itself into my memory. The execution of the attack by Born Crazy and Crunch Bunch was as flawless as many of the attacks we had waged in the past in our own neighborhood. It was the closest I would ever come to catching a severe beat-down at one of these Halloween battles.

They must have heard us coming as we marched up 231st Street, attacking anyone who happened to be on the streets and raiding the fruit stands just off Broadway. And then we suddenly found ourselves under a vicious attack of eggs and we could hear car windows breaking.

Eggs don't break car windows, do they?

A second later, I saw a golf ball hit the stairwell of a building and ricochet toward my head. Either reflex or dumb luck kept me from being hit.

"Oh shit, they're throwing golf balls at us!" I heard someone yell.

One guy got hit from a ricocheting golf ball and fell to the ground.

I didn't know him, so I just kept on running—although even if I did know him, I still would have kept running. It was every man for himself. I never saw a crew so big break so fast. It was as if the block had parted in half and half the guys managed to escape, while the other half—my unlucky group—huddled under the cover of buildings or cars. I was waiting for the golf balls to stop raining down so I could make my dash back to the projects. Born Crazy was coming out and attacking whoever was left in their neighborhood. It wasn't enough for this crew of crazy-ass white boys to attack us from the roof; they wanted to get their hands on us, too. I wasn't worried about the golf balls anymore, and I began a fifty-yard dash like Carl Lewis back to the safe haven of Bailey Avenue. I ran a few blocks and met up with my cousin Herman, who was planning on standing his ground there and attacking any Born Crazy or Crunch Bunch members who came running toward our neighborhood. However, before we got the chance to retaliate, the sirens began to get closer and louder and the running started all over again. We made it back to the safety of our neighborhood, our home, and we would laugh at all that madness for years to come. I'll never forget the fear a bunch of flying golf balls put into some of the toughest guys I ever knew.

This is my last real memory of those Halloween wars. The last few years I lived in New York, the NYPD really began to crack down and the wars began to disappear. The Giuliani administration changed things. Two hundred Hispanics and blacks holding eggs and fruit today would be met with a hundred squad cars. I don't believe these wars can exist today on the levels they once did. I remember stopping by my cousin Richie's block on Halloween in 1992. I was getting ready for my night-shift job at the World Trade Center and I saw the younger kids gathering their crew up, getting ready to wage war against the same neighborhoods we had once battled. There were about fifty of them.

But the war of '92 would never take place, at least not around Kingsbridge Road. Just as I was getting into Richie's car to leave, the NYPD came roaring up the block with sirens blaring. They pulled up with three task force vans and detained every kid on the block. Every youth with a pair of gloves, a mask, or eggs in their hands was grabbed and thrown into the vans. I later found out the NYPD held the whole crew until midnight and then let them go home with tickets for loitering or disorderly conduct. The citizens of New York had finally had enough.

The problem was that our parents had very little control over us. Most of us came from single-parent homes, and if our mothers weren't working, hanging with their friends, or out on a date, they were busy getting high and drunk themselves. There was not much for us to do after we'd outgrown trick-or-treating. The youth seemed to have very little supervision. The school system, community programs, and law enforcement were set up to be reactive, not proactive.

No matter how you look at it, we had about an eight-year run and caused some serious destruction in our own neighborhoods. In hindsight, destroying our own communities was a ridiculous way to behave. I knew someone would be killed as a result of these All Hallows' Wars, and eventually I read about an innocent victim.

On October 29, 2005, at approximately 9:15 P.M., Joey Padro was on his way to work. He was driving near his home in the Mott Haven section of the Bronx. His van was suddenly pelted with eggs by teenagers behaving exactly the same way my crew and I had behaved over a decade earlier. Padro, the brother of an NYPD detective, pulled his van over to confront the teens. Some members of the media reported that Padro chased the teenagers toward a building while screaming, "You better wash this shit off my car!" People from the neighborhood later said that Padro actually said, "I don't want no trouble, I just want someone to clean this mess off my car."

No one really knows the truth, but some say Padro gave chase toward the lobby of a building in the infamous Patterson Houses projects. Other witnesses say there was no chase—rather, Padro calmly walked into the building looking for the teenagers who had agreed to wash his car. There was a fifteen-year-old male lying in wait, and he pumped bullets into the back of Padro's head, arm, and back. The New York *Daily News* reported that the young gunman allegedly screamed, "Yeah, we'll wash this shit off your car."

The fifteen-year-old gunman, known on the streets as Hell Rell, was trying to earn a reputation and murdered an innocent man. Joey Padro was pronounced brain-dead at Lincoln Hospital and eventually taken off life support. He left behind a wife, Maria; and two sons, Jeremiah, three, and Joseph, twelve. It would have been nice if the same neighbors who showed outrage after the incident had called the police earlier in the evening, when the teenagers first began victimizing their neighbors with eggs and threats. It might have even saved a life.

But who are we kidding? No snitching allowed in the hood. Remember? Not even if it means saving the life of a law-abiding citizen on his way to work.

DJ Red Alert with members of the Crazy Young Criminals.

UL MATE MY HEART'S SOUL MATE MY HEART'S SOUL MA
Y HEART'S SOUL MATE MY HEART'S SOUL MATE MY HEAR
UL MATE MY HEART'S SOUL MATE MY HEART'S SOUL MA
Y HEART'S SOUL MATE MY HEART'S SOUL MATE MY HEAR
UL MATE MY HEART'S SOUL MATE MY HEART'S SOUL MA
Y HEART'S SOUL MATE MY HEART'S SOUL MATE MY HEAR
UL MATE MY HEART'S SOUL MATE MY HEART'S SOUL MA
Y HEART'S SOUL MATE MY HEART'S SOUL MATE MY HEAR
UL MATE MY HEART'S SOUL MATE MY HEART'S SOUL MA
Y HEART'S SOUL MATE MY HEART'S SOUL MATE MY HEAR
UL MATE MY HEART'S SOUL MATE MY HEART'S SOUL MA
Y HEART'S SOUL MATE MY HEART'S SOUL MATE MY HEAR
UL M.   SOUL MA
Y HEAI   IY HEAR
UL MA   JL MATE

My Heart's Soul Mate

In the mideighties, I would sit alone in my bedroom, on the stoop of my building, or the rooftop and get lost in my thoughts. I've always been the type of person to spend most of my time alone, letting that voice in my head converse out of control. Most times I found myself wondering why the hell I was born in what seemed like such a cold place. I'd experienced so much poverty, despair, and violence at a young age and my mind wouldn't allow me to look past the negative or see that there might be light at the end of every dark tunnel. But life has a funny way of showing us light even when we don't know we are searching for it.

My mind-set would forever be altered when I met the one person in this world I felt I could confide in deeply and without fear of being judged. It seemed that this person, who would come to love me so wholeheartedly, looked right into the center of my soul. Her eyes pierced my physical being and penetrated the deepest core of my heart. I was just a child, but this was no puppy love. This was the real thing. The type of love they say some people never get to experience in their entire lives, the kind of love that makes people do crazy things. More important, the sort of love that gave me a reason to love life—something I cannot recall ever really doing before then.

I can't remember the exact date, but it must have been sometime around Christmas of 1986, possibly even 1987, when I first met the little girl who would change my world forever. Lori DeSoto was a petite thirteen- or fourteen-year-old whose background was Puerto Rican, Italian, and Portuguese. I thought that mix bred some of the toughest and most beautiful women in the world. This little girl would steal my heart and give me the reason I needed to live and breathe for the next few years, until I found my own identity, my own manhood. I can still see Lori's big hair (I think all the girls had big hair around that time), and I can still conjure up the feeling of my heart stopping when I first laid eyes on her. The connection for me was instant.

It was my cousin Herman's birthday party, and my cousin Tony, who has since passed away, was DJing, playing the old "Sixteen Candles" song, along with the Pee-wee Herman rap song that was out at the time. As Herman walked into the house, Tony mixed a slow record with a rap record and blended the two sounds into one. Tony would play "Happy Birthday" and then cut "Herman, Herman" into the song to make the turntables sing happy birthday to Herman. Lori was there that night and she had my undivided attention. I watched her from the corner of my eye all night. I'll never forget that first memory of her. Although we didn't really "meet" that night, my heart was already hers and would remain hers for the rest of my life.

After Herman's party, I started walking the twenty city blocks home, from one end of Kingsbridge to the other, instead of letting the Sacred Heart bus drop me off in hopes of getting a glimpse of the girl I had become infatuated with. Sacred Heart was the Catholic school my mother enrolled me in after I left Aviation High School in Queens. I didn't feel welcome at Aviation after being chased to the subway for my leather coat one day after school.

One afternoon I was walking up Suicide Hill with my hockey skates and book bag when I finally ran into Lori and her girlfriend Natalie.

I said hello and Lori said, "You're Johnny's cousin, right?"

"Yeah," I said.

"What are you doing with ice skates?" she asked.

"I play hockey for Sacred Heart."

Here I was, starting off the relationship with a lie. Truth of the matter was, I never made it to tryouts, because my boy Steve, whom I went to school with, hadn't picked me up that morning. Fuck it—talking about my skates and my fictitious sporting life was a good icebreaker, and I was off to the races with that shit.

"I don't know any Puerto Ricans who can ice skate. Are you good?" Lori probed.

"Yeah, you know I'm nice with mine," I said with a cocky grin on my face.

I wasn't lying about being nice on a pair of ice skates. Ever since I got my first pair of stolen Bauer ice skates I was a natural. I remember going up to the Burlington Coat Factory in Westchester County with my boys. We'd all chip in a few bucks, except for me because I never had any money, and we'd buy one pair of skates. Then the next guy would go into the store with the receipt and the empty bag in his pocket. He'd put a nice pair of new skates, box and all, in the empty bag and walk out with it. We'd repeat the cycle until we were all headed back to the Bronx with new skates. Then we'd take off to Central Park to go ice skating in Wollman Rink and have some fun.

Before I knew it, we had reached my building on Creston Avenue and Lori and I exchanged phone numbers.

"I hope to see you soon," I said.

"I'll give you a call sometime," Lori said as she walked away.

But she never called. Sometime later I was on the rooftop at 60 East 196th Street, where I'd escape from the world, and I saw Lori and her friend walking up Creston Avenue. She was actually coming to visit me. We spent a few hours that afternoon talking about ourselves and getting to know each other's worlds.

We would become boyfriend and girlfriend for the next three or four years. I believe we experienced the kind of love most people dream about.

I remember borrowing friends' dirt bikes or walking to visit Lori on the other side of Kingsbridge—170 West Kingsbridge Road, to be exact. When I go back to visit the neighborhood as an adult the distance seems so small, but when I was young it was like traveling to the other side of the Bronx each time I set out to visit her. I rarely had two nickels to rub together, so on our one-month anniversary, I brought Lori one red rose. I continued that trend for at least six months. Afterward, it got difficult for me to afford the roses and the trend died out, but I always tried to show Lori how much I loved her, even if I had to steal stuffed animals from my sister's collection.

When you are raised on welfare it leaves a lasting impact on the way you think about money, clothing, and anything else having to do with finances. I always felt like an outcast when I walked up to the counter of the bodega to pay for my groceries with a purple five-dollar food stamp or an orange ten-dollar food stamp. It's as if I was begging the old Spanish guy behind the counter to give me the food for free. And God forbid my friend walked in to see me getting change counted out in what looked like Monopoly money. Everything slowed down as the bodega man counted "U-n-n-n-n-o-o-o-o, d-o-o-o-o-s-s-s, t-r-e-s-s-s," until I felt like screaming out, "Just give me my fucking money, man."

How was I supposed to focus on school when my stomach often broke out into a gangster rap song with the lyrics "Feed me bitch, feed me bitch," playing on heavy rotation in my head? I started to question my entire existence because I couldn't feed myself and I couldn't help my family. I couldn't help my mother pay a light bill. I couldn't get my little sister the dress she begged my mom for. I couldn't buy those new Bo Jackson Nikes everyone in the neighborhood was rocking. And I began to feel worthless.

Leaving school never hurt me because the second I got that first paycheck I was going to give Moms some money and hit my little sister off with a few bucks. My brother was good, he had a job. And when I eventually received that first paycheck I went straight to the fucking candy store and bought every piece of neatly packaged sugar rush I could get my hands on and I paid for it all with green money.

Fuck welfare and fuck school. It was time for me to be a man. I wanted to help my mom out with a few bucks. I didn't want to ever go back to that purple five-dollar bill.

I had a mini nervous breakdown in the living room the night I told my mother I could no longer handle the stresses of school.

"Mom, I'm not a bad kid, I'd give anyone the shirt off my back, the last dollar in my pocket. But the problem is I never have a dollar in my pocket and I can't deal with it anymore."

I told her that all I really wanted was to save the world and make a difference in a place I saw as nothing more than just evil. My mind had been altered by everything I'd seen in the streets and I didn't care about school or anything else at that point in my life.

"Maybe I should join the Army, Ma; I really don't know what else to do, I feel lost. I need some time to think about what I'm going to do next in life, and if I don't drop out of school now I'm going to end up killing myself because I can't handle it."

My mother dreamed that all of her children would graduate from high school and had sacrificed so much to assure us a good start in life by putting us in Catholic school. And here was her middle child having a nervous breakdown. She took my dropping out extremely hard, but I guess the crying, coupled with the argument that I was going to off myself, was enough for her to agree to allow me to leave school.

"Mom, I'll go back one day, I promise." It would be a promise I kept almost twenty years later when I graduated from college.

What I wanted more than anything was to have things I could call my own and to be accepted by the neighborhood thugs. Once school was no longer an obligation, I began to spend all my time in the streets with the local drug dealers, graffiti artists, car thieves, and stickup kids.

I lost a little piece of my soul every day as I dabbled in petty crime, trying to earn a reputation as a tough guy. At five-foot-nothing and one
hundred pounds, it was hard, but as guns appeared, it became easier
for a little guy to level the playing field. I held myself pretty well and
earned respect from the neighborhood guys. Of the thirty-two years
I've spent on this earth, these are probably the years I regret the most.
So many things could have been done differently. I made many bad decisions along the way and I hurt many people, including Lori, the closest person to me at the time. Hindsight is a funny and painful thing.
You can look back, but you can't change a damn thing.

Early in 1988, my mother came home from work and saw Terrell
and me having a fight with two guys over a graffiti beef Terrell had gotten into. I'd known Terrell since he was two or three years old. He lived
next door to my *titi* Vilma and he was always in her house while his
mother worked toward a nursing degree. He was like a little brother
to me and my cousins and I'd do anything to protect him. If you have
ever seen the movie *Boyz n the Hood* and remember the speech Laurence
Fishburne gave in the middle of the street, then you can imagine what
my mother did that day on the corner of Creston and Morris. She
was a strong woman and taught us how to stand up and fight for the
"right" thing, but we fought only because we liked to fight. My mother
didn't understand why we all wanted to kill one another, and she let
the whole neighborhood know it that day. This was shortly before she
witnessed two men shooting at me and finally left the Bronx. I was dating Lori at the time and I was part of a crew, so I wasn't going anywhere.
After my mother left, Lori would become my entire life.

Without Lori, I probably wouldn't have lasted as long as I did. She
fed me, clothed me, and gave me the love and support I needed to survive being virtually alone on the streets.

In those days, Lori was one of those crazy-in-love teenage girls. She
used to sneak out of her house and walk across some rough neighborhoods at night to come see me, bring me food, and keep me company.

She would cut school and spend the entire day with me, and once again she would bring me food. When I think about how hungry I was sometimes—no job, no money, and nothing to eat—I'm not sure what I would have done if I didn't have her taking care of me. Lori's sacrifices at such a young age spoke volumes about how much love she must have had in her heart for me. She helped me appreciate life and feel secure. I never felt alone when I was with her and I was passionate about her in return.

It was a year after my mother left that my brother Bill and my cousin Richie moved out. This is when I went into business with the Jamaicans and turned the apartment into a stash house. I mentioned that Chippy, the Jamaican who ran the stash house, was murdered when his crew tried to rob the rapper Slick Rick, but I didn't mention that I was supposed to be a part of their team. Instead, I'd gone to visit my mom that weekend.

I planned the robbery with Chippy and two other guys, who shall remain nameless. We were supposed to rob Slick Rick's house while he was out on tour. As in any other job, there was an inside man. I guess the inside man screwed up and ended up getting Chippy killed and another guy shot. It's no secret now that Slick Rick went after his cousin after the robbery and ended up doing some time of his own.

I could have ended up dead had my mother not driven up to New York for a weekend visit after months of my not seeing her. I remember she took me shopping for a coat at the same Burlington Coat Factory I had robbed the ice skates from. Bill and I went inside with Mom, and after I picked out a new beige parka I handed it off to my mother and told her I was going to look around.

Bill and I went over to the shoe section and my brother looked out for me while I stole a pair of Timberland boots. I took off my old sneakers and put them in the box and off I went with my new laced-up boots, looking for Mom. We were standing in line waiting to pay when my mother noticed the new boots. My brother and I both looked at her, and shook our heads as if to say, "Mom, please stop looking before you get us busted."

When we made it to the car, my brother and I jumped in the back and burst out laughing while Mom cursed us in Spanish. My stepfather, Jesse, had no way of knowing he was the getaway driver. I don't think he would have been too happy, as he was a federal officer in Virginia.

Later on that evening, over dinner, my mother pleaded with me to come visit her in Virginia for a week or so. I really didn't want to go, but she cried and I felt like shit. It was the least I could do after she bought me a new coat and watched me steal.

"Okay, Mom, you got me for one week, but that's it," I said. My mother smiled and it felt good to make her happy. That visit would save my life.

The time I spent in Virginia helped to clear my head. I also realized how much I truly loved and missed Lori. We talked on the phone often, and she offered me a place to stay. Apparently her mother had agreed to let me live with them for a little while so that I could try to find myself and fix my life. Living with Lori and her mother was a great experience and something I've never been able to repay them for. I decided to go straight and found a great job with a brokerage house on Wall Street and Broadway as a computer operator, processing and printing stock exchange reports. Life was going pretty well for a while, but Lori and I started to fight more and more about less and less, and I was physically abusive to her. It would destroy not only my relationship with Lori, but also the beautiful friendship we had.

The machismo that exists in the Latino community is a horrible legacy passed down from generation to generation. I remember seeing my biological father beat my mother the few times he stopped by for a visit. Years later, I would learn that he was beating her because she refused to have sex with him in exchange for the fifty or so dollars he was dropping off to feed his three kids. Although I'm emotionally scarred to this day by the images of seeing my mother beaten, I turned around and abused this little girl the same way—the girl who cared for me, supported me, and even convinced her mother to take me into their household and offer me shelter. It does not matter how long I live, I will never be able to forgive myself or forget what I did to Lori.

She was the only person I was able to confide in. She took care of me like no other person in this world. The way I thanked her was with verbal, physical, and emotional abuse. I wasn't a grown man; I was only sixteen or seventeen years old. Even though I witnessed the men in my family commit these atrocities on their girlfriends and wives, I can't blame anyone but myself. I should have been, and I wish to God I was, strong enough to respond to Lori with compassion and morals when we were fighting. This is one of the greatest regrets in my life.

The abuse started out with me grabbing her wrists or arms to stop her from walking away. Eventually I was pulling her hair and then moving on to slapping her in the face. One day, while she tried to run away, I hit her in the back of the head and knocked her down a flight of stairs. I remember running into her friend's boyfriend on University Avenue and telling him about what I'd done. He then turned and told his boys, "This kid is crazy, son. He kicked his bitch down the stairs and beat the shit out of her."

I laughed right along with the group of thugs on the corner. I didn't think anything of it then. I remember slapping Lori in the face several times one night because she was outside and not in the house when I felt she should've been. I was on my way to go bowling with my boss, Tommy, and my cousin Richie. When I got in the car, I joked with them about kicking Lori's ass. It was unimaginable and inexcusable, and I could never see myself doing it today.

I never got help for this type of behavior. I merely outgrew it when I had a daughter a few years later with Stormy, who would become my wife. I remember looking at my daughter, Heaven, the night she was born and thinking about what I'd put Lori through. It was Lori I called the night Heaven was born. The situation at the hospital had been tense. I hadn't been there for Stormy throughout the pregnancy, except financially, and her mother didn't call me at work when Stormy went into labor. Her mother hated me, and I blamed Stormy for her mother's behavior and for letting her cause me to miss my daughter's birth. I called Lori for comfort and she was still there for me, even after everything I'd put her through.

Our relationship, so volatile and dramatic, would eventually end in a ridiculous way. My mother was visiting from Virginia and I wanted Lori to spend the night with us at my aunt Iris's house. She refused.

I finally said, "If you don't stay with me, I'm never coming back to your house again."

Lori wouldn't come and I left her house, but worse than that, my stubbornness kept me from going back. It was probably the best decision Lori ever made in her life.

Shortly thereafter, I moved to my cousin's home at 2520 Bailey Avenue to the same apartment where I had first seen Lori. Although the memories of her were everywhere and I saw her everywhere, I tried hard to forget about her. At the time, I remember thinking she was the wrong girl for me, that she didn't really love me, because if she did, she would have come with me to my aunt's house to visit my mother. We talked occasionally and she cried on the phone a lot, but I still didn't believe that she really loved me—even after feeding, clothing, and sheltering me.

At the time, my warped mind believed that if Lori wasn't completely and utterly submissive to my every wish, she didn't love me. There was no such thing as *no*. It was either *yes* or *you don't love me*, no in-between. I was too immature to understand compromise. I watched the Latino men in my family be served dinner first, call their wives for a can of Budweiser even though they were sitting right next to the refrigerator, and slap their wives down in front of whomever was present if they were spoken to in a manner they saw as disrespectful. I was emulating the behavior I witnessed growing up, and shamefully it was what I believed a relationship to be.

Had my mother stayed in New York, I don't believe I would have found the balls to behave this way. My mother would have killed me if she had seen the way I treated Lori. She'd been the victim of domestic violence from very early in her childhood and she wouldn't have stood for her son perpetuating it. I know it's an excuse most men use, but the truth was I might have loved Lori a little too much. I just didn't know how to deal with the emotions.

I met Stormy a few months after breaking up with Lori, and it was Stormy who became my wife. I had no idea that Stormy and Lori already knew each other. When they found out they had me in common, I figured they would dislike each other. I thought Stormy was very cute and she reminded me a lot of my mother. (I know it's sick, but isn't that what we look for, a mother figure?)

Stormy and I hadn't been dating for long when Lori called and told me she'd run away to my mother's house in Virginia. She wanted us to get back together and she wanted me to leave the streets and move to Virginia. She told my mom and me that she was pregnant with my child. In all fairness to Lori, she doesn't remember telling me she was pregnant. Lori also told me she was coming home and that her dad, whom I cared for deeply, said we could live with him as we tried to work things out.

The problem was, I was already living with Stormy. I was a hobo and bounced around quite a bit in those days. I needed time to think about whom I was going to spend the rest of my life with. Who would make me happiest? I went back to the only place I could, the old drug house on 196th Street. The beef over the stolen drugs had died down, and I went to stay there for a few days to make my decision. In the end,

I chose to move in with Lori and her dad and give our relationship one more chance. I was happy with my decision. But I never did go through with it.

About a year earlier, I had found Lori speaking with a friend, Kassim, and I smacked him. A few days later, he came back with Lori's ex, Mark, and all of his cousins from the Castle Hill section of the Bronx. They headed over to Lori's house thinking I'd be there, but she begged them to leave me alone. That night, Lori and I were in her mother's apartment talking and crying together. It was one of the most intense and passionate conversations I've ever had with another human being. We talked about how much we meant to each other and how deep our love was. She had this look I'd never seen before. She was scared for me.

That night we made a pact that no matter where life took us or whose arms we ended up in, we would always try to find our way back to each other. I will remember this moment with sterling clarity for the rest of my life. The conversation, the memory of loving someone that much, will never fade. This pact was one of the reasons I decided to get back together with Lori even though I was with Stormy. I was becoming a man, holding down a job, and thinking I just might be able to have a good future after all. Then I made a phone call to Stormy that would change everything.

Stormy was crying uncontrollably and told me I was a bad person for walking out after she'd given her heart and her body to me. Going back to Lori meant breaking Stormy's heart, something I didn't want to do. I told Lori we shouldn't get back together. It just seemed like the easier thing to do. I really believed Lori would always be there when I was ready to go back, but I couldn't have been more wrong.

One of my biggest regrets is that I was never able to introduce Lori to the responsible me, the changed man, the man who had found his compassion and enough love to do the right thing all of the time. The man who would have chosen with his heart and said, "Lori, I want to be by your side forever. I want to cherish you, protect you, and care for you."

There is nothing worse than losing a person, especially a best friend. What you are really losing is a confidante, the person you come home to and laugh with at the end of the day. The person you hug and cry with when things are not going your way. What you lose is the comfort you feel when they hold you and the security of being in their arms.

I thought I would at least have Lori's friendship, her love, for a lifetime. After all, I was her first love, right? Nope. I was a great friend though, right? Negative. On Christmas Day 2003, I called Lori on the phone and got into the whole "I wonder what would have become of us" discussion, something she no longer wanted to talk about with me. During the conversation, Lori told me that not only was I not her first love, I wasn't even a good friend. She told me many things I didn't really need to hear, many things I deserved to hear, and many things that really broke my heart. Sixteen or seventeen years after I first met her, here I was sitting in my truck waiting to go upstairs and play with my daughters on Christmas morning and all I could do was sit there and wonder what might have become of us had I never met my wife.

Our hearts have a funny way of choosing their own soul mates. We don't have the option of turning off our love when things are not working out in our favor. Definitely not! So every time the plane I'm on starts making funny noises, I think about her. Whenever I accomplish something great, I think about her. She will always hold a small piece of my heart and I have absolutely no control over those emotions.

Lori once told me to stop living in the past.

I've read biographies in which great men have said, "You shouldn't live in the past."

I've seen great movies where the lead character says, "If I live in the past, I won't be able to see my future."

I wish I could agree with them, I wish I could live by those words and those examples, but I can't. My past is my only teacher. My past is my present and it dictates my future. I don't want to let those memories fade.

Lori is my history. She's one of the most important people in this world to me. She loved me when I was nobody, a thug, a heartless little boy who had no future to speak of and no hope of accomplishing anything in life. She loved me when I was lost, when I was physically abusive, inconsiderate, a cheat and a drug addict. She loved me when I was poor, tired, and weak. She loved me at my worst. How can I ever get over that? Lori did find a real man to call her husband and she is expecting her first child in 2008.

In the movie *A Bronx Tale*, Sonny tells C that when it comes to love you only get three great ones in your lifetime. He'd met all three of his when he was sixteen years old. Not unlike Sonny, I met all three of my great ones before I turned eighteen. My first was Lori. My second great one was a girl named Yanira Valentin, with whom I've since lost all contact. My last great one became my wife, Stormy.

Stormy taught me how to transition into being a man. She taught me the meaning of forgiveness, of understanding, and of unconditional love. I'm a better person today because of the life lessons all three girls taught me and for the love they showed me when I was at my worst. However, I'm only a man because Stormy saved my life and gave me the opportunity to become a man. She stood by me even after she found out I had been keeping so much of my heart closed off to her in hopes that one day Lori and I would reunite. She stood next to me as a rock when I failed to succeed in life no matter how hard I tried to find my calling. I never settled for Stormy—Stormy settled for me. I never deserved Stormy, but I earned her love. She was the best thing that ever happened to me, and she made me realize the true meaning of love. There was a chance I could have left Stormy for Lori, but I chose not to.

In the end, I discovered that my wife owned my heart and my soul, and deservingly so. The person I married is my heart's soul mate, the person I had with me the whole time. I was just too blind to see what was right in front of me. The heart is a crazy thing.

IVE piece for my girl Yanira on the rooftop of 60 East 196th Street.

Stormy, Heaven, and me on the subway.

HER ZEN THE GODFATHER ZEN THE GODFATHER ZEN THE G
THER ZEN THE GODFATHER ZEN THE GODFATHER ZEN
ODFATHER ZEN THE GODFATHER ZEN THE GODFATHER
HE GODFATHER ZEN THE GODFATHER ZEN THE GODFATH
EN THE GODFATHER ZEN THE GODFATHER ZEN THE GOD
HER ZEN THE GODFATHER ZEN THE GODFATHER ZEN THE G
THER ZEN THE GODFATHER ZEN THE GODFATHER ZEN
ODFATHER ZEN THE GODFATHER ZEN THE GODFATHER
HE GODFATHER ZEN THE GODFATHER ZEN THE GODFATH
EN THE GODFATHER ZEN THE GODFATHER ZEN THE GOD
HER ZEN THE GODFATHER ZEN THE GODFATHER ZEN THE G
THER ZEN THE GODFATHER ZEN THE GODFATHER ZEN
ODFATI   ATHER
HE GO   GODFAT
EN THE   HE GOD

The Godfather Zen

John Gotti is often referred to as the last don, or the final godfather of organized crime in the twentieth century. In our neighborhood, there was only one man who held the respect, fear, and power to be considered the godfather of Creston Avenue. If the Creston Posse, as we were known at the time, had been an organized crime family, then Zen would have unquestionably held the title of godfather, or *capo di tutti,* as the Italian Mafia families say. He was the first, the last, and the only godfather figure to ever walk the streets of 196th Street and Creston Avenue in Kingsbridge.

His birth name was Zenun Berisha, and he was of Albanian descent. He stood a powerful six feet two inches tall, and he was as wide as Sammy "the Bull" Gravano. If Zen was ever afraid of anything in his life, or was ever afraid *for* his life, he never let any of the neighborhood guys see it. He was a living testament to the philosophy "Never let them see you sweat." His fearless nature and physique made him a man we could all follow into battle. We fought many battles in our neighborhoods, and I can recall as if it were yesterday how secure I felt going into these battles knowing Zen was our fearless leader, heading up the pack ready for whatever came our way.

My first introduction to the Albanian guys in the neighborhood wasn't a pretty one. As with any situation in our neighborhood, news of violence spread quickly, and with each recital of the story the violence always increased tenfold. If a guy got stabbed, you'd hear he got his head nearly cut off. If a neighborhood guy got into a fight with two guys, it would almost certainly be reported back that he fought a crew of twenty. Don't get me wrong, there was real violence at times, especially as we grew older and the crew got larger and more fearless. However, at times the stories would just be exaggerated beyond all reasoning. There was no mistaking the stories about the violent Albanians around the corner, though. When you heard a story about those guys, it was usually right on point.

The story goes like this: Karen was a few years older than me and lived downstairs in apartment 4F. Hers was one of the last Irish families to stay behind during the Great White Escape, and she became a close friend of my family. Her older brother, Mike, got into a verbal confrontation with an Albanian kid named Sal. At the time of the confrontation, Sal happened to be picking garbage out of the gardens in front of the building around the corner. If you have ever spent time in a park in New York, you have seen the guys walking around with big wooden sticks with a sharp metal spike on the bottom. The tools are used to pull the trash out of the dirt without having to bend down and pick it up, and they can penetrate almost anything. Unfortunately for Mike, Sal happened to have one of these weapons in his hand the day of their confrontation. As things escalated, Sal decided to plunge the metal spike into Mike's leg, and the legend of violent Albanians around the corner grew to mythical proportions. I spent my earlier years steering clear of the Albanian guys for fear of being stabbed, but they would eventually become great friends of ours and a huge part of the neighborhood crew.

I can recall being especially intimidated by Zen, as he was a very big guy and he never made eye contact with me. Zen never even acknowledged my existence until one day when a good old-fashioned burglary would introduce us to each other and make us friends until the day he died.

It was just after dusk, with a slight chill in the air. As we had done countless other times before, a bunch of us were standing on the stoop in front of my building at 60 East 196th Street. There was a Jamaican drug house on the first floor. For some reason, Zen noticed that all of the lights were out in the drug house. He spent some time trying to figure out if we knew whether the apartment was actually empty. In retrospect, Zen had a look in his eyes like, *There is no way they left this apartment unguarded.*

For the first time, Zen focused all his attention on the smallest guy in the group, which happened to be me.

"Aye, little man, if I push you in that window, will you unlock the door for me?"

It took me a few minutes to catch my breath. Not only was I overwhelmed that Zen was talking to me, but he was asking me to break into the apartment of the most violent guys in the neighborhood. Sure, the Albanians were tough, but the Jamaicans would put a few bullets in you with no hesitation at all. I know they call them "Colombian neckties," but the Jamaican guys were just as quick to slash your throat and pull your tongue out through your neck. They had killers on their payrolls—I knew this for a fact—and here was Zen asking me to put my life on the line so he could rob their apartment.

I think I surprised myself when I said, "No problem, Zen, I've got this."

No sooner did I speak the words than I found myself thrown through the first-floor window of a known drug location. It would go down as my first and only apartment burglary, if you want to call it that. Even though I didn't do much burglarizing, I guess you could say I was the main accomplice.

Just as soon as the four deadbolts on the door were undone, Zen and a few other neighborhood guys came running in.

"Little man, unplug the TV and get it to your house now," came the command from Zen.

And just as soon as the leader gave me an order, I was off to the races, carrying a twenty-five-inch color television up five flights of stairs. Things were moving so fast, I really didn't have time to be scared, but I remember my heart beating out of my damn chest. I was helping the most powerful guy in the neighborhood pull off a small-time heist. I knew this was my in to the crew. I'd be known as a fearless hood, and I was damn proud of myself for it. The adrenaline must have given me strength as I carried the Jamaicans' heavy-ass television set up five flights of stairs.

These be one of those times I really wish we had an elevator in the building.

I don't know what else was stolen from the house in the time it took me to take that TV upstairs, but it must have been everything. The funniest thing was hearing the Jamaicans curse up a storm when they found out they'd been robbed. Drug houses would no longer get any respect and I didn't care about the Jamaicans.

Although the neighborhoods around Kingsbridge were hodge-podges of ethnicities, the Jamaicans didn't seem to have loyalty to any one neighborhood. We policed ourselves and looked after one another. The Jamaicans' loyalty was to the almighty dollar, their customers, and their suppliers. If they didn't like you, they'd slit your fucking throat in the lobby of your building even though they lived only a few doors down. When they came in, they brought a new level of ruthlessness with them, and their violence would ultimately change the character of our neighborhoods. In an effort to protect themselves, everyone else had to step up his own violence, and New York saw an epidemic of crimes the likes of which had never been recorded in its history.

The Jamaicans turned us against one another, as some of the guys went to work with them and some continued robbing them. This was the first in a very long list of ugly happenings that would take place in our neighborhood. However, on this night, all ended well. A lasting friendship was born between Zen and me.

We'd sit on the stoop and laugh after we told the Jamaicans, "Damn, we have no idea what happened. Whoever robbed you must have been good, we never saw them."

Not only did my reputation grow within the Creston family, Zen now protected me. He was always putting his arm around me and seeking me out when he arrived in the neighborhood. I had always felt comfortable on Creston—I grew up there—but now I felt *protected*, and there was a big difference. I was getting too bold for my own good, but I knew my crew had my back no matter what, and they always did. Through all the little neighborhood scuffles, skirmishes with the hoods from Walton High School, battles on the Grand Concourse, and fights with the boys from Morris Avenue, I always felt safe when Zen was there. He would have made an unbelievable leader in the military. He never left a man behind. Zen saved my life on at least two occasions.

The wars we had on the block were never about race, color, or creed. Our wars were more territorial. It wasn't a rare thing to see a group of Hispanics, blacks, and Caucasians fighting a group of Hispanics, blacks, and Caucasians. It just meant we were from different neighborhoods. If you stomped through our neighborhood and you weren't from there, you had to be very fucking quiet. Any noise perceived by us as disrespect would have P-Funk's mother throwing baseball bats out the window and us kicking the living shit out of you, win, lose, or draw.

There always seemed to be a small group of illegal Mexican immigrants walking through 196th Street, and it became second nature for us to pick on these guys. We were second-generation New Yorkers and as American as any of the white boys in the neighborhood. At the time, I saw myself as an American, not as an immigrant. While some racist white boys might have called me *spic* very early on, it wasn't something that continued for any length of time. I only felt like an immigrant in Brooklyn or Staten Island. Looking back on how we treated these Mexican men and understanding my own history leaves me with a sick feeling. We verbally abused the shit out of these men. Men who worked hard for their chance at the American dream.

We used to sing a song every time they walked by us on Creston Avenue. I'm not sure who made it up. Real animated and drawn out, we'd sing, *"It's the Mexican Americans."* It wasn't exactly a song, more like a one-liner or a hook, but we would sing it every time these guys walked by. It didn't matter if there were thirty of us on the corner or two. Like I said, it was second nature.

One summer afternoon, Vincent and I were standing in front of the building and a group of four Mexicans walked by. As the guys got within a few feet of us, Vincent and I began belting out *"It's the Mexican Americans,"* just as loud and animated as always. As soon as they realized there were only two of us, they came after us with fists flying. Vincent took on two of them, I hit one of them, and I noticed the fourth pulling a large object from under his shirt. It took me two seconds to realize it was a very large knife. I yelled to Vince that there was a knife and we set off running around the corner to Morris Avenue.

They chased after us. I managed to dodge the knife-wielding Mexican a couple of times, but when his fast little partner ran around a parked car, I realized I was about to be boxed in. I was standing in the middle of the street up against a car and I realized I was finally going to have to face the music. Seconds after I realized I was about to be stabbed, I saw a car pull up in the middle of the street and I saw my good friend, my savior, coming at full speed. As if in a movie, the knife was coming up toward my chest when Zen kicked the Mexican guy who was holding it. Zen kicked him right in the middle of the chest.

The guy went down hard and so did the knife. Normally, I would have teamed up with Zen and beaten this guy half to death, but a part of me knew this was ridiculous and we'd started it. After a few punches and kicks, I managed to pull Zen away and walk back across the street to the stoop as the Mexicans ran off. This was the last time I made fun of the Mexicans and it was the first time Zen saved my life. I was sixteen years old.

A year or so later, I was almost killed by Barney, the leader of the Jamaican drug crew who had taken over the stash house in apartment 5F after Chippy had been murdered. I had borrowed some of their weed and hadn't paid them for it. It didn't take long for Barney to realize that I was smoking a lot, wearing $120 Nike Air Maxes, and rocking new gear. The name "Barney" may not be very scary these days, with the popularity of the big purple dinosaur, but trust me, this guy was no one to fuck with.

Barney was hard-core, six foot four, and his eyes were a dark yellow. He looked like he had death in his soul. And he wasn't looking too happy when he caught up with me in the lobby of the building as I was hanging out with Zen and Zef, another fearless Albanian who dabbled in crimes that would have anyone else seeing the inside of a prison cell for five years.

I had been avoiding Barney as much as possible, but my luck ran out that afternoon. Barney was walking right toward me with a look that could have killed me on the spot. He was yelling a hundred Jamaican curse words at me. I started to feel brave because I wasn't alone.

I yelled back, "Fuck you. You guys owe me money for turning my apartment into a stash house!"

Before I could put two sentences together, Barney's unbelievably huge hands were around my throat and I was being lifted off the ground.

I was being choked to death in the lobby of the building where I had lived since I was seven years old. It seemed like a shitty way to die, but I had no way of overpowering the huge Jamaican who was suffocating the fucking life out of me.

Zen came to my rescue. With the help of Zef, he managed to pull Barney off me and talk him down. At this point, Barney was calling me a "bumba clot rasta" and telling me I was dead the next time we crossed paths.

I probably would have died. As I gasped for air, I thanked God that Zen was there to save my ass.

Not long after the Barney incident, I left Creston Avenue behind and started sleeping with a gun. I feared for my life—and with good reason. Zen had been murdered, and I knew I didn't have my body-guard anymore. A few months before Zen's death, there had been a situation on Creston Avenue. My brother and his partner, Frankie, had stolen an Audi. The guy whose car they had stolen was a very well-known drug dealer and gunrunner named Tony. Although Zen and I had nothing to do with the theft of the Audi, we would be caught in the middle when the guy came to claim either his car or somebody's life.

It was straight out of the wild, wild west. Just after dark one night, Zen, Frankie, and I were standing in front of the building and noticed that 196th Street was being virtually shut off from the rest of the Bronx. Two cars had parked at the end of the block, on Morris Avenue, so that they cut off 196th. Two more cars had done the same thing on Creston Avenue. Exiting the cars were a bunch of young tough guys holding a lot of big guns. The kind of shit one thinks only happens in the mov-ies. These guys were dead serious, and they were making sure no one escaped. Frankie managed to slip inside the building, where he lived in the basement apartment. Later, he told us that he had a shotgun ready to go by the window if they had started shooting. Zen had a little gun on him, I believe a .25 semiautomatic he carried because he could conceal it easily. On this night, he never even bothered trying to pull out the weapon, and I was just kind of standing there saying to myself, *Damn, these guys are good!*

I was frozen with fear before I realized who the guys were. I knew most of them. They were from Davidson Avenue over by Fordham Road, and I had bought guns from them, hung out with them, and was very close to a guy—also named Frankie—who ran with their crew. These guys didn't ask questions; they let their guns blaze and smacked up whatever witnesses were still breathing for information. I knew that Tony himself thought of me as one of the cool little niggas from around the way and that I'd helped make his partner J.R. some money. This is probably what saved our lives that night.

Tony walked up to within five steps from me and Zen with a big-ass gun in his hand and said, "Come here, little man."

"Yo, what's up, Tone, what's all this about, man?" I asked while trying not to let my voice shake.

"The only degenerate car thieves stupid enough to rob my shit would be you stupid-ass motherfuckers from Creston," said Tony in a heated voice.

I started to tell Tony I didn't know what he was talking about when he abruptly cut me off.

"Listen, man, if I didn't know some of you niggas and do business with a few of you, I would have already lit this block up. I'm gonna say this one time and one time only, so shut up and pay attention. If I don't have my motherfucking Audi back, with all my fucking music in it, I am going to come back here and kill anyone and everyone standing on this block."

Tony continued, "Your mother, your father, your brothers and cousins, your kids. Whoever is here when I come back is going to get hit. So tell whatever faggots stole my shit I want it back in a few days or they are going to see what I'm about."

All Zen and I could do was agree to pass the message along to the thieves who stole his Audi. To this day, I don't think Tony knew my brother was directly involved, but his partner Frankie was a well-known car thief in the Bronx. It wasn't hard to track him down to our neighborhood. Tony made it clear that if he didn't get his car back, there would be no talking when his guys returned. Needless to say, Tony got his car back, with his five-thousand-dollar stereo system still intact. I've never seen, and I hope to never see, another scene like that. These guys were good, and they set off a conversation that night between Zen and me that I would never forget, a conversation that gave new meaning to the phrase *here today, gone tomorrow.*

After the guys with guns cleared out of the neighborhood, Zen and I stood on the corner smoking a small joint. Zen was trying to teach me how to roll a joint, but I just didn't have the patience for it. When the weed began to take effect on me, I looked at Zen and joked that if Tony's boys had killed him, I would have taken all his jewelry and kept it. Zen had some very nice custom jewelry and it was good-quality gold, which always made his jewelry shine more than the ten-karat shit most of us bought on Fordham Road.

When I finished joking with Zen about taking his jewelry, he looked me dead in the eye and said, "If anything ever happens to me and you're around, please make sure my kids get my jewelry. It's the only thing I have to leave them and it belongs to them."

I will never forget those words. Barely three months after he shared those words with me, Zen was killed on Fordham Road—just a few minutes after I left him to go upstairs.

There are some things you can never forget, no matter how hard you try. Zen being killed was like that for me. I had grown to love this man like a brother. He protected me. He looked after me. And he respected my heart. He once told me that he didn't have a problem getting into a fight with me around because he knew I wouldn't run away. He was right; no matter what the odds were, I wouldn't leave my boys. In that respect, I was like Zen. It was from him that I learned never to leave a guy from my crew behind. Hearing Zen tell me he believed in me like that was very important to me. How could the most powerful guy in the neighborhood be dead? At the time I couldn't really grasp the reality of losing Zen.

The story would be told a million different ways a million different times. Muhammad, Sal's brother and another of the craziest Albanians in the neighborhood, had been there and told us what happened when Zen died. The guys were on their way to get something to eat on Fordham Road. They were pulling up to a red light on the corner of Webster Avenue and Fordham Road when Zen almost hit a guy who was jaywalking. The guy banged on the hood of the car and began cursing at Zen, Muhammad, and one of the neighborhood girls, who was sitting in the front passenger seat. He then approached the passenger-side window and spit on the girl. Zen and Muhammad got out of the car. The pedestrian pulled out a butterfly knife and plunged it into Zen's chest. The knife hit very close to Zen's heart, and it didn't take long for him to die from the internal bleeding.

Zen was the biggest, strongest, most respected member of the Creston Posse, yet a puny little Fordham University prep student killed him as if it was nothing. Zen had survived untold numbers of battles with some of the toughest crews in the Bronx. All it took was a blade held by a small hand to kill the most feared member of our crew. I was in a daze when I heard. More important, my heart was truly broken. Zen, who had stopped a guy from plunging a blade into my own chest a few years earlier, had died in just that way. I lost one of my closest friends that night, and I would never get over Zen's death. In some ways, it scarred me for life, and it erased what little innocence I had left in my seventeen-year-old heart.

In the days leading up to the funeral, I replayed our last conversations in my head, like an endless loop. No conversation stood out as much as the one we had shared about the jewelry. To this day, I will not joke about death or even talk about it out loud because Zen was killed shortly after our conversation. I felt like I had jinxed him by discussing his death, and that feeling stayed with me for a very long time. I remember the day of the funeral as if it were yesterday, and I remember the Albanian guys telling us not to cry over the corpse. Albanians believe that if you cry over a body, the dead person will spend eternity filled with sadness. I wanted to make sure I didn't have anything to do with Zen spending his eternity that way.

It was very hard for me to see his son yelling, "Daddy, wake up. Wake up, Daddy!"

I refused to go up to his corpse to say goodbye. I was afraid of letting a tear slip down my cheek and onto his face. Eventually, I found the strength to walk up to the casket and kiss Zen goodbye, one of the hardest things I've ever done. I can still feel how cold his head was when I kissed him goodbye. He was the first guy from our crew to be murdered. The terrible thing was that Zen was living on the straight and narrow path. He worked two jobs, took care of his family, and would only stop by the neighborhood to see his friends late at night, after his family had gone to bed. He was twenty-six years old, almost a full ten years older than me.

To this day, if you ever walk down 196th Street and Jerome Avenue, there is a testament of just how powerful Zen was. Nearly twenty years later, his memorial graffiti piece is still on the wall untouched. It is almost unheard-of in the Bronx for a memorial piece to last this long. The piece has been redone a few times, but his name is still on the wall even though there are new guys running the block. This is a huge statement to the power and respect Zen's name has retained throughout all these years.

The Fordham prep student who killed Zen was never convicted of the crime. *New York Newsday* made it seem like Zen was a bully deserving of death. This was my first lesson in not believing everything you hear or read in the media. The media didn't know that Zen had cleaned his life up and was working two jobs to take care of his family. They didn't know that he took care of every person he ever met. They didn't care to find out. The more dramatic story was that a Fordham prep student defended himself against a big, bad street thug and that the murder was justifiable homicide. No need to investigate the student who was tough enough to hit the hood of a car, spit on a girl, and then plunge a butterfly knife into a man's chest.

I will always remember the good times I was able to spend with Zen. I will remember the life lessons he taught me, as well as his heart, and I will always remember him as a great man. If Zen taught me anything, he taught me how to have undying loyalty for my friends—how to face my fears and stare them down when it came to backing those I ran the streets with. Zen never ran from a challenge, no matter what the consequence, and there would be many times in my life when I'd have to take a deep breath and say to God, "God, if you don't get me out of this, I understand. Just take me with you when these guys are done with us and let me have the strength not to turn and run from my boys who need me right now."

It didn't really matter at the end of the day if you lost the fight as long as you didn't run. Losing a fight was something you could get over immediately, but running from a fight and leaving your boys behind was something you could *never* live down, and no one taught me that lesson better than Zen. Zen never got to see me become a man; that wouldn't come for another three years until after my daughter was born. But his character and the way he carried himself stayed with me to this day. And if I listen closely enough to those distant memories, I can still hear him laughing about all the stupid shit we did.

I can still hear him say, "Aye, little man, if I push you in that window, will you unlock the door for me?"

To the media he may have been a bad guy, but to the Creston Posse he will always be the Godfather Zen, the godfather of Creston Avenue.

REST IN PEACE, ZEN.

Zen graffiti memorial I did with Zef (RIP) on 196th Street.

NE SECONDS GONE IN FIFTY-NINE SECONDS GONE IN FIF
ECONDS GONE IN FIFTY-NINE SECONDS GONE IN FIFTY-NII
NDS GONE IN FIFTY-NINE SECONDS GONE IN FIFTY-NINE SE
ONE IN FIFTY-NINE SECONDS GONE IN FIFTY-NINE SECOND
FIFTY-NINE SECONDS GONE IN FIFTY-NINE SECONDS G
TY-NINE SECONDS GONE IN FIFTY-NINE SECONDS GONE I
NE SECONDS GONE IN FIFTY-NINE SECONDS GONE IN FIF
ECONDS GONE IN FIFTY-NINE SECONDS GONE IN FIFTY-NII
NDS GONE IN FIFTY-NINE SECONDS GONE IN FIFTY-NINE SE
ONE IN FIFTY-NINE SECONDS GONE IN FIFTY-NINE SECOND
FIFTY-NINE SECONDS GONE IN FIFTY-NINE SECONDS G
TY-NINE SECONDS GONE IN FIFTY-NINE SECONDS GONE I
NE SE   IE IN FIF
ECONE   FIFTY-NII
NDS G   .   -NINE SE

Gone in Fifty-nine Seconds

In 1986, one out of every 159 cars in the United States was stolen. In New York City, car thieves worked very hard to ensure that their reputation as some of the best in the world preceded them. Just one year later, in 1987, the Kingsbridge section of the Bronx would be introduced to one of the most talented car thieves in the history of New York. I know this because I had the pleasure of witnessing him at work, and he could literally steal a car as if he had the keys in his pocket.

His name was Frankie and his tales are the stuff legends are made of. The title of this story is a testament to the talent he had somehow managed to acquire in the streets. Frankie never saw a car he couldn't take. Alarms, chains, cutoff switches, the Club, removing the steering wheel from your car—these were merely slight challenges for him. If your rims caught his eye or your stereo system caught his ear, he was surely coming for the vehicle just as soon as the sun went down. At the time, I felt lucky to accompany him on some of these expeditions.

There were really only two ways to become part of our neighborhood crew if you were not born and raised in the neighborhood or one of the surrounding areas. The first was to be introduced into the crew, sort of the way the Mafia does it—"He's a friend of mine or a friend of ours." If someone vouched for you, it was usually a ticket into the crew. The second way was to move into the neighborhood: If you hung out with us for a while, you would become a part of the crew by association. Frankie's way in was to move into the basement apartment at 60 East 196th Street with his girlfriend, Jackie, and his craziness made him fast friends with the neighborhood tough guys. There is a saying in the street: "Game recognizes game." If being a criminal was the game, then Frankie would come to be recognized by the guys on Creston Avenue as a key player.

Frankie drove a 1987 Toyota Supra that was rust-colored. You could always hear Frankie coming home at 2 A.M., just as you might hear him after a long night of car thievery blasting his system at six in the morning. One morning, I looked out the window after hearing Frankie screaming; he was poking his speakers with a screwdriver and trying to rip them right out of the hatchback of his car. Not much technique involved, just brute force. He managed to pull a twelve-inch speaker out of the car and slam it on the ground.

That was when my brother and I yelled out the window, "Frankie, what the fuck are you doing?"

He yelled at us to go back to sleep and continued to scream at his car. We would later find out that Frankie was just tired of the sound coming out of the brand-new, state-of-the-art speakers, so he decided it was time to dispose of them. If he couldn't have them he didn't want anyone to have them, and this would prove to be Frankie's personality for as long as we knew him.

I cannot really put a date on when my brother and Frankie became fast friends, but I know it was sometime in late 1987. Will never really spent much time on 196th Street—he usually hung with our cousins on Bailey Avenue—so when he started hanging out on the block, I soon realized he was part of Frankie's car thief organization. One day Will would come home with a new system in his Mustang; a few days later he'd put new rims on the car. I knew he wasn't buying this stuff.

Soon enough, our bedroom became a storage space for all the stolen rims and car-stereo equipment my brother was collecting on these car-shopping trips. Ten years later my stepfather, Jesse, would say he knew we were a criminal enterprise the first day he walked into the house. However, with my mother working two jobs and having her own life, she paid little attention to the mini chop shop in her boys' bedroom. In her defense, even if she'd asked, we would have only lied and said the stereo systems and rims belonged to friends.

In the beginning, I lost a lot of sleep at night as I worried that my brother wouldn't come home after a car theft gone wrong. If a drug dealer didn't shoot one of them dead, I figured the NYPD would get their hands on Will and Frankie and put a stop to their criminal ways. It wasn't long, though, before I was asking to come along for the ride. At first they laughed off my request, but one night they needed me to be a lookout and they came calling. It was the night I realized that shit was fun.

It was a rainy night and it must have been close to 1 A.M. We used to do a call that sounded kind of like *whoo-a-whooop,* and we'd do it over and over to get guys to look out the window. We used this call if we were getting ready to go out for the night, if there was some type of problem in the neighborhood, or to just rally the guys if we were going to a public pool early in the morning. This was long before the days of cell phones being affordable, so I guess you could say this was our mass communication in the neighborhood. I must have been in a deep sleep, because I dreamed that someone was doing the "call" to get my attention.

When I finally awoke, I faintly heard "Yo, Ive" following the call.

When I looked out the window, my brother, Frankie, and Macho were standing outside, motioning for me to put on some clothes and come downstairs. Macho was a guy I'd met while working at a mobbed-up Top Video store in the Bronx. At the time, my mom was dating a guy who was either connected or a made guy, and he helped my mom get me a job at the video store. It was a front for the illegal numbers that were run in the back.

As I was racing to get dressed, my heart was beating a hundred miles a minute. I knew they weren't calling me down to play spades. I knew this was going to be an exciting night. In the back of my mind, I hoped we all came back home safe.

When I got to the stoop, they told me they were getting ready to rob the audio place—not just any audio place, but the one that had just opened up on the block. I was surprised, because Frankie not only stole for the guys who owned the shop, but he seemed to be close friends with them as well.

But that was just the way Frankie was. He would rob his mother for a dollar (although I never once heard Frankie say he even had a mother). I think he was raised in group homes or something like that, because he never once mentioned family. You could tell he had had an extremely hard life from his cold demeanor and the lack of loyalty he would come to show down the road.

Anyway, it didn't really matter to me who we were robbing. I wasn't there to ask questions. I was asked to be the lookout, and I was going to make damn sure I had my brother's back as well as the backs of Frankie and Macho. This was just the opportunity I had been waiting for—to get on Frankie's team—and I was going to do whatever it took to prove myself a valuable team player.

I stood in front of the audio place, trying like hell not to look nervous. My job was to wait for the guys to tap on the gate, letting me know they were ready to come out with another load of audio equipment. This must have gone on for two or three hours. Once the car could hold no more goods, we would unload it at a garage my brother rented across the street from our building on Creston Avenue, the same garage that held the rest-in-peace memorial for Zen, and go back for more.

Damn, I couldn't believe we were emptying out the entire shop.

On the last run, it was starting to get a little light outside. By the time I got comfortable with the lookout role, I was also getting a bit nervous about the sun coming up. Then, with little warning, a garbage truck rolled up from around the corner. I banged real light on the gate as I saw the truck in the distance.

Frankie lifted the gate and told everybody, "Let's go," but my brother was still inside and didn't seem to care that the garbage truck was getting close. It would take only seconds for the garbage truck to reach the front of the store and catch us in the act.

I finally stepped into the store and said, "Let's get the fuck out of here."

My brother was collecting grills, which were used for decorating around the speakers. They had emptied the entire store, and here was my rocket scientist of a brother risking all of us going to jail for some ten-dollar grills. By the time we were leaving the audio place, two garbagemen were walking right toward us, asking what the hell we were doing there. At that point, my brother and Frankie both started threatening them and throwing the speaker grills at them. To this day, I laugh about the fact that they actually began throwing the grills at the garbagemen. Here I was, scared out of my mind, while Frankie yelled at the garbagemen, telling them to mind their fucking business and daring them to call the cops. The garbageman ducked the grills and yelled at his partner to do just that.

To make our escape, we hopped into my brother's car—which was loaded with the last stock of audio equipment we had just swiped—and drove down Creston Avenue, headed toward 198th Street. Once we hit Jerome Avenue, we doubled back and argued about whether we could make it up 196th Street in time to stash the car in the garage prior to the cops showing up on the scene. We decided to go for it, and as we raced up 196th Street toward the middle of the block, Frankie hopped out and opened the garage door. We all jumped out of the car, shut the garage door, and ran up the stairs of the building just as the sound of

sirens grew louder. They seemed to be coming from the Grand Concourse, Creston, 196th Street, and Morris Avenue. I'm sure the cops
never knew they were probably twenty seconds away from bagging the
whole crew running up the stairs to enter the building. We spent hours
watching the cops from our fifth-floor window as they walked up and
down the block and even stood right in front of the very garage where
most of the stolen goods were stashed. Had they thought to open that
garage door, I might be writing this book from jail.

After I sold my share of the audio equipment, my payment for the
lookout job was two thousand dollars, but more important, I earned a
coveted spot on Frankie's team as well as the respect of my brother and
the neighborhood guys. At the time, I never had any regrets about this
robbery; after all, most of the stuff in that shop was stolen from somewhere else to begin with. The guys who owned the shop were bigger
crooks than we were. We were just thieves stealing from thieves.

Over the next two years, Frankie's reputation would grow and grow.
Eventually, people from all over the Bronx came to Frankie to steal shit
for them. This was good for business, but it was bad for the neighborhood. We always had drug dealers and other thugs rolling through,
looking for their cars after their shit was stolen. There was really only
one time when Frankie and my brother had no choice but to return a
stolen car, and that was Tony's Audi, when Tony came through 196th
Street and shut down the whole block wild-west style. And still, twenty
guys with guns would not be the scariest thing I'd experience dealing
with Frankie.

One night we were standing around and someone joked to Frankie
about stealing a limo. The problem was, Frankie never took a joke as
anything less than a challenge, so we were off a few minutes later en
route to stealing a limo. I remember driving around for about half an
hour, looking for a limo to steal, when we ended up around Westchester Avenue, where there were many nightclubs. Frankie spotted a limo
around the corner from a reggae club. I just knew we were about to be

fucking with a bunch of crazy Rastafarians again, and I wasn't happy about it. I got an uneasy feeling as Frankie told me to walk up to the corner and keep a lookout while he tried to hotwire it. This was one lookout job I wasn't excited about—these Jamaicans like to shoot at people. But like the good soldier I was, I headed to the corner to take up my post.

I could hear the limo's engine turn over once, twice, but it wasn't catching for some reason. As Frankie tried a few more times to start it, the Jamaicans started to walk toward the only little Puerto Rican sixteen-year-old standing on the corner of a very tough neighborhood. I stood my ground for a few seconds, as I still hoped Frankie could get the limo started so we could hop in and go, but as I turned the corner I watched Frankie take off like a bat out of hell—in the limo.

Damn, what a miscommunication this was. I had about half a city block's worth of head start on the eight Jamaicans, who were now running toward me as fast as they could. I knew that if I let them catch up, I'd be one dead Puerto Rican that night. When I turned the next corner, there was my guardian angel, Zef, on his Ducati motorcycle—telling me to hop on. Just like that, my life was spared again, and we were doing a hundred miles an hour, headed for the safety of the neighborhood.

When we reached the block, I had all these visions of telling Frankie what an asshole he was for leaving me behind to be killed. But soon we were all laughing, joking, and sitting in front of the building, playing with the TV and stereo in the limo. It was just another stupid thing that made us who we were—young, dumb, and fearless. At least I knew for sure that Frankie was fearless; I just did a good job of hiding my fear. But even with all the laughter, I felt that Frankie had betrayed me, and I understood where his true loyalties lay.

But then who the fuck was I anyway, that Frankie should feel some kind of loyalty to me? I was the littlest dude in the neighborhood, the youngest in the crew, and he was now one of the most respected and feared, so he didn't have to give a fuck about me. But then, neither did anyone else in the crew, and that didn't stop them from taking care of me. How could I expect Frankie to give a fuck about me, though, when he never gave a fuck about himself?

One night we were on Creston Avenue in the Fordham Road section of the Bronx. Frankie had been trying to steal this car with a monstrous sound system for weeks, but the kid had an alarm Frankie just couldn't get around. The problem for the owner was that Frankie didn't even want the car; he had heard the kid's sound system and was convinced he had some Harman Kardon amps in the trunk, which were very expensive and put out a real sharp, distinct sound. This night Frankie wouldn't take no for an answer, so he took a tire iron to the guy's hatchback windshield. In the dead of the night, there's no sound much louder than the crash of a tire iron going through the back windshield of a Toyota hatchback. Coupled with the blaring alarm, we had managed to wake the entire neighborhood up out of bed in two seconds.

As Frankie, my brother, and I all struggled to pull this huge, ridiculously heavy audio box out of the broken car window, apartment windows started flying open and people started yelling at us to get the fuck out of their neighborhood.

We just tuned them out and kept tugging at the bolted-down box until someone said, "I'm going to blow your fucking heads off!"

I was about a second away from running to the getaway car when Frankie shouted back, "If you had a gun you would have shot us already! Shut the fuck up and go back to bed!"

When we finally got the box free, my brother and I ran back to the car with this sixty-pound speaker box. I remember looking back and seeing Frankie throwing cassette tapes at the guy's window on the second floor of the building. He was yelling, "Get some better music. This shit sucks."

I will never forget thinking to myself, "This guy is really fucking crazy," and that perception I had of Frankie would never change.

One day, Frankie and Macho showed up in the neighborhood looking like modern-day rap stars. The gold chains they were wearing around their necks were monstrous gold cables. Their chains looked like they had been stolen right off the necks of LL Cool J or Biz Markie. They must have been five-thousand-dollar chains, and judging from the gaudiness of the pendants, I had a feeling they came straight off some poor drug dealer's neck. However, the story I would hear from Macho was unbelievable. Even after seeing Frankie do some of the craziest shit ever, this story took first place.

Apparently, Frankie and Macho were riding around doing everyday shit when they spotted two Jamaican drug dealers in the middle of the street around the Pelham Bay section of the Bronx. It was broad daylight, and the glare of the chains coupled with the light summer gear the Jamaicans were wearing made Frankie come to the conclusion that the dealers couldn't possibly have guns hiding under their clothing. Armed with only a tire iron and a pulley that Frankie used to pop ignitions when he couldn't bust the steering columns to steal cars, Frankie and Macho performed the very definition of a strong-arm robbery. Macho told me that Frankie hit the Jamaican guy a few times on the head with the pulley. The Jamaican guy told Frankie he could have the jewelry if he just stopped hitting him. So Frankie and Macho were now the owners of some very expensive jewelry. Although Frankie never displayed this type of violence in front of me, I always knew he had to have it in him to be so utterly ruthless in the car-theft game.

The end of my relationship with Frankie would come just as suddenly as the beginning. Shortly after Frankie stole the Audi belonging to Tony, the big drug dealer, and ended up having to return it, my brother told Frankie that my connection with those guys was most likely the reason they didn't come with guns blazing. P-Funk told Frankie that I had introduced these guys to the neighborhood as my gun connection, and Frankie took that to mean I must have more loyalty to Davidson Avenue than to my own neighborhood on Creston. Not only that, he thought I was some kind of rat. Frankie wondered how else they could have found out that he and my brother had stolen the Audi in the first place. He was too stupid to realize that everyone knew he was the only one with the skills, balls, and stupidity to pull off that type of theft.

The truth is, I didn't know Frankie and my brother had stolen that car until the shit came down, and I was just as pissed that they would bring the heat down on Creston Avenue like that. I knew J.R. and Tony through an acquaintance and I found them to be real cool cats. I was looking forward to rolling with some real rich drug dealers, and these guys were big in the gun-running game. I had hooked them up with people from Creston for quite a few gun sales and the relationship was strong. The bottom line was that I was upset that Frankie and my brother had flushed my opportunity to make money with these people down the toilet, but I would never have dreamed of going against my family, my boys, or my neighborhood. Therefore, what was done was done.

Frankie went so far as to grab me by the throat one night and accuse me in front of a bunch of guys I grew up with. I think Frankie forgot that I had been in this neighborhood all my life, and the guys quickly pulled Frankie off me and asked him what the fuck was wrong with him. I went upstairs and told my brother I was going to kill Frankie and that I didn't appreciate him calling me a rat or attacking me the way he did. My brother always came to my defense, and this time was no different; he went straight downstairs and told Frankie never to put his hands on me again. Frankie apologized to me and gave me a hug, but things between us were never the same after that. I couldn't trust him anymore and I saw him as an enemy, so I kept my distance.

Frankie's car-theft career would come to an abrupt end one day due to his uncontrollable violence. I heard the story from my cousins Herman and Johnny, who had joined Frankie's inner circle after being introduced to him by my brother. Apparently, Frankie had some beef with some guys over money. When he went to collect, he was met with guns. Never being one to lose a battle, Frankie returned in a custom van he had stolen weeks earlier. He came back with a shotgun and his new fifteen-year-old sidekick. Frankie unloaded a few shots into the crowd. As soon as he was done shooting, he heard sirens and proceeded to take off.

The car chase went on for miles. Odds were on Frankie getting away from any police chase, as he had done so many times before. This time, the problem was that his heart overruled his street sense and he pulled over to let his sidekick out of the stolen van. I often wonder whether he would have done this for me during one of our many criminal outings. The answer is that I simply don't know. However, this day, Frankie decided to stop to let the kid out of the van. By the time he took off again, the police had bridged the gap and were closing in fast. Frankie ran right into a police roadblock and decided the van would be able to bust through.

After the van crashed through the police cars, it flipped onto its side and Frankie was trapped inside. Months later, from a jailhouse phone, Frankie would tell my cousins the story of the cops pulling him out of the van by his broken arm and beating the shit out of him. He said the cops were merciless with him as they cursed and pummeled him with fists, boots, and police-issue batons. Not only had Frankie just run a police roadblock and shot up a neighborhood with a shotgun, but the van he was driving belonged to a police sergeant. That most likely led to the ferocity of the beating.

I saw Frankie once after he did his three-and-a-half-year sentence and he was very cordial with me. We reminisced a little bit and talked about some of the good old days. We drove around with Frankie and my cousins in Frankie's freshly stolen customized van and we laughed a lot about all the capers we had pulled off in the past. When Frankie pulled up to my cousins' neighborhood, we exchanged "laters" as I stepped out of the van. I would never see Frankie again after that day. His story is one legends are made of. Through the years, I heard rumors of what he was up to or which jail he was in, or which funeral home he was in, for that matter. I don't really know whatever became of Frankie, but I know for sure he was one of the greatest car thieves to ever come through the Bronx.

Frankie and his gang were directly responsible for hundreds of stolen cars between 1987 and 1989. I was there to witness and even participate in many of those thefts. When Frankie laid eyes on your ride, it was sure to be gone in fifty-nine seconds or less. Even if you were a sergeant with the New York Police Department.

ROFIT THIEVERY DRUG PROFIT THIEVERY DRUG PROFIT T
RUG PROFIT THIEVERY DRUG PROFIT THIEVERY DRUG PROF
RY DRUG PROFIT THIEVERY DRUG PROFIT THIEVERY DRUG
HIEVERY DRUG PROFIT THIEVERY DRUG PROFIT THIEVEF
ROFIT THIEVERY DRUG PROFIT THIEVERY DRUG PROFIT T
RUG PROFIT THIEVERY DRUG PROFIT THIEVERY DRUG PROF
RY DRUG PROFIT THIEVERY DRUG PROFIT THIEVERY DRUC
HIEVERY DRUG PROFIT THIEVERY DRUG PROFIT THIEVEF
ROFIT THIEVERY DRUG PROFIT THIEVERY DRUG PROFIT T
RUG PROFIT THIEVERY DRUG PROFIT THIEVERY DRUG PROF
RY DRUG PROFIT THIEVERY DRUG PROFIT THIEVERY DRUC
HIEVERY DRUG PROFIT THIEVERY DRUG PROFIT THIEVEF
ROFIT   PROFI
RY DRL   Y DRUC
HIEVER   THIEVEF

Drug Profit Thievery

The sales of narcotics in inner-city neighborhoods has made a lot of young men and women rich. It is the hood's version of the American Dream. Two of the neighborhoods I called home for twenty-one years—Creston Avenue and Bailey Avenue—were no different. But there were differences in the way the guys from these neighborhoods went about profiting from the illegal drug trade. Some folks chose to distribute illegal drugs on the street corners and others chose to make the money overnight by robbing the drug dealers of their profits. Either way, there was a shitload of money to be made.

   This story revolves around the biggest payday I would ever witness in our neighborhood, and also the end of a few guys from our crew.

   I first met Toothless Rob when I was in grade school at Our Lady of Refuge School in the Bronx. Toothless Rob always looked like a bum. The kid's gear was always outdated and disheveled. His clothes never met an iron and always looked dirty. He wasn't an attractive guy, either, and he earned his nickname for a reason: He had quite a few teeth missing. I wouldn't consider Rob one of my closest friends growing up, but he was one of the extended crew, and I never had any problems with the guy. He wasn't a power player, but he was always around the neighborhood.

Then there was Angelo, who went by the nickname Cockzolio. I can't remember when I first met him; he just kind of appeared on Creston Avenue one day and became a part of the crew. He was a big guy and he liked to joke around a lot, not unlike the rest of us. We would stand on the corner of 198th and Creston for hours on end, or sit on the stoop and crack jokes all day when we weren't playing spades or blackjack for money on the hoods of cars. Cockzolio went to the same school of style as Toothless Rob. If Rob deserved to be sentenced to eight years for fashion crimes, Angelo would have been sentenced to life without possibility of parole, no questions asked. The guy weighed 250 pounds and wore neon spandex biker shorts and old tennis shoes. Cockzolio wasn't out to impress people.

Albanian Danny was brand-new on the block, and he only spent a very short time hanging out with us before the huge payday. Unlike Toothless Rob and Cockzolio, Albanian Danny looked good before the robbery, and he was flashy as hell. He showed up on the block driving a brand-new, metallic-blue Toyota Celica GT with a sunroof and a nice sound system. It was no Mercedes-Benz, but it was a brand-new ride; and at the time that was a significant status booster. The kid always dressed fresh to impress, and he wore expensive bulky jewelry. I can't say where he got the money to drive a nice ride and wear nice jewelry, but I would learn that he was all about his money and all about getting paid.

There was one other guy involved, but he wasn't from the neighborhood and I never learned his name. This ragtag bunch made up the unlikely robbery crew that would benefit from the riches of a $750,000 payday in one night. These guys were by no means major players in the neighborhood, but they would team up to rob one of the richest drug dealers in the Bronx. Timing is everything, and I've often wondered where my timing was on that night. Where the hell was I when they came looking for the fourth guy to help them carry the safe out of the stash house?

The robbery was planned by Cockzolio and the unknown associate after being tipped off by an inside man who knew how much cash the stash house was holding. At the last minute, Albanian Danny was brought in to monitor the drug dealers' habits. It was an around-the-clock job learning who was coming in and going out of the stash house, figuring out who lived in the house and who visited. The team had to be sure that when they walked into the stash house of one of the most powerful Dominican drug dealers in the Bronx, they weren't going to be surprised by a gun in their faces. I'm not sure how they managed to pull off this type of surveillance without arousing suspicion, but they managed to get it done.

I understand they scoped out the house for three months before the opportunity to make their move finally presented itself. And the entire time they were planning this robbery, they kept it very quiet to the rest of the neighborhood crew. There was going to be a lot of money made that night, but they didn't want to share it with the world. This was going to be their big payday, and the fewer people they had to divvy up the money with, the more profit for themselves. I remember thinking afterward what selfish bastards they were—all that money, but not enough to share with their boys in the neighborhood.

In addition to the profit issue, the drug dealer they were robbing was a very close associate of our friendly neighborhood drug dealer, P-Funk. Had P gotten ahold of the news that this robbery was being planned, he might have tried to intervene. You can't mess with people's money that way, especially that type of money and those types of violent people.

It rained very hard the night of the break-in, which was perfect for the robbery crew. Under the cloak of rain and the noise that the rain makes, you are much less likely to run into people in the street. All criminals love to commit their crimes on rainy days. Our crews were no different.

After somehow discovering that the stash house was going to be vacant that night, the three guys sprang into action and put their months of planning to work. It was time to get an inside look at the house they had been watching for so long from the outside. Their lives would never be the same when they entered through a back door, but I'm sure they had no idea just how much their lives would change.

The story told to me by Cockzolio himself was that they entered a darkened two-story house that had four bedrooms and numerous other rooms. They had absolutely no clue where the money was hidden, but they knew for a fact that this was the Dominican's main stash house. That's all they needed to know, and armed with that information, they were not leaving until the money was found or they were forced out. They rummaged through the house for more than two hours; at one point they were even planning on giving up and leaving the house empty-handed. The money was hidden so well they had no hope of ever finding it.

On their way out of one of the bedrooms, one of them flipped a bed upside down in anger. There was money taped underneath the box spring—a great deal of money. After they discovered the money under the box spring, they looked a little closer at a closet in the same room and noticed a small lump in the carpet. When they ripped the carpet up, it exposed a small trapdoor and a safe. The safe was what they were searching for, but they didn't have the tools to remove it. After loading the money under the box spring—estimated at one hundred thousand dollars—into garbage bags, the guys hit the road. When they got back to Cockzolio's apartment, they thought there had to be a way to go back and get the safe. This is where Toothless Rob would benefit—at least in the short term.

Toothless Rob happened to be in front of his building when Albanian Danny and Cockzolio came walking out with crowbars. They told Rob that if he didn't help them out they were going to beat the shit out of him. Toothless Rob was frightened of helping out, but he was probably more scared of getting his ass kicked by the neighborhood guys, so he grudgingly agreed to take part in removing the safe from the stash house. The crew drove back to the house and scoped things out for a little while to be sure no one had returned. When the coast was clear, they went back in and got to work ripping the safe out of the floor in the closet. It didn't take them long to rip that floor to shreds and lift the safe out.

When the safe was cracked open early the next morning, they would discover more money than anyone in my neighborhood had ever seen. They had taken part in the biggest drug-money heist we had ever heard of, and they had done it with no violence and, more important, no witnesses. I'd never seen $10,000 in cash, much less $750,000 in cash, but I can imagine what was going on in their heads as they counted the money. We were a bunch of welfare kids who made money on the streets any way we could. It had to be a dream come true.

After the money was divvied up, each one got between $175,000 and $190,000. I'm not sure how long it had taken the drug dealer to make three quarters of a million dollars, but I know it only took the crew four hours to take it all away. With the exception of Albanian Danny, who always looked nice, these guys just went from bums to made men, or as Notorious B.I.G. once said, they went from "ashy to classy" overnight.

At the time of the robbery, I was spending a great deal of time with my girlfriend, Lori, down by Bailey Avenue, so I wasn't on the block. I missed the most exciting part of what happened next.

Apparently, Cockzolio had seen one too many commercials and when somebody asked him, "Cockzolio, you've just stolen three quarters of a million dollars from a drug lord. What are you going to do next?" the only thing Cockzolio could reply was, "I'm going to Disney World!"

I'm not sure the question was actually asked, but the truth of the matter was that Cockzolio *did* go to Disney World. And he took about eight guys from Creston Avenue with him in—you guessed it—his brand-new Mercedes 190e and drop-top BMW 325i. The Creston Posse, straight from the streets of the Bronx, many of whom had never left the neighborhood, were headed to Disney World, and they were going to enjoy every minute of the free ride.

Cockzolio didn't buy only one car immediately after the robbery, he bought three. He also bought my good friend Zef a Ducati motorcycle—the most gorgeous motorcycle I've ever laid eyes on. That was the same Ducati Zef used to save my life the night I was being chased for stealing a limo outside the Jamaican club.

And me? For years to come, I had to listen to the stories about how much fun my boys had in Disney World and how much money they spent and threw around on that trip. My timing had been off, and I was probably arguing with my girlfriend while these guys were living the life and enjoying the fruits of the big drug-money heist.

Money changed many things for Cockzolio, but certainly not one thing—he never learned how to dress any better. He would wear a Rolex watch and a ten-thousand-dollar diamond ring with the same neon spandex biker shorts. I guess it didn't matter anymore. The guy had some beautiful jewelry and some beautiful cars and the women would ignore the rest, although I'm not sure why.

Albanian Danny left immediately after the robbery and I never saw him again, although recently I've heard rumors that he has been seen back on the block. My understanding was that Albanian Danny moved back to Albania, where the exchange rate for the U.S. dollar was eight to one. If you do the math, this means he took his $175,000 dollars out of the country and became an instant millionaire when he touched down in his motherland. Every now and then, he would send a post-card with no return address to say, "What's up, fellas?" Albanian Danny was the smartest one in the robbery crew. By leaving immediately, he managed to keep his life. I heard he went on to purchase a lot of property in Albania.

If you have been adding up the items purchased by the rocket scientist known as Cockzolio, you will no doubt understand that he spent his share of the profits pretty damn quickly. Purchasing three $40,000 vehicles and a $15,000 motorcycle had him at $135,000. With the purchase of the Rolex and diamond ring, he was quickly closing in on his original bum status, and with the $20,000 trip to Florida, he was really asking to be back on the block, broke and sitting in his expensive cars with no money for gasoline. This is pretty close to what actually happened, too. But I will get back to Cockzolio's demise a little later.

"I Got It Made" was a rap song by Special Ed that was popular around the time of this drug money heist. The song spoke about having enough money to buy an island in Tahiti and anything else Special Ed desired. Toothless Rob made that his theme song, and you could hear the song from four blocks away before you ever saw his "Batman" Corvette come driving up the street. It was a $60,000 candy-apple-red, custom-designed Corvette convertible with a system that would blow your eardrums out even if you weren't sitting inside the car. The reason we called it the Batman Corvette was that it had these futuristic side skirts on it and a huge Batman wing on the back that made it look like it could fly. Both sides of the car had chrome siding, and written on the chrome were the words ABOVE THE LAW. Toothless Rob had truly made it to the big time and he wanted the Bronx to know.

The Creston Posse didn't lie low with the money. If you drove through 196th Street and Creston, you would see two hundred thousand dollars' worth of exotic cars and a Ducati motorcycle straight from Italy.

Hmmm . . . I wonder who stole my money?

Legend has it that Toothless Rob was the first to get snatched up by the drug dealer.

Toothless Rob must have told a pretty convincing story—how he was just a bagman and was only used to help carry the safe out of the stash house and wasn't involved in the actual planning of the robbery and how sorry he was. These are all my assumptions, of course. I wasn't there. However, word on the street a few years later was that Toothless Rob had agreed to set up Cockzolio and the silent partner no one knew about in exchange for his life.

Why the hell not?

Sammy the Bull made a similar deal to give up John Gotti in exchange for his life. However, there *would* be a problem with Toothless Rob's master plan, and he would have to answer for that.

Cockzolio ended up sitting on the block in his exotic cars with no money for gas, just as predicted. But he damn sure knew what time it was, since he still had the Rolex to tell him that. It was time to find the next drug dealer to rob. After all, it was so easy and the payday was ridiculously lucrative. But there was a problem. He wanted to get paid fast, and he didn't want to watch another stash house for months. That lack of planning and patience would be Cockzolio's downfall. And when I say downfall, I mean he fell as hard as he possibly could.

Cockzolio and his new team decided to pull off a strong-arm robbery. Cockzolio's brother, who was an NYPD officer at the time, outfitted them with bulletproof vests, weapons, and shirts that read NYPD in bold letters. They had what they needed to rob the next stash house without having to do it when no one was home. The plan was to pretend it was a drug bust, and once inside they would take the money and run. The problem was the drug dealers realized the bust was fake, and one of the guys jumped out of a four-story window to escape the robbery. He crawled to a passing vehicle in the street to summon help and the real cops arrived shortly thereafter.

The front page of the New York *Daily News* read FAKE COPS IN REAL BUST, and Cockzolio was on the cover, wearing a long black trench coat and handcuffs. Here was a guy who had just made almost two hundred thousand dollars less than six months before, and now he was headed to jail—thirty years to life. The charges included robbery and the rape of one of the victims in the apartment that day, as well as impersonating a police officer and a host of other offenses. I guess you could say what goes around comes around.

It didn't take a genius to figure out that with Albanian Danny far removed from the neighborhood and Cockzolio on his way to the penitentiary for a very long time, it would be almost impossible for Toothless Rob to make good on his promise to deliver the culprits to the Dominican drug dealer.

A short time after Cockzolio's bust by the NYPD, Toothless Rob was sitting in a restaurant having lunch. Two masked men walked into the restaurant and shot him nine times. Rob didn't survive the hit, and although it isn't known if the Dominican drug dealer was involved in Rob's murder, the fact is that Rob had become the victim of the same type of setup he was trying to pull off on Cockzolio. Just as in the song, Toothless Rob truly did "have it made," but he only managed to live on top of the world for a short time. Rob was the first guy to drive a Lotus through Kingsbridge Road, years before hip-hop stars made enough money to drive those types of imports. I can't imagine Rob saying it was worth losing his life for.

Cockzolio would go on to escape from the penitentiary, but he was caught and eventually sentenced to an additional thirty years to life, to run consecutively with his first sentence. He might see daylight if he lives to be eighty-five years old, and I'm sure he will still be scheming to get rich quick when he gets out. I wonder if he would say the crimes he committed paid off?

My brother in-law, Jorge, recalls a conversation he later had with P-Funk about how the Dominican drug lord felt about losing his ill-gotten gains. He told P-Funk, "Those bastards took all the vacation money I was saving for the summer."

I wonder if he was planning a trip to Disney World. The poor little drug dealer lost three quarters of a million dollars of vacation money.

I guess my timing was good after all. Had I not been so busy arguing with Lori, I most likely would have been one of the guys called on
to remove the safe from the stash house. It would have been an offer I
would have gladly accepted at the time, though it would've sucked to
collect the nine bullets that would come as a result.

REST IN PEACE, BOB.

Rooftop behind Kingsbridge Road.

HAT YOU LOOKING AT? WHAT YOU LOOKING AT? WHAT YOU
G AT? WHAT YOU LOOKING AT? WHAT YOU LOOKING AT
)U LOOKING AT? WHAT YOU LOOKING AT? WHAT YOU LOOK
HAT YOU LOOKING AT? WHAT YOU LOOKING AT? WHAT YOU
G AT? WHAT YOU LOOKING AT? WHAT YOU LOOKING AT
)U LOOKING AT? WHAT YOU LOOKING AT? WHAT YOU L
? WHAT YOU LOOKING AT? WHAT YOU LOOKING AT? WH
)OKING AT? WHAT YOU LOOKING AT? WHAT YOU LOOK
HAT YOU LOOKING AT? WHAT YOU LOOKING AT? WHAT YOU
G AT? WHAT YOU LOOKING AT? WHAT YOU LOOKING AT
)U LOOKING AT? WHAT YOU LOOKING AT? WHAT YOU LOOK
HAT YOU LOOKING AT? WHAT YOU LOOKING AT? WHAT YOU
G AT?   KING AT
)U LO   YOU L
? WH/   AT? WH

What You Looking At?

The New York City Police Department should keep statistics on how many people have been beaten, robbed, stabbed, shot, or killed over these very dangerous four words: *What you looking at?*

In Kingsbridge, when someone looks you in the eye and says, "What you looking at?" or "What the *fuck* are you looking at?" it's a modern-day challenge to a street duel.

I cannot even begin to count the number of times I used these very words when dealing with people in the streets, cars driving by the block, or other crews when I was young. These words were etched into my brain like my name, address, and phone number. I would throw the question at anybody who decided they wanted to get into a staring match with me—anywhere, anyplace, and anytime. When I think about it now, I'm surprised these words didn't cost me more blood, or my life. They did eventually end up costing me a great deal.

My sophomore year in Sacred Heart High School in Yonkers, New York, was sure to be tough. I had spent the summer ditching summer school. I had never gone to summer school in my life, and I wasn't thrilled about having to make the two-hour trek each day to Iona College to take a course in—of all things—*religion*. After spending my entire nine years of schooling in Catholic school, my dumb ass had failed Religion in ninth grade. I guess I should have explained to the nuns in the school that God wasn't a very popular figure in my neighborhood. Because I had only made it to three summer-school sessions, I was going to have to take the same class in high school again, but I was going to have some explaining to do to the school officials at Sacred Heart.

I would be enrolled in all tenth-grade courses, except for ninth-grade religion, and I would have to find a way to finish tenth-grade religion by the time the school year was over. This left me with a real chip on my shoulder and only deepened my hate for school and magnified my love for the streets. Around this time, I wasn't trying to stay in school any longer, but dropping out wasn't an option. My mother worked hard to put us through Catholic school, and years later I would find out that my uncle Joey, a prominent attorney in Queens, helped my mother with the tuition. Joey would eventually find himself on very hard times due to his cocaine addiction and was later convicted on money-laundering charges. I guess even the most educated in my family found ways to fuck things up.

The bus stop to get to Sacred Heart High School was underneath the number 1 train on 231st Street and Broadway. It was the bus stop where I'd already been involved in two fistfights, most likely for my "What are you looking at?" attitude.

The first time, my ex-girlfriend's new boyfriend came walking by one morning and just started throwing blows out of nowhere. His street name was Sonic, and we had a real hate-hate relationship. He was already a full-time street thug and had probably just come from hanging out all night. He must have had a rough night, because he came at me like a rabid dog. It was six-thirty in the morning and I was definitely caught off guard. Because of the sneak attack, I got my ass kicked pretty thoroughly that morning, or maybe the guy was just that much better at fighting than I was—a real strong possibility.

While I tried in vain to fight Sonic off, my brother fought with one of his homeboys. The guy with Sonic was much bigger than my brother, but my brother was doing a pretty good job of not getting his ass kicked as badly as I was. I recall getting on the bus and calling all of my schoolmates punks for not coming to our defense. I would have thought a few of the guys would have come to our aid that day, but for whatever reason they chose not to. Maybe it was just too damn early in the morning to fight.

The second I returned home from school that day, I put in a phone call to my cousins and told them what happened. My cousin Herman went right after Sonic and his partner, who was named Ivan too. He found them walking by the handball courts in the Marble Hill projects, where he lived. And he didn't even bother to wait for me to show up to let me get my blows in. I later heard that Herman grabbed one of our boys, Victor, who was great with his hands, and told him they were going after Sonic and Ivan. When they caught up to Sonic and his boy, Herman and Victor beat them viciously. Herman pounded on the bigger guy, Ivan, who had fought my brother at the bus stop, and Victor smashed Sonic's head into the mailbox. All the while, Herman was screaming, "If you ever fuck with my cousin again, I'll kill you."

I never had any problems out of those guys again. I later found out my ex-girlfriend, Isabel, had dated both of us at the same time. I had started dating Isabel in the seventh grade, after we met at a mutual friend's sweet sixteen party. Even though at the time it seemed like we lived on opposite ends of the Bronx, we still managed to have a nice on-again, off-again relationship leading up to high school. She would be the last girl I would date before getting serious with Lori. Her two-timing was partially the reason Sonic came after me that morning.

That bus stop was always bad fucking luck for me, and one chilly morning in November would be no different. I was standing there with a few friends when the first school bus pulled up. The first bus always held freshmen and the less popular students, so it wasn't a bus I ever rode. I was standing right by the door when it opened, and a young Dominican kid and I locked eyes. The kid wouldn't turn his face.

"What the fuck are you looking at?" I asked.

The kid started talking all sorts of shit and I tried to board the bus to kick his ass right on it, or to pull him off. But the bus driver told me to step down and drove off. The kid and I yelled at each other that we would settle things at school.

By the time I arrived that morning, I was all pumped up—ready to find this kid and pound him into the holy ground of Sacred Heart High School. I was surprised to hear that a fight had already broken out involving the kid, two of his cousins, and my brother, Bill, who was by himself.

I grabbed the small hammer I used to carry in my book bag and ran as fast as I could to where my brother was fighting all three of the Dominican kids.

I approached the hallway and could hear the commotion. I couldn't believe two of my friends, Joey and José, were fighting my brother. Now I'd have to fight my friends over a situation that probably could have been settled had I only known the freshman on the bus was their cousin. They were swinging wildly at my brother and he was fighting José straight up. I turned the kid from the bus around with a hit to the side of his head from my miniature hammer. He went down quickly. I was going down after him when Joey came between us. The school officials ran toward us and we all took off in different directions. I dumped the hammer a few hallways down.

Half an hour later, I was called out of my classroom and summoned to the dean's office. When I walked in, everybody involved in the fight was already there. What was supposed to be a discussion on how to resolve our differences quickly turned into a "This isn't over" threatening match among all of us. The school officials had to move us into separate rooms, and we were then called in alone. When it was my turn, the dean asked what my role was in the situation. I told him what had happened at the bus stop and that when I got to school some girls told me my brother was in a fight. I was protecting my brother. The dean asked me if that was it. I told him it was. He then told me that they had over twenty witnesses that placed the hammer, which was now on his desk, in my hands. I could be permanently removed from the school for using a weapon during a fight.

My brother and I were both suspended for a week while the officials decided what the next step would be. Because Joey, José, and their cousin were bloodied, they were made out to be the victims.

After my one week's suspension, I learned I wouldn't be thrown out. Instead, I was put on strict probation. The smallest incident would get me kicked out of school for good. When I returned to class that day, José and I looked at each other. I told him I was sorry and that I didn't know the kid was his cousin, but he told me that my brother had no right and that it wasn't over.

Before he finished his last sentence, I walked over to his desk and swung at him, connecting on quite a few blows and knocking him out of the chair. After we were pulled apart, I immediately knew my education at Sacred Heart High School was over. I was free.

A few days later, Joey showed up in my neighborhood with about three carloads full of goons, looking to carry out their form of street justice. I was standing in a bodega with my ex-girlfriend Isabel. They entered the store one by one with baseball bats.

I was petrified that I was about to have my skull bashed in with a baseball bat, and I was defenseless against a car full of guys. I never made a habit of being cornered, but these motherfuckers had me cornered in the store and there was simply no escape. I thought I was about to get the beating of my young life and I really didn't see any way out.

There was a big guy in the store named Boobie, who was a karate champion and a well-known fighter in the Marble Hill projects. Boobie didn't know me, but he knew Isabel. Because she was crying and begging the guys to leave me alone, Boobie got involved. As the guys pushed me out the door and prepared to beat me to death, Boobie threw a karate kick at one of them and snatched the baseball bat right out of his hands, all in one move. God is my witness, the truth is that Boobie saved my ass that day. He pushed me behind him and stood in a karate stance, keeping the ten or so guys at bay. He calmly told them they'd have to come through him if they wanted to get at me.

Seizing the opportunity, I started talking all kinds of crazy shit.

"This shit ain't over, motherfuckers. I'm going to get you for this."

That's when I heard Joey say, "His brother works at Burger King a few blocks away. Let's get him."

With that, they were gone just as fast as they had come.

I told Isabel to call my cousins, who lived a few blocks away, and ran as fast as I could with Boobie to Burger King. By the time we got there, the cars were peeling off because the police were in the neighborhood. Ten minutes later, my cousins Herman and Johnny showed up with about fifteen guys. We ended up waiting hours for the guys to come back, but they never did. By the time I got home that night, Isabel called to tell me she had seen my cousins being handcuffed and put into a police car. I told her she had to be wrong. There had been no fight and there was no way Joey and his crew had come back after I left.

Soon as I hung up, I called Titi Vilma. I found out they really had been arrested for a fight.

After I left, another of my cousins, Bobby, had gotten into a staring match with some big white boy inside the Burger King. Once again, words were exchanged, and I bet the first words out of Bobby's mouth were "What the fuck you looking at?"

The white guy and two of his buddies squared off against Bobby, Herman, Johnny, and the other guys who came with them. The two groups exchanged blows. One of the white guys was trying to get away in his car when Johnny smashed his window with a baseball bat. This caused him to crash into a pillar underneath the 1 train. They pulled the white guy out of his car and continued to beat all three guys until the police from the 50th precinct showed up. Everyone involved was arrested. I'd left only a few minutes before.

I guess my cousins didn't have enough of an adventure with the big fight outside Burger King, because two days after that drama, we were on our way to Sacred Heart High School again looking for Joey, José, and his cousin. Just out of jail, my cousins were adamant about us finishing this thing off. They wanted to send a message to everyone that this type of shit wasn't going to fly in our family and we would always be the last to respond to any kind of conflict. Herman and Johnny knew no limits when it came to being crazier, more conniving, and more violent than anyone else in the streets. It is the reason they had such a solid "Do not fuck with these guys under any circumstances" reputation in such a large area, covering most of Kingsbridge. There were a lot of bad motherfuckers running around back in those days, but Herman and Johnny almost always proved to be the baddest of the bad. They always had to be the last crew standing, period.

As we pulled up to the school, we parked the car a few blocks away, facing the direction of the highway so we could make a clean and fast getaway. We then stood on the corner, hidden by the building, and waited for them to walk through the area that separated the school from the bus stop. I could feel my heart beating one hundred miles an hour. Not only were we getting ready to wage a war outside a Catholic school, but we were also in Yonkers, and everyone knew the reputation of the racist cops in Yonkers. If we were caught, we would surely be up shit creek without a paddle. The anxiety was killing me.

"There they are," I said to my crew.

I could see the fear in Joey's eyes as he realized he was now alone and looking at my five guys. He didn't have karate champion Boobie there to save his ass. When I think about it now, I feel bad. I know how afraid I was when his crew had me cornered.

Herman was the first to react. He set upon Joey like a wild animal. The first few punches spilled blood that completely covered Herman's yellow sweatshirt. He had broken Joey's nose with one of his first punches. When one of Joey's boys tried to intervene, Bobby and I began our own ass-whipping on the would-be savior.

After a few minutes of us beating these two guys into the ground, someone said, "Let's go," and we headed to the car and were on our way back to the safety of our block. We somehow managed to make a clean getaway, but we damn sure deserved to go to jail for what we did that day.

This was my last memory of Sacred Heart High School—really, my last memory of high school altogether. I bounced around in a few public schools after that, and very shortly thereafter I dropped out for good. I still remember it like it was yesterday, returning to Bailey Avenue that afternoon and joking about the serious beating we had just laid on Joey and some Good Samaritan trying to save his ass. But inside the guilt was killing me, and I felt terrible every time I looked at my cousin's yellow sweatshirt, completely covered in Joey's blood.

And then Herman snapped me back to reality.

"You're buying me a new sweater, motherfucker."

There was no room for a conscience in the streets. Only the strong survived, and if you felt you were tough enough to ask someone what the fuck they were looking at, you had better be tough enough to back that shit up. In our neighborhoods you kept your eyes in check, and if you didn't you had to deal with whatever came your way. That's just the way it was. It was an urban law ingrained deeply into our systems.

The media took to calling us animals, and in some sense of the word we *were* animals, trying to prove our dominance on the streets. A man can see any fear when he looks into another man's eyes. It's the reason you keep your eyes in check in our neighborhoods. To do otherwise is to challenge the next man's dominance.

This was our reality on an almost daily basis, and the reason eye contact was a bad idea in the Bronx.

Last MoRican with my cousins Herman and Johnny.

High-Fashion Heist

The only reason anyone in my crew ever got a legitimate job was to gain an in, because once you were in, your real job began. The real job was to figure out how to rob an establishment undetected. This was the mentality I had for many years, and I can remember casing quite a few locations where I worked—the Mafia-owned video store; the Target of our day, which was called Odd Lot; and the Burger King. I was never successful in trying to find a way into any of these places, although I came very close to figuring out Odd Lot. Moreover, I never came close to getting the codes to the alarms or the combinations to the safes. That is, until I started working at a Korean-owned clothing store on Kingsbridge Road named Vital Fashions.

My brother, Willie, had been offered a job at the fashionable clothing store, and he was ready to start the following Monday. That very same weekend, Willie decided it would be in his best interests to move his girlfriend, Tina, and his daughter, Meghan, to Virginia Beach, where my mother was living.

I was shocked, because my brother had been taking care of me, for the most part, after my mother fled the Bronx.

What the hell was I going to do to get by? How was I going to eat? My brother and my cousin paid the bills in apartment 5F at this time.

My brother told me about the job in the clothing store. He said that I should stop by the following Monday morning and tell them he was leaving the state. Maybe they would give me the job. It sounded easy enough. I followed his advice, went down the block to Vital Fashions, and got the job that morning.

There was a minor problem, however. I'd been hired only after I told them I could speak fluent Spanish. Though my brother wasn't fluent, he'd picked up much more than I had, since he mostly stayed with our *titi* Vilma down on Bailey Avenue. Here was a Puerto Rican kid from the Bronx who couldn't speak a lick of Spanish, but I wasn't going to let them know that. I had to eat and this was my only prospect, so I was going to have to hope I could play this one off.

The first few weeks were a cakewalk. I learned how to fold clothing nicely and hang things up. Things were going well, and once I got comfortable I started watching the old Korean man punch the alarm code into the system. I knew once I had the code there would always be a way to get in and rob the store after hours. I was growing up around some very talented career criminals on Creston Avenue and I was confident that with the codes they could get us inside.

One afternoon, I was sitting on a stool in the corner of the store and I heard the old man calling my name. With his thick Korean accent, the way he said it sounded more like "Iban." He needed me up front. As I walked closer to the front of the store, I could hear a man speaking in Spanish to his wife.

Oh, shit!

The jig was up and I was about to be found out. As I approached the couple, I knew enough to say: "No hablas ingles?"

The reply was, "Sí, un poquito."

I was thinking, *Okay, I have a little bit of Spanish here, and the wife has a little bit of English. This'll be a piece of cake.*

My plan was to drag the Spanish-speaking couple clear to the back of the store so the old man wouldn't hear my broken Spanish and wonder if he had been bamboozled.

"Ven conmigo."

I practically grabbed the woman's arm and dragged her to the back of the store. I think she wanted to buy her husband some dressier clothes, but those were in the front of the store by the old man, so I was going to have to put her husband in some AJ jeans and a nice rayon shirt with polka dots on it. I knew how to say *camisa* (shirt) and *pantalones* (pants), so I was doing okay.

The woman began speaking so quickly that I started to sweat, trying to make out at least every third word she said. Once I lost track of what the hell she was saying, I just started pointing at items and saying, "Sí?"

After a grueling exchange of broken Spanish and halting English, we finally got her husband an outfit and I got them up to the counter. Once again, the woman began talking rapidly, and I just replied, "Sí. Sí. Sí."

Once the couple left with their bags, the old man approached me and asked, "Iban, what happened to your Spanish? It sounded like you were having a really difficult time with the language."

I thought for a second and wondered if I was about to get fired.

Then I calmly replied, "It was the weirdest thing I ever heard. I think they were speaking some form of ancient Mexican dialect."

The old man asked, "Isn't all Spanish basically the same dialect?"

"No way," I told him. "There is Dominican, Mexican, Puerto Rican, and Colombian."

He thought for a second and said, "Oh, I think I understand."

That had been close, but I still had my job and I was still going to be able to case the joint. When the old man told me he understood, he probably meant he understood that he had been bamboozled. Maybe he felt sorry for me—a bad move on his part. He should have thrown my conniving ass out of his shop that very same day. It would have saved him a lot of heartache.

Most of the time, I just stood around outside the shop. It was a great place to meet girls, as the foot traffic on Kingsbridge Road provided plenty of opportunities. I met a beautiful young girl named Diana, whom I had seen in the area many times. She seemed to walk by the store often and make eyes at me more and more, even though I never thought I would have a shot with her.

Eventually I would begin having "relations" with Diana, and I really began to like her a great deal. She came by my apartment a few times to hang out. Early one afternoon, I was upstairs with my girlfriend at the time, Lori, and I heard Diana downstairs screaming my name. I tried to pretend that I didn't hear anything, but Lori kept asking me who the girl was downstairs calling my name. Finally, Lori jumped out of bed and ran downstairs to confront the girl. They argued and that was the last time I saw Diana.

I started to really enjoy working in the clothing store, and the Koreans began treating me like part of their family. They would buy me lunch almost every day, and when we worked late they would buy me dinner. This was huge to me, because I didn't make a lot of money, and there were many times when I went without eating much more than a slice of pizza a day. I was really starting to care about them, but I still had an inside job to do. I guess I have to say I cared about the payday a hell of a lot more than about them. I wasn't there to make friends and I wasn't there to make a career out of retail. I had to stay focused on the reason I took the job and remember that eventually this was going to be a nice payday for me if I was able to pull off the heist.

Being the youngest guy in the neighborhood really had no perks. I was always being beat up by the older guys when we'd try to work out in my building's small boxing gym. I was always being left behind when the guys went out clubbing. When they were fighting with grown men, I could barely contribute enough to get any kind of real respect from the older guys. I had earned a decent amount of respect from the guys over the years, but they were pulling off heists on a weekly basis and I was never invited to partake in the extracurricular activities that earned them all nice cars, flashy jewelry, and the latest gear. In order to be invited into *that* circle, I was going to have to prove that I too was capable of pulling off a heist on the next level.

I was always around when the little events took place—the petty crimes and the smaller fights—but this would be different. This was my heist, my plan, and my in. If I could pull this off, I would get respect and finally be in the position I wanted to be in.

The problem was that I couldn't get any of the older guys to take me seriously. Most thought I couldn't pull off the job, and the rest didn't see the value in robbing a store full of clothing and leather coats. The only guy who really believed in me at the time was Zef. For some reason, Zef had faith that we could pull off the heist and that it was worth his time and energy.

Zef was about four years older than I was. He had a great deal of respect on the block, and I pitched this robbery to him as if I were selling an idea for a start-up business. I was relentless in my pursuit for a partner in crime. If I could talk Zef into this job, I knew he would be the link I needed to help us get inside the store. Zef told me to work on the code and think about the best way to enter the store. He suggested I go to the back of the store and see if there was any way to enter through the roof, like an air-conditioning unit, or any other form of entry besides the front door. There was no way we were going to get in through the front. Even at two o'clock in the morning, police patrolled up and down Kingsbridge Road, and even if there were no police the traffic from passing cars would be too heavy for us to go in undetected.

With Zef's advice and backing, I had the confidence I needed to go through with the heist. I began spending a lot more time in the back of the store looking for the in, and one day a lightbulb went off in my head. I literally saw sunlight coming into the store from outside the building. When I moved a few boxes, I noticed a huge metal plate on the back wall, between the first floor and the roof. The plate had been welded to the back of the store, right on the brick of the small building.

Apparently, the clothing store had been hit before, and the best they could do to fix the hole in the wall was a metal plate with some rivets in it. I finally had the muscle and the in to the clothing store. It wouldn't be much longer before I put the last piece of the puzzle together, the code to the alarm. I would need the code to turn off the motion sensors that were on the first level of the store, where most of the clothing was located.

I had been watching the old man punch in the code a few times a week when I opened the store with him in the morning. Usually he left me outside with the gate halfway down, but after six months of me working there, he was taking me inside the store as soon as the gate came up.

4-5-0-9 . . . I couldn't believe my eyes as I watched the old man punch the code into the alarm-system panel. After all the planning, hoping, and dreaming, I was finally going to see my plan come to fruition. It had been months since I had mentioned anything to Zef, as Zen had been murdered in the meantime. It was a very down time for the boys on Creston Avenue. We had lost our leader, and we were at an emotional low in the neighborhood. When I saw Zef standing in front of the building that day, I could hardly conceal the oversize smile on my face.

Without me saying a word, Zef said, "You have the code, don't you?"

After going through the details and checking out the metal plate one night, we were positive we could knock it off the wall with a few strong guys and crowbars. The rest would be up to me. I was going to have to be the one to go inside and turn off the burglar alarm, not only because of my size but because this was *my job*.

Zef recruited Vincent and Cockzolio. Cockzolio had just finished pulling off the $750,000 robbery, yet there he was six months later, completely broke from blowing all of his profits. I never really liked the guy, nor did I trust him, but he was huge and I knew that he and Zef would be able to get that metal plate off the back of the store. The plan was in place, the muscle was in place; all we were doing was waiting for the right night to pull off the robbery—a rainy night. Once again, under the cloak of darkness and rain, we would be out in the Bronx trying hard to get paid while the rest of the city slept. It was time to do what we did best and what we enjoyed the most—robbing something.

I don't recall what night of the week it was, but we knew it was going to be a long, dark, rainy night. We got our tools together in my apartment on East 196th Street. We had our masks and gloves and two crowbars. I would only have sixty seconds to turn the alarm off. I had to come in on the second floor of the building, get down the staircase in the dark, and shut off the alarm. I was a nervous wreck, and I'm not sure how I kept from vomiting on myself.

One of the things I always loved about our neighborhoods in the Bronx was the way the alleyways would take you from one side of Creston Avenue to the other side of Morris Avenue. They would take you from 196th Street to Kingsbridge Road and everywhere in between. You could disappear in an alley on one side of Kingsbridge and not be seen for hours. It was an endless maze of escape routes, and we knew that maze as well as we knew the backs of our hands. We had been playing there since we were in the first grade, and the mazes had helped me escape everything from a beating from a rival crew to cops giving chase during the All Hallows' Wars. I always boasted that if I made it into the alleyway, there was no way a cop or anyone else could ever catch me. I was little, I was fast, and I knew exactly where to run and hide. One time the cops chased me into my building on Creston Avenue. I ran up to the roof, jumped onto the roof of the next building, took the elevator down, and ran through the alleyways all the way to Kingsbridge Road. Then I jumped in a taxicab and went to my cousin's neighborhood on Bailey Avenue until things cooled down.

An Albanian friend of ours named Mario lived in the building we needed access to for this heist. The building was actually owned by his dad. Mario's dad was a tough old Albanian with rumored connections to the Albanian mafia; he kept his building and the alleyway gates locked down tight to safeguard the building and its tenants. We needed to get through his alleyway to access the back of the clothing store undetected, and we could then spend as much time as we needed removing the metal plate from the back of the building. Zef managed to secure a key from Mario that gave us access to the alleyway, and we were on our way, with the rats running right by and right over our feet. I didn't even think about the rats, because I was nervous about being the first to enter and having to punch in the alarm code in sixty seconds or fewer, with hands that shook like I had Parkinson's disease.

We walked into the building on the intersection of Morris and Kingsbridge and climbed out the second-floor window and onto the adjoining roof of the Chinese restaurant. All of the store roofs on Kingsbridge were connected, so all we had to do was walk from roof to roof until reaching Vital Fashions.

It seemed to take forever for Zef and Cockzolio to remove the metal plate from the back of the store. They knocked at it as if they were mad at the world while Vincent and I looked up at the windows facing the alleyway. The noise was deafening and we needed to be sure no one looked out the window. It sounded as if someone was holding a bullhorn right next to the rivets as Zef and Cockzolio removed them one by one. Once the third rivet popped off, the metal plate swung around and hung by the last rivet. I had an entryway. It was time for me to go to work.

I was climbing into the hole when someone must have thought it would be funny to push the hell out of me. I went flying into the store and fell on a bunch of boxes. It probably took me twenty seconds to crawl out of the pile of crushed cardboard. After I regained my bearings, I finally made my way to the staircase.

The only light I had was the little bit of light coming into the store from the alleyway, so I felt my way around, trying not to break my neck on the stairs on my way down. I finally made my way to the panel of the alarm system and slowly entered the code. The second I saw the green LED read DISARM, I ran behind the counter and removed the video tape from the VCR that was hooked up to the camera monitoring the store. The only thing left to do was to empty the store.

I passed the VCR tape up to Zef and took off my beige Woolrich coat, putting on a brand-new black fur coat. Not only did I think the fur coat was the greatest coat in the store, I figured if I had to run I'd at least have a nice fur coat to show off. Looking back now, I probably should have taken the black leather trench coat. I would probably still wear that today with my business suits and ties. When Cockzolio was arrested a few months later after trying to rob a drug dealer, he was wearing a black leather trench coat from the heist that night. I still recall chuckling when I saw him on TV being brought out of the precinct handcuffed and wearing the trench coat.

Since I was the only person small enough to fit through the hole, I had to pass box after box out through it. I was carrying tons of boxes up the stairs and throwing them out of the hole to Zef, Vincent, and Cockzolio as fast as I could. The plan was for them to bag everything up in garbage bags, so we could throw them off the roof into the alleyway, and then bring the car up to the side of the alleyway and fill it up when the coast was clear. After more than an hour of doing this, I knew we must have hundreds and hundreds of clothes and jackets. The stuff in that store was nice—and very pricey. I was about to be the best-dressed person on Kingsbridge. The adrenaline rush was incredible. It's the power one feels getting something for nothing, when most of us never had anything to begin with.

All of a sudden it got very quiet, and I couldn't find anyone to pass anything to. I tried calling out to Zef, Vince, and Cockzolio, but there was no answer. I was also trying to be very quiet and I figured that maybe they were loading up a car.

After standing there for a few, I finally heard Zef say, "Get the fuck up here right now."

As soon as he said it, I threw myself through the hole like Superman. I remember looking back as I was jumping off the roof and seeing what seemed like hundreds of garbage bags full of clothing and coats still sitting on the roof of the store. I had been passing items up for close to two hours and most of them hadn't been moved much farther than the rooftop.

No time to think about that.

We could hear sirens everywhere, and it was a race against the clock to get back to our building, to our home base, to safety.

The most dangerous move we had to make was from the darkened alleyway of Mario's building to the corner of Creston Avenue, around the corner, and into the building on 196th Street. We waited until the sound of sirens died down and came out of the alleyway very slowly and very low to the ground, so that if we saw a cop car we could lie down and try to hide ourselves using the parked cars. We'd done this many times. As we turned the corner of Creston, we could see a cop car with no sirens on racing up 196th Street from Jerome Avenue. We lay down behind parked cars and after it passed us by, we got up and ran for the entrance of the building. I've never been so happy to see the lobby of my building as I was that night. We'd escaped. That was a good feeling. A feeling that soon turned to anger when I thought about the payoff.

"What the fuck happened?" was pretty much the first thing out of my mouth when we reached the lobby.

Zef said someone must have seen us on the roof and called the cops. Cockzolio had brought his police scanner along and he heard the call go out for "Robbery in progress on Kingsbridge Road," so they had no choice but to abandon everything we had emptied the store of.

"Everything is gone? We left everything behind? You have got to be fucking kidding me!" I shouted. The months of planning had been for nothing.

"Tell me you got one carload out of there," I asked them.

"We got nothing, man, we got nothing," Zef replied.

I thought I was in the middle of a bad dream. We got safely back to my apartment, and after about twenty minutes we went to the roof of Mario's building to watch the cops and see what was going on. After all the planning, all the dreaming I had put into my first big heist, we were now watching the cops remove everything from the roof. One by one, they threw the garbage bags down and loaded them into the police cars. I watched as all my dreams of owning ten closets full of designer clothing and leather and fur coats drove away. I'd wanted to share those clothes with the neighborhood guys. I wanted to give out leather coats as Christmas presents to my family members. And finally, I didn't even have my black fur coat. That's right: I'd taken off the fur coat in the store because I got so hot lifting all those boxes. And worst of all, I'd left my own beige Woolrich coat in the store.

"Fuck me! I left my coat in the store."

"You have got to be fucking kidding me," said Zef. "You left your damn coat in the store? Tell me you didn't have any ID in there." I definitely didn't have any ID in the coat, but the old Korean would know it was mine. I only wore it every day in the winter.

Zef told me to call in sick the next day and gave me one hundred dollars to go buy the same exact coat the next morning. He wanted me to show up to work the following day, wearing my coat and pretending I had no idea that the store had been robbed. It was genius, but there was no fucking way I was walking back into that store ever again so long as I lived.

A few years later, I would learn that Zef, Vincent, and Cockzolio had taken me for a ride. The youngest guy on the block, the one who made the heist possible, was still shown no respect. I heard through the grapevine that the leather trench coat wasn't the only thing Cockzolio came away with from the heist that night. They filled three carloads with garbage bags full of clothing and coats and then sold them to one of Cockzolio's contacts and split the money up among themselves. I never saw Cockzolio again after that night.

It didn't matter. The truth was, I didn't deserve anything from that robbery. I had no business robbing those hard-working Korean people, who made a living working sixteen-hour days, and I'm glad I didn't profit from the robbery.

Three years later, I was walking on Kingsbridge Road and went right past the store. I'd always avoided the store, but for some reason I'd forgotten about the robbery. The second I walked by the store, the old Korean man came running out, yelling, "Iban! You stay right here. You very bad man, Iban, very bad man. I call police on you, Iban. You rob my family."

I swear I could see his eyes welling up. I don't know if those tears were from anger or the hurt he felt at being robbed by someone he'd treated like family. Probably both. He went inside the store to call the cops and I made a mad dash for Morris Avenue and back to the safe haven of my neighborhood—one city block away.

He was right, I was a piece of shit, but it wasn't until I became a real man that I realized what I had done to him and his family. At the time, the neighborhood thugs felt exactly like Calogero in *A Bronx Tale,* when he tells his dad, "It's true what Sonny says. The working man is a sucker, Dad."

It would be years before I understood that the working man was no sucker and how great a sacrifice it is to wake up early every morning and work long, hard hours to give your children the life you felt they deserved.

Mr. Kim was right: We were all very bad men. This was one of the low points of my life, and I felt very sorry for what I did to that family after the way they had treated me. I'm just glad I didn't profit one red cent from my High-Fashion Heist. Who knows? I might still be looking for the next in.

And as for Zef, I loved him too much to care about his betrayal. It was just another lesson. A few years after I left the Bronx, I would learn during a phone conversation with my brother-in-law, Jorge, that Zef was murdered by a Jamaican guy—in the very same lobby where he and Zen had saved my life. I only wish I could have been there to help save his life the way he helped save mine.

ZEF . . . REST IN PEACE

Creston Avenue and Kingsbridge Road.

EIGHTS BEEF WITH THE HEAVYWEIGHTS BEEF WITH TH
AVYWEIGHTS BEEF WITH THE HEAVYWEIGHTS BEEF WIT
IE HEAVYWEIGHTS BEEF WITH THE HEAVYWEIGHTS BEF
ITH THE HEAVYWEIGHTS BEEF WITH THE HEAVYWEIGHT
EF WITH THE HEAVYWEIGHTS BEEF WITH THE HEAV
EIGHTS BEEF WITH THE HEAVYWEIGHTS BEEF WITH TH
AVYWEIGHTS BEEF WITH THE HEAVYWEIGHTS BEEF WIT
IE HEAVYWEIGHTS BEEF WITH THE HEAVYWEIGHTS BEF
ITH THE HEAVYWEIGHTS BEEF WITH THE HEAVYWEIGHT
EF WITH THE HEAVYWEIGHTS BEEF WITH THE HEAV
EIGHTS BEEF WITH THE HEAVYWEIGHTS BEEF WITH TH
AVYWEIGHTS BEEF WITH THE HEAVYWEIGHTS BEEF WIT
IE HE,   ITS BEI
ITH TH   WEIGH
EF W   E HEAV

Beef with the Heavyweights

In Kingsbridge, even fisticuffs between girls had a tendency to turn bloody as hell. Bronx girls could be brutal. And at ten years old I witnessed just that during a fight that took place between my female cousins and one of their female neighbors.

The fight took place at the corner of 196th Street and the Grand Concourse and involved my cousins, Lulu and Fufi, who were just barely in their early teens at the time. During the altercation, Lulu wrapped her dog's leash around her hand and proceeded to beat a girl in the head until the girl's face was covered in blood. To add insult to injury, Lulu's Chihuahua, Macho, proceeded to bite the girl as she was being beaten by Lulu and Fufi.

I don't know what that fight was about, but the girl on the receiving end of the beating that day learned a lifelong lesson—bring a weapon to your next brawl, even if it's just the family pet. The girls in the neighborhood could fight just as dirty as the boys and wouldn't hesitate to do so.

Shortly after the brawl, my cousins were relocated out of the Bronx by their dad, my uncle Cisco, to the safe haven of New London, Connecticut. It was the smartest decision my uncle would ever make in his lifetime. The girl fights in the Bronx would only get bloodier and bloodier as the years went on.

One of the worst girl fights I've seen took place several years later at the intersection of West Kingsbridge Road and Sedgwick Avenue between two girls from the neighborhood. What happened that fateful day wasn't just a fight between young teenage girls, it was a fight that would turn two neighborhoods against one another for close to two decades.

Tangie was a young Puerto Rican girl from Sedgwick Avenue with a hot temper who was dating the whitest thug in the neighborhood. The great white thug was known as Rich Buddha and he was one of the holdovers from the sixties and seventies, when Kingsbridge was awash in Italian and Irish immigrants who had migrated from lower Manhattan looking for a quieter place to call home. In the late eighties and early nineties, there were very few white boys left in what had become predominantly black and Latino communities surrounding Kingsbridge. You couldn't tell Rich Buddha to his face that he wasn't black or Latino, and the way he dressed, walked, and talked never gave us reason to question where his heart was at or how in touch with the streets he truly was. He was one of us.

My first impression of Rich Buddha was that he dressed real fly. He always had on the latest Timberland boots and matched them impeccably to his colored Champion hoodies. He sold weed out of his apartment and in front of his building, and his mom smoked weed with him—with us, too, for that matter. It was the first time I met a mom who actually got high with her son and his friends. It was obvious he got his name, Buddha, from the amount of weed he smoked and supplied to the neighborhood as "pharmacist." I liked him from the moment I met him, mostly for his unapologetic honesty and the way he carried himself with confidence. He was a real street cat and he was always real cool with me.

He would also be the reason many young lives were lost well before their time.

It was a warm afternoon and school was just breaking up. Earlier in the day, Tangie had gotten into a fight with a girl from her school named Lisa. The beef was over nothing more than two teenage girls not really feeling each other. And although Lisa might have thought the beef was over, Tangie had other plans when she caught up with her later in the day.

Tangie knew Lisa had to walk by Buddha's building to get home from school, so she tied her hair back, put Vaseline all over her face, and placed a box cutter in her back pocket. People knew it was on. Girls tied their hair up and put Vaseline on their faces to prevent whoever they were fighting from grabbing ahold of their hair or scarring them. This we saw all the time. What we hadn't seen was a teenage girl packing a box cutter.

Lisa walked up Suicide Hill and eventually made her way to the front of Rich Buddha's building, where Tangie confronted her. As the argument grew louder, Tangie and Lisa began to throw blows at each other. The fight took mere seconds to escalate into uncontrollable violence. To this day, only Buddha knows whether he was merely trying to break up the fight and pull Lisa off Tangie, or trying to help Tangie beat Lisa. But I know that what Buddha did that afternoon started a war to rival any the Bronx had ever seen.

Buddha pulled Lisa off Tangie, and while he was holding Lisa's hands behind her back, Tangie used the box cutter on both sides of Lisa's face. Tangie repeatedly slashed Lisa and blood began to gush from the freshly opened wounds. Over four hundred stitches were required to close the wounds and her beautiful face would be forever scarred.

At the time, Lisa was dating a young buck from Heath Avenue named Chino. Chino was no stranger to beef, as the crew on Heath Avenue, or the Heavyweights, as we called them, were making a name for themselves in the gun and drug business and never hesitated to pull out the pistols and shoot up a rival neighborhood. There was no way

Chino was going to let sleeping dogs lie and he was on the hunt for Rich Buddha, ready to bring down the gavel of street justice.

My introduction to the Heavyweights took place a few months before the fight between Tangie and Lisa. I just happened to be returning from the midnight shift at my job in Manhattan and had done some shopping before getting back to the Bronx. It was around eleven A.M. and several crewmembers were hanging out on the block, including my cousin Herman and one of my closest friends at the time, Rico.

We were standing on the stoop snapping on one another, joking about one another's clothes, mothers, and hairstyles, like we always did to kill time. That's when we noticed someone being chased right toward us. Although most of us were thugs at some level, we never let anyone get beat up in our neighborhood unless it was us doing the beating. When the person being chased got close, we grabbed and pulled him behind us, and when the people chasing him reached us we looked at them and asked what the problem was. That immediately sent them in the other direction. At the time, we had no way of knowing that the guy we protected was the little brother of one of the drug dealers from Heath Avenue. When I realized this, I knew we'd done a good thing. There was a chance that Bailey Avenue and Heath Avenue—two of the most powerful and violent neighborhoods in the area—would be unified. We had rescued a member of a rival clique and I was sure it would benefit us in the end.

The guy was named Lent, and he told us that this was the second time these kids had chased him and that he planned on catching up with them after school broke that afternoon. We decided to join in the fun and told Lent we had his back; we would roll with a few members of the Heavyweights to the school to hand out a couple of beatings to his enemies. Five guys from Heath Avenue and five guys from Bailey Avenue loaded into two cars and headed for the other side of the Bronx to dole out a little payback. This time we'd be the ones doing the chasing.

Mount St. Michael Academy was a Catholic high school for boys located on Murdock Avenue. There is a misconception that Catholic school kids are goody-two-shoes types, but I can tell you that many thugs put in their time at different Catholic schools across the city. I spent ten and a half years in Catholic school and, aside from not being able to cut school very easily, there was nothing goody-two-shoes about us. I may not have turned out to be the toughest kid in the Bronx, but I went to Catholic school with boys who became cold-blooded killers and some of the biggest drug dealers and gunrunners New York has ever seen. Trust when I say we learned that God would forgive any sin with eight Our Fathers and eight Hail Marys.

When we arrived at Mount St. Michael Academy, we parked the cars a few blocks away and talked about a quick getaway. Besides high school security, there were always cops close by just in case anything happened. My hands began to shake a little as I waited for Lent to point out the people that he was having a beef with. I was never one to throw the first punch, but for some reason, on this particular day I was itching to hit someone and hit him hard. As hundreds of high school kids poured out of school, we watched them walk by ten at a time until I finally heard Lent say, "There they are."

When I looked up, I saw two Puerto Rican guys walk out side by side. One was short, the other tall. I looked back at Lent and then at the two people in front of me, saying, "Are you sure this is them?" The second Lent said yes, I turned toward the taller guy and threw a punch with everything I had in my short, 120-pound frame. I've never forgotten the punch I threw that day, because it was the first and only time I've ever knocked someone down with just one punch. I'm not sure if I hit the guy square on the jaw or caught his nose, but he went down like a ton of bricks. I felt someone getting close to me and I turned my face just in time to see another person coming to his defense. With less than a second to spare, one of the Heavyweights hit him square in the back with a walking stick. I heard the stick crack as it connected with the guy's back, immediately followed by an awful scream of pain. But I felt no remorse, because this same guy was about to lay me out on the concrete.

This was by no means a fair fight. Ten thugs stomped four people into the ground, two of whom were only trying to save their Mount St. Michael brothers. Finally, after a few minutes of beating these people with bare fists, booted feet, broken sticks, and a handy metal garbage can, we heard the sirens getting close and ran.

The escape plan went out the window when I saw the car I was supposed to leave in pulled over by the cops moments before I reached it. I made a beeline left and ran through a small park that was next to the school. I felt people running with me, and when I turned around I was relieved to see that it was two of my boys, Rico and Ronnie. They had also seen our car being pulled over by the cops and decided to follow me even though I had no clue where we were or where I was headed. Every time we saw or heard a police car from a distance, we would crouch down behind parked cars. After running for what felt like a few miles, we finally saw the Nereid Avenue entrance to the number 2 train. I was just happy to have escaped the back of a police cruiser, and even though I had no money for the train, we jumped the turnstiles and headed back to the security of Bailey Avenue.

We had to go well out of our way to make it back to the number 1 train, which would eventually get us to 225th Street and West Kingsbridge Road. When we finally arrived in the park, my cousin Herman, who had jumped into a car with the Heavyweights, was already drenched in sweat after playing a couple of games of handball. Most of the crew thought we had been arrested, since they had already been on the block close to two hours. They were relieved to know we escaped, though they had not been so worried that they couldn't enjoy the beautiful day playing handball in the park. Talk of the knockout blow I had thrown that afternoon was already growing to mythic proportions. I had never felt so tough. Truth be told, I was one of the worst fighters in the neighborhood, but the Heavyweights would only know me as the kid who threw one hell of a knockout punch—a punch that had been thrown to help protect one of their little brothers and redeem the reputation of their neighborhood—and that was cool with me.

A few days later, a brand-new, shiny white Nissan Pathfinder with chrome rims and a system you could hear from a mile away pulled up on the corner of Bailey Avenue, where I was standing with one or two other guys from the neighborhood. I recognized the Pathfinder as belonging to Jay, the most powerful man on Heath Avenue. At seventeen years old, he wasn't actually a man, but he was definitely the man behind the gun and drug empire Heath had built over the last few years. Although Jay didn't say anything to me that day, a few guys from Heath piled out of the truck and gave me half hugs and pounded me on the back.

Lent's big brother came out last and said, "Yo, I heard what you did for my little brother at his school. Good looking out, son, if you need anything come see me on the block."

With that, my introduction to the guys making a great deal of money by selling a great deal of drugs and moving a great deal of guns in the area was complete. My reputation with the Heavyweights was secure, and I was happy to have made that type of connection. I knew it would benefit me in the near future. Crazy as we were on Bailey Avenue, it was rare we made any actual money, and I knew it was only a matter of time before the Heavyweights would help us change all that.

I was excited about the possibilities and looked forward to being a part of a team that knew how to get paid on the streets without getting caught. The actual name the Heavyweights went by in the streets was AFO, which stood for "All for One," and they were most definitely a team I wanted to be a part of. A team made up of loyalty, trust, mutual respect, and honor. At a time when every guy on Bailey Avenue had slept with his friend's girlfriend at least once, AFO was about family, and that type of behavior was strictly forbidden by their crew. I guess in that regard they fashioned themselves after the same strict codes the

Mafia obeyed, and I respected them more for actually upholding those rules.

When the invite came for the crew from Bailey Avenue to go to a house party on Heath, I was excited about seeing how these cats got down. They didn't disappoint; the party was crazy. The drugs, liquor, and girls were in abundance at the house party, and we danced all night. At one point, when House of Pain's song "Jump Around" came on, we all jumped around like a bunch of wild-ass thugs, breaking into a chant of "CYC and AFO." Crazy Young Criminals and All for One had united that night, and the union would be powerful for the Kingsbridge section of the Bronx. The coming together of these two crews would allow us to have the numbers, the craziness, and the artillery to go unchallenged. We'd have no problem taking over the drug trade of the sloppily run Marble Hill projects a few blocks away, as well as any parts of Kingsbridge we wanted to control.

An unfortunate turn of events would cause the marriage between Heath Avenue and Bailey Avenue never to make it out of the engagement period, as the fight between Tangie and Lisa would test loyalties on both sides and set up bloodshed and violence for years to come, with no end in sight.

The weekend after Tangie went postal on Lisa's face, one of the young guys from our neighborhood, Frankie, was throwing a house party in his crib. We never turned down a chance to wreck someone else's house and get drunk and high safe from the streets and the cops' ever-present eye. I didn't make the party that night because it was one of the few times I actually decided to go to work. So while shit was getting ready to jump off in the Bronx, I was downtown at my job, working the midnight shift in the World Trade Center. Even though I wasn't there, I got the play by play on just how deadly the party almost became from Manny the next morning.

Chino, Lisa's boyfriend, had found out Rich Buddha would be at the party. His chance to kill Buddha would never be better. When you are raised in the streets you can be proud to a fault, but Puerto Ricans especially have a way of taking pride and using it to justify very stupid actions. Chino's reputation was on the line. He had no choice but to get revenge.

Although I wasn't there when the Heavyweights were gearing up to go find Buddha, I have been in the midst of a modern-day lynch mob getting ready to go to war with another neighborhood. They would have been puffing blunts and getting liquored up while loading their guns. Chino most likely would have been talking shit like "I'm gonna kill that motherfucker Buddha and anyone who tries to stop me," trying to get his boys pumped up. They would have been talking about respect and how their neighborhood wasn't gonna be fucked with. They had to maintain their honor in Kingsbridge and this was going to be one way of doing it.

Shooting up a house party on Bailey Avenue and hopefully killing Rich Buddha would have quickly made them feared and respected.

The boys from Heath rode an elevator up to the roof of an adjacent building, climbed over to the roof of Frankie's building, and made their way down into the building via the rooftop door.

Sometime after midnight on the night of the party, eight people all dressed in black made their way from the rooftop into the building where the party was taking place. They all had on black ski masks and gloves. Some held Uzis and TEC-9 submachine guns; others held two 9 mm handguns, one in each hand. The guys from Heath meant business, and only an act of God would prevent them from slaughtering everyone in the house party.

My cousin Johnny and another member of our crew, Manny, were on their way back to the party after returning from the bodega to get some forties and Phillies Blunts. They ran into the eight masked men. Johnny and Manny now found themselves pressed up against a wall with pistols trained on their heads; there was nothing they could do to prevent what was about to occur inside an apartment packed with their people. Manny in particular was desperate to make it back inside because the mother of his child, Jessie, was inside dancing with some of her friends. With a gun pointed directly at his head, Manny kept trying to push his way into the apartment to rescue Jessie. One of the gunmen pushed a nine-millimeter closer to his head and told him if he kept fighting to get back in, he would die.

Manny would later tell me that after all eight men got into the apartment through an unlocked door, he heard more than a hundred shots fired. Manny knew many of the partygoers, most of them members of the Bailey crew, were being slaughtered right along with his wife. Manny's gun was inside his coat in one of the bedrooms and he was helpless to do anything.

Hitman and my boy Macho from back in the day would tell me how Rich Buddha hid in one of the back bedrooms the second he saw the gunmen come in. Buddha knew that Chino was looking to kill him. He was lucky to end up in the same bedroom with Hitman. That was the only reason Buddha lived.

With Chino leading the gunmen, they opened fired into the bedroom. As they approached the bedroom door, Hitman stuck a sawed-off shotgun out the door and without looking fired into the crowd. The shot must have scared the hell out of the Heavyweights, because it sent them running out of the apartment and back to their neighborhood, a few short blocks away.

Hitman told me later how scared he was after firing the round from the shotgun. "I only had one shell in the shottie. If they had kept coming, I would've been out of fucking luck and I wouldn't have been able to do anything else to stop them," he said with a nervous laugh.

I'd never seen or heard Hitman be nervous about anything, but when he was talking about that night, I clearly saw he felt lucky to be alive.

The gunmen were smart not to shoot Johnny or Manny. Had that happened, they would have started a war not only with the guys from Sedgwick Avenue but with everyone on Bailey Avenue. The guys from Heath knew what Herman, Johnny, Will, and Hitman were about and their beef was with Buddha, so there was no reason to start a war with another neighborhood. It would have meant a much higher body count down the road on all sides.

After the gunmen fled, Manny and Johnny ran in expecting to see a massacre, but everyone was alive. Miraculously, not one person at the party had been shot, despite all the bullets fired. I don't believe they wanted to hit anyone other than Buddha. Some people had been cut by glass from an entertainment center and television that had been shot up, but everyone walked away. Dozens of bullet holes decorated Frankie's mother's apartment. The fellas on Bailey Avenue were beyond upset that the Heavyweights would disrespect our neighborhood and shoot up one of our parties. We all talked about retaliating, but the Heavyweights were after Rich Buddha and didn't hurt anyone in our crew. Bailey Avenue decided not to start a war. It was a wise decision. We had some crazy members in our crew, but we didn't have the guns the guys on Heath had and we damn sure didn't have the unity they had.

That night would be the first time the Heavyweights tried to murder Rich Buddha, but it wouldn't be the last, and unfortunately they wouldn't always miss their intended targets, as their targets eventually grew from Rich Buddha to anyone associated with his crew.

A few weeks later Buddha found out where Chino lived, and he set out to send a message that Heath Avenue wouldn't be the only ones shooting.

Buddha and a few members of his crew from Sedgwick Avenue drove down to Heath to shoot up the block and anyone who looked like they were down with All for One. There was no one on the street to shoot at, so Buddha jumped out of the car and fired several rounds from a shotgun directly into Chino's first-floor apartment. By the grace of God, no one was injured, but the message was loud and clear. Buddha was not going to run away from the beef and he was going to bring it not only to Chino's neighborhood but to his front door.

Around the same time Buddha was shooting shit up on Heath Avenue, my cousin Johnny was looking for Ronnie to beat him down. Ronnie hadn't been down with our crew on Bailey Avenue for more than a year. He actually lived on Heath but took to hanging with the guys on the block. He wasn't the typical thug, though. Shit, I wouldn't call Ronnie a thug at all. He was more of a pretty boy and never really looked to get into trouble.

Johnny was convinced Ronnie was with the gunmen from Heath the night they shot up Frankie's party. Ronnie was one of us and Johnny couldn't see why he would betray his own neighborhood to get in good with his new crew. Ronnie and I were the two that were most excited about being down with Heath Avenue. We both knew how large we could get if we ran with them, but my loyalty was with Bailey Avenue, and Ronnie seemed to forget where his should have been. As far as Johnny was concerned, Ronnie should've warned us that Chino was planning to shoot up Frankie's party. Ronnie was a traitor, an enemy. Johnny's anger only grew stronger and more intense.

It was close to seven on a Friday night, and I was standing in front of the Chinese restaurant on the corner of Bailey when I saw Ronnie walking up the block right toward me. I wanted to walk over and tell him that Johnny was looking for him, but I hadn't seen Johnny for most of the day, so I thought I had plenty of time to warn Ronnie to stay away from the neighborhood until Johnny had time to calm down. I was upset with Ronnie, but I understood that he was trying to earn a reputation with his new crew and he had the same vision I had. We both knew we had a better chance of seeing real money with the guys from Heath than we ever would with the guys on Bailey, and I couldn't find fault in that.

Ronnie gave me a hug with a pat on the back, which was the way we always greeted each other. I asked him what had happened the night of the party.

"Yo, Ive, I didn't know shit was going to go down like that, son," he said.

"Ronnie, what the fuck, how you gonna roll on your own niggas like that?" I asked.

"I was there, bro. We all talked about dressing in all black and finding Buddha to fuck him up. I didn't know they was gonna shoot shit up like that. I swear to fucking God, Ive." Ronnie spoke as if I was the one he had to convince.

"Were you one of the guys with the two nine millies in your hand?"

"Ive, I'm the one who kept Manny and Johnny from going inside the apartment, man."

"My man, you need to stay the fuck off the block for a minute. These niggas ain't happy about this," I said, as I shook my head in disbelief.

I was about to tell Ronnie how heated Johnny was and how he wanted to beat him down, when Johnny appeared out of nowhere and slapped Ronnie in the face with everything he had in him. If Johnny thought you were a pussy and wouldn't fight back, he would slap the shit out of you. He reserved throwing punches for men. Judging from the way he was slapping Ronnie around that day, he thought Ronnie was a bitch. Johnny slapped him with both hands and Ronnie hunkered up against the steel gate of the Chinese restaurant, trying to block the slaps.

I tried to pull Johnny off Ronnie. Then a few more guys showed up to help me break them apart. Ronnie never took a swing at Johnny, not because he was soft, I think, but because of the respect and love he had for him. As Ronnie rose from the ground, he yelled at Johnny about how much he loved him and how he thought of him as a brother. Tears streamed down his face as he continued telling him how he felt about him and the neighborhood he grew up in.

Johnny told him to get the fuck off the block and return to them Heath bitches. He told Ronnie if he ever saw him again he would beat him worse until he stopped coming back to the neighborhood.

"You're not welcome in the Chinese restaurant. You're not welcome in the bodega. And you damn sure better not come back to this fucking block, or I will kill you next time."

I'd never seen so much pain in my cousin's eyes. He truly felt betrayed by Ronnie. Later on my cousin would tell me how helpless he felt the day the party was shot up. That one of our own helped a crew of outsiders was an unforgivable sin. I can't say that I ever blamed Johnny for that, no matter how I felt about Ronnie as a friend. Blood was thicker than water always, and I would have to side with Bailey Avenue in this fight.

Eventually the beef between Heath and Bailey would die down, but the beef between Heath and Sedgwick avenues intensified. The streets around Kingsbridge Road were about to be turned into bloody red rivers, and no one had any idea just how deep those rivers would run.

The Heavyweights tried to kill Rich Buddha several times, but one of Buddha's boys from Sedgwick Avenue would be the first to spill blood. It would be a teenager with a gun, flawless aim, and a reputation to build. Nando was an up-and-coming tough guy from Sedgwick who always struck me as kind of soft. I'm not sure if it was his quiet demeanor, but when I heard the name Nando it didn't register on my respect meter. This was in direct contrast to hearing the name Hitman. In order to survive on the streets we all had reputations to earn and to protect, and Nando was no exception.

In an act that has been repeated by others many times over before and since, Nando set out to earn his. He loaded his gun and sought out the first person on Heath Avenue who had anything to do with the beef between the two rivals. Cesar never saw Nando creeping up from behind, and in an instant Cesar was shot once, twice, ultimately six times.

As Cesar lay on the hard sidewalk, spilling blood, Nando made a mad dash back to the safe haven of Sedgwick Avenue.

Cesar was one of the main thug niggas on Heath Avenue. I never really liked the kid, but that was mainly due to the fact that we had experienced an earlier beef with Cesar by way of a fistfight with my cousin Herman. If there was one thing I knew about Cesar it was that he wasn't a punk. Anyone who stood toe-to-toe with my cousin Herman and lived to smile about it was a hard motherfucker. But even the hardest motherfuckers fall when bullets enter their body.

Nando became a street legend, most notably on Sedgwick Avenue, and his rep still stands today. Nando was quickly arrested and convicted on attempted murder charges. He paid with eight and a half to fifteen years in prison for an instant reputation in the streets. Although Nando was successful in drawing first blood in the feud, which had now transferred from the girls to a bunch of hooligans with guns, he was a failure in his own life. He was on his way upstate to serve his time in the New York State correctional facility. Nando was the first to go to jail in the ever-growing feud started by a vicious girl fight, but surely not the last.

On December 26, 1998, several years after Nando went to jail, guys from Sedgwick Avenue found themselves in the same nightclub as guys from Heath Avenue. When Hefty, a member of the Sedgwick crew, entered the restroom, several of the Heavyweights followed him inside. Hefty couldn't do anything to fend them off. Six men armed with knives stabbed Hefty repeatedly, as if they were in prison shanking an inmate labeled a child molester or a snitch.

Moe, perhaps the toughest and most feared member of the Sedgwick Avenue crew, heard the commotion and went in after Hefty. Moe took out the knife he had in his coat pocket and started stabbing some of the Heavyweights. But he was outnumbered and they stabbed Moe several times, though not before he ripped into Jay's face. Unfortunately, Moe was too late to save Hefty's life.

Hefty died two days after Christmas because of blood loss. Moe would end up wearing a colostomy bag, and Jay required plastic surgery to repair the damage Moe did to his face. Everyone involved would go to jail for different lengths of time, but no one would spend more than seven years in prison for Hefty's murder. There's no snitching allowed in the streets. No one was talking. The beef between Heath and Sedgwick would go into the new millennium.

I knew Hefty from the neighborhood and when I received word from back home, I felt a great deal of remorse. The war had been going on for eight years. I said a prayer for Hefty and felt justified in having left the Bronx five years earlier. I had a five-year-old daughter named Heaven and a three-year-old daughter named Starr, and I couldn't imagine raising them in that environment. An environment that seemed predisposed to war.

It was as if the battle cries never stopped calling in Kingsbridge. And whenever the war drums called us, our pride always caused us to feel the need to respond.

Fort Independence was just a few blocks away from Heath Avenue. According to Bronx historians, several cannonballs unearthed back in 1915 were identified as coming from the days when George Washington commanded the fort. Actual wars had been fought on Heath Avenue, and we seemed doomed to repeat the bloody history of the neighborhood. We were street soldiers.

I always felt like the neighborhood was cursed. No one ever seemed to do good things with their lives until fleeing the place they grew up in.

It didn't make sense to me that I had to run away from the place I called home, the place I loved. Make no mistake about it, I loved my streets—*el barrio mio.* But I owed it to my daughters to live and fight another day. And the fight I wanted to take up was a fight to succeed at life, so that I could provide my daughters with a father they could be proud of. I no longer wanted to fight against a bunch of thugs with guns in an environment that made it easy to throw bullets at one another all day. The sad truth is, I had to leave to save my sanity.

I guess I've proven I'm no different than the Irish and Italians who fled when they saw what they perceived as negative changes that they couldn't control taking place around them. They must have seen that the neighborhoods would deteriorate, and when they fled they helped that assumption to manifest itself by not being there to help prevent it from happening. When all the good people flee, there is no one left to clean up the mess being made of society. And now I was guilty of being one of those to flee. But the killing never seemed to end, so what choice did I really have?

Just two and a half years after Hefty's murder, his brother Brolick would meet the same fate at the hands of the Heavyweights. On July 10, 2001, Brolick was hanging out with his cousin and some of the fellas from his crew in front of the building on Fort Independence known as F.I.P. The sound of gunfire erupted quickly and seemingly out of nowhere, shattering the sound of summer and sending Stone and the rest of the fellas scrambling in search of cover and weapons. I'd known Stone practically all my life. He was one of the little guys on Creston Avenue while I was growing up out there, even younger than me. Eventually he grew up to become one of the most respected and feared guys on Kingsbridge, but he always showed me a lot of love and respect when I went back home to visit. He said it was due to the fact that I bought him candy when he was young and treated him like a little brother.

When the gunsmoke cleared, Stone was desperately in search of a weapon to return fire with. But with their weapons not strategically placed, there was no time to shoot back. As the shooter fled on foot, Nando, just home from jail after shooting Cesar, gave chase with nothing more than a few bottles of beer. Once the shooter reached his getaway vehicle, he jumped in and the car raced off as Nando threw the bottle.

After Stone retrieved a gun from the stash, he returned to the street to see his cousin Brolick lying in a pool of blood. Brolick had been murdered in cold blood, in broad daylight, in front of his cousin, and Stone had now lost two of his cousins because of the war with the Heavyweights. There was no telling how many more bodies would pile up.

It was later rumored that a young man named Khalid was paid two thousand dollars and a pound of weed by the Heavyweights to execute Brolick. It was a professional contract. It would be Khalid's first and last contract killing, though. He would be murdered not too long after carrying out the hit on Brolick, shot to death walking down Webb Avenue in much the same way he murdered Brolick. An eye for an eye.

What goes around always comes back around. Sometimes it takes a while to run its course, but it always runs its course.

Close to twenty years after that fateful afternoon and the fight between Tangie and Lisa, the boys from Heath Avenue and Sedgwick Avenue are still shooting at one another. Shortly after September 11, 2001, I went back home for a visit. I stopped on Webb Avenue to take a few pictures of the graffiti memorials erected for Brolick and Hefty. All that was left of two brothers, two human beings, was a wall of spray paint. It just didn't seem to add up.

Two undercover cops had been staking out the memorial, looking for people willing to talk about the crime, and when they approached me that afternoon I could offer no information. All I could do was tell them I knew the two brothers what seemed like a lifetime ago. Even as the outsider I had become, I knew better than to exchange information with the police. No snitching allowed—the streets police themselves, take themselves to trial, and execute themselves. I was just in the Bronx on a weekend pass, so who was I to get involved?

I guess I've been gone too long, and I no longer carry around the kind of hate in my heart that one needs to survive on the streets. I don't understand how killing one another makes sense. My mind can't comprehend it. So I can no longer condone it.

In 2006, I got a phone call telling me that some people I grew up with shot at the Heavyweights. I still get these calls even though I no longer travel in those circles. They are all random phone calls, and most of the time I have no idea whose voice is on the other end of the line. I'm no longer connected, but I'm still associated.

The war is worse these days, because it has been passed down to another generation, a younger generation that picks up guns sooner than we did and shoots more than we ever thought was okay. Wars went from fists to bats and knives to guns.

We didn't kill each other to earn respect. In the beginning, we turned to guns to protect ourselves from others. But as with all things, the gunplay escalated and the trigger fingers got itchier. In the Bronx, you could no longer hold down your block without shooters. And today you can't hold *yourself* down if you yourself aren't a shooter. It's a new game, but the funny thing about this game is that nobody ever wins.

SURVIVAL 101 SUBWAY SURVIVAL 101 SUBWAY SURVIVA
Y SURVIVAL 101 SUBWAY SURVIVAL 101 SUBWAY SURVIV
BWAY SURVIVAL 101 SUBWAY SURVIVAL 101 SUBWAY SU
1 SUBWAY SURVIVAL 101 SUBWAY SURVIVAL 101 SUBWA
AL 101 SUBWAY SURVIVAL 101 SUBWAY SURVIVAL 101 S
RVIVAL 101 SUBWAY SURVIVAL 101 SUBWAY SURVIVAL 10
Y SURVIVAL 101 SUBWAY SURVIVAL 101 SUBWAY SURVIV
BWAY SURVIVAL 101 SUBWAY SURVIVAL 101 SUBWAY SU
1 SUBWAY SURVIVAL 101 SUBWAY SURVIVAL 101 SUBWA
AL 101 SUBWAY SURVIVAL 101 SUBWAY SURVIVAL 101 S
RVIVAL 101 SUBWAY SURVIVAL 101 SUBWAY SURVIVAL 10
Y SURVIVAL 101 SUBWAY SURVIVAL 101 SUBWAY SURVIV
BWAY   3WAY SU
1 SUE   SUBWA
AL 1C   AL 101 S

Subway Survival 101

New York City's subway system isn't just one of the most efficient modes of transportation in the world; it can also be one of the most dangerous ways to travel, especially after the rush-hour crowd has found its way home at the end of the day.

In the early nineties, crime on the subway was skyrocketing, averaging more than eighteen thousand felonies every year, with the majority taking place after the sun went down. With fewer riders and less police presence on the subway cars after dark, the subway was a prime location for criminals. Most New Yorkers would warn tourists to avoid eye contact on the subway at all costs. My warning would be that if you had to ride the subway after dark, carry a weapon and pay attention to your surroundings at all times. The subway was its own world and the rules were different; having street smarts wouldn't always carry you through. Shit, in some cases not even having a weapon would help you survive if you were caught sleeping without one eye open.

From 1989 to 1993, I worked the midnight shift for a brokerage house in the financial district. It was the pre-Giuliani era, before the crime statistics system CompStat was introduced to help reduce subway crime. When you put your token in the slot, or hopped the turnstile as

I often did, you might have been caught off guard by the ENTER AT YOUR OWN RISK graffiti sign posted in the Kingsbridge subway station. I was a nonpracticing Catholic boy and always crossed myself when no one was looking and asked God to get me to my final destination in one piece.

My cousin Richie taught me that the best way to survive the subway at night was to be prepared. I carried a big-ass knife. I heard a rumor that it was legal to carry a four-inch folding knife, but I carried an eight-inch folding knife. If I ever needed to stab someone, I wanted to do it from a distance. My cousin Richie once told me that stabbing someone the first time was the most difficult, but the next time was no different than beating them with your fists. Although I carried a knife for protection, I was never involved in any beef while carrying. So I never had a reason to stab anyone. I was never forced to graduate to that next level of violent behavior.

Maybe I'd do it to save my own life.

It was around 8:30 A.M. when I exited the number 4 train at the Kingsbridge Road station after a long night of work. I was exhausted, walking with my head down avoiding eye contact. I didn't see the swarm of police officers in the station that morning, grabbing everyone and anyone they thought looked suspicious. An officer had to repeat himself a few times because I didn't realize he wanted to talk to me. I'd just left the subway car peacefully and my only thought was of going home to catch some sleep after ten hours of printing stock-exchange reports.

The cop took me to a room in the back of the subway station. When I walked inside the dimly lit room, I noticed four other young Hispanic and black males being interrogated.

The first thing the cop asked me was, "Are you carrying any weapons, son?"

I thought about it for a few seconds and looked around the room. I knew I was about to be searched and there was no way around the fact that I was holding.

"Yes, Officer, I have a knife inside my coat pocket."

I raised my arms while he ruffled through my pockets. His eyes got big when he realized just how big a knife I was carrying. I knew I'd be catching sleep down at central booking while waiting to be processed on weapon-possession charges. The officer asked me why I was carrying the knife and I told him it was for protection.

"Protection from what?" he asked.

"Officer, I ride the trains at midnight to work downtown. I've seen some crazy shit on the trains; I ain't trying to be nobody's victim."

"So you think you can just stab someone before they stab you?"

"If I had to protect myself, sir, I would," I said in a respectful tone. "I'm just trying to feed my fiancée and get ready for the birth of my child. I'm not a punk, Officer. I work hard for a living. You know how the streets are."

After showing him my World Trade Center ID, he not only told me I was free to go, he handed the knife back to me. I turned to see another young Hispanic male being handcuffed. It turned out he had been carrying a handgun. I thought he was probably a student at Walton High School, a rough public school located on Reservoir Avenue. Even so, getting caught carrying a concealed gun meant he was on his way to the precinct for processing. I'm not sure which was worse, jail or Walton High School, but I got lucky that morning.

I had a lot of fun working the graveyard shift in the World Trade Center. I had the entire Thirtieth floor of Tower Two to myself. I'd walk around for hours, going through people's desks and imagining what their lives were like. I'd find pay stubs that read seven thousand dollars and think to myself there was no way someone could make that much money every two weeks. My favorite office had a huge mahogany desk and was covered in New York Knicks paraphernalia. I used to spend hours in the office, taking naps and looking through the guy's telescope.

One night I took all the fellas from the block to hang out with me and signed them all in as visitors. We spent a few hours playing hide-and-go-seek, but no one could find anyone else because the place was too big. When I found Ray a few hours later, I noticed a bulge in his jacket.

"Yo, Ray, what you got in your coat, kid?" I asked.

He opened his coat and said, "I only got a few things, man, nothing no one will miss," as he displayed about a thousand pens and a radio.

"Son, I don't give a fuck about the pens, but you gotta put back the radio. I can get fired over this shit," I said in all seriousness.

I could steal anything I wanted on the streets of New York, but when I was at work I almost always knew how to behave accordingly. I say *almost* because I always wrote graffiti wherever the fuck I went, especially inside the buildings I worked in.

"And if any of you other motherfuckers are thinking about stealing big shit," I said to the rest of the crew, "don't do it, man. You'll get me fucking fired."

Everyone I ever took up to the World Trade Center to hang out with me, including Stormy, always said the same thing: "The place is haunted."

I always felt spirits roaming on the thirtieth floor, and I'd see shadows and shit from the corner of my eye walking the hallways. After a while I got used to the presence and I wasn't afraid of it. But the place always felt eerie, and after the attacks on 9/11 I'd think about that presence and wonder if it was a sign of things to come.

Shortly after my brother moved to Virginia Beach to start his new life, he quickly realized he wasn't going to be able to keep his girl, Tina, happy on a Burger King salary. He called me one afternoon to tell me he discovered how easy it was to buy guns in Virginia. He asked me to set up some buyers in New York and we'd split the profits.

After making a few runs back and forth to Virginia, my brother was slated to bring a large shipment of tech nine submachine guns to the Bronx one night. He called right before he left to tell me he had a bad feeling in the pit of his stomach and didn't want to make the run.

"Yo, we got people waiting on these guns, man. You got to deliver," I said, with no regard for his feelings.

"I'm telling you, Ive, I got a bad feeling that something isn't right," he said.

"Bill, I got a bad feeling I'm going to get fucked up by the people we promised these toys to if I don't deliver. It's just your nerves, man. Get the fuck on the bus."

As my brother drove around Virginia Beach contemplating what his next move should be, he was suddenly surrounded by ATF agents in unmarked cars and arrested. He would later be charged with intent to distribute firearms across state lines and serve three years in a federal penitentiary. My brother never spoke of my involvement to the ATF. Even though they knew I was involved, without my brother's willingness to cooperate and testify against me they had no case. Once again, I had dodged a bullet.

One of the lessons Zen taught me was, When one brother gets locked up, the other has to stay clean to be around to support Mom. But I didn't heed Zen's advice, and with my brother locked up I took to carrying a black .25-caliber semiautomatic handgun on the train. I didn't always have the luxury of having a weapon for protection, but when I did, it set my mind at ease. Before I had the gun, I had to use my subway smarts to protect myself. Subway smarts were, in theory, street smarts applied to a more confined space. Street smarts included never turning your back on anyone, always being aware of your surroundings, picking and choosing your battles according to which ones you thought you could win, and never underestimating anyone. However, one of the most important elements of street smarts couldn't really apply to the subway system, simply put because it was the subway and not the street.

My cousin Freddie taught me one of the most important rules of the street—always leave an escape route. Needless to say, it would be tough to jump off a moving train, so you had to know which subway car to ride in. Even though I usually had a weapon to protect myself, there were still no guarantees I'd be able to survive a mob of twenty guys on the train out to rob. So I usually sat in the middle of the train, on the same car as the conductor. It was common knowledge to New Yorkers that it was the safest car on the train.

There was no escape once the subway car pulled away from the station. I always kept a mean face on to make the other person think I was the one looking for trouble and I made sure no one intimidated me. I used to fall asleep on the train with my hand wedged in my jacket pocket, tired from a long night's work.

If you have ever seen *The Godfather*, Al Pacino's character, Michael Corleone, pulls this off when he stands in front of the hospital with Enzo, trying to protect his father from the men coming to kill him. The old hand-in-the-pocket trick I picked up from watching the movie with my boys is one of the reasons I'm still here to tell my story. I'd fall asleep on the subway train for the hour-long ride from the beginning of the Bronx to the end of Manhattan. I knew it was dangerous, but it was my reality and I found a comfort zone after a few months. I'm sure it didn't hurt that I carried myself as a thug from the Bronx, which often left other passengers feelings uneasy.

Even though I worked in Manhattan, the midnight shift allowed me the freedom to dress the way I dressed in the neighborhood. Baggy jeans, a Carhartt jacket, and Timberland boots were the uniform of a Bronx thug at the time, and that was all I wore. The Port Authority police always raised their eyebrows when I walked the halls of the World Trade Center. But I'd pull out my black all-access ID badge and they'd let me walk through.

I remember waking up on the train to see some thug who looked like me sitting across from me, staring at my hand in my pocket and wondering if I was strapped. I guess he never saw the need to test me and chose instead to move on to easier prey. Why run the risk of messing with someone who might be tougher than you are, or someone who could possibly be armed? Most criminals go for the easier score, so I fronted and was left alone—for the most part. I wouldn't always be so lucky.

I fell asleep one night while riding the number 1 train on the Broadway line. I opened my eyes and I saw I was at the 137th Street station, about midway through my ride to work. When I looked directly across from me I saw four young toughs staring directly at me. I looked to my left and saw one guy sitting really close, and there was another guy to my right. It looked like six guys were getting ready to pounce on me. I was sure they would do it the second the subway car rolled out of the station into the darkness of the tunnel. I only had a few seconds to figure out how I was going to handle the situation. I had a gun with me, but there were six of them and they could overpower me and take my gun if I didn't better position myself in the subway car. There would be no escape once the doors closed and I wasn't about to be a sitting duck.

As the doors closed, I jumped out of my seat and walked backward to the door to my left. While I reached down into my pants to pull my pistol out, take the safety off, and load a bullet into the chamber simultaneously, I heard them saying, *"Deja para robarlo,"* which means something to the effect of *Let's rob him.* The two guys closest to me got up and walked toward me but I raised my gun and aimed it at chest level. They froze midstep and seemed confused about what to do. I had moved so fast they barely noticed me pulling the gun out. I'm not sure if they thought I couldn't understand them plotting their move in Spanish, but I heard them loud and clear. I just stood there staring at all six guys while holding the gun, now pointing straight down, as if I were a police officer or had authority to be standing in a subway car holding a loaded .25-caliber pistol with a bullet in the chamber.

I'd never shot anyone, but I'm pretty certain that if any of them had made a move toward me I wouldn't have hesitated to unload my clip into each and every one of them. At least I'd unload the seven bullets I had in the clip and hope whoever wasn't shot would scatter. I didn't want to be a victim that night. They had picked the wrong guy on the wrong subway car to test. The funny thing was, we all sat back down and they stayed in the car with me for the next four or five stops. I tucked the gun into the waistband of my pants; I knew they were no longer looking for trouble. I kept the safety off in case they made another move. All of a sudden, two of the guys started fighting; they bloodied each other up while the rest of their boys rooted them on. I don't really know what the beef was about—I only picked up every third word of the Spanish they were speaking—but it seemed like they were snapping on each other. This kind of fight happened often in our neighborhood. Two guys would start talking about each other's mothers or whatever, and when someone's ego got bruised, blows would be thrown.

Bloodied and not being able to rob me, the six got off the train at 86th Street and Broadway. As the train pulled away, one of the guys punched the window and showed me his middle finger. I laughed the rest of the way to work. I didn't feel tough, but I had survived. It was almost like I'd been in *The Godfather*; it was a huge adrenaline rush, one I wouldn't have minded reliving.

Rule number one when carrying an illegal firearm: Don't pull it out if you don't intend to use it.

I would have definitely used it that night, no questions asked.

I felt like stabbing someone was too up close and personal. You could shoot a person from a distance, so it wasn't as personal. You didn't necessarily have to be tough to shoot someone, but in my eyes you had to be tough to get up close and stab someone. If they overpowered you, they could take your knife and use it to kill you.

Having a gun made me feel protected, but it also caused a lot of stress for me throughout the years. I feared another morning raid by the NYPD, some random search where I would be caught and locked up for carrying a concealed weapon. The stupidest thing was that I was hopping the turnstile with a pistol in my waistband, risking going to jail for a few years to not pay a buck twenty-five for the subway.

One morning I dozed off on a subway car on my way home from

work and woke to see twenty or thirty police officers sitting and standing all around me. I thought I was having a nightmare. Then I realized I was actually sitting in a subway car carrying a gun, staring at more police officers than I'd ever seen in such a confined space.

My heart was racing and I was sweating. I wondered to myself whether the officers noticed the sweat now dripping down my face.

I watched the officers get off two at a time at every station from 59th and Columbus Circle to 225th and Broadway. There were a few times after that morning that I'd run into the same routine. I finally realized that the officers met for briefings somewhere downtown and then hopped on the subway to spread out across the city. Unfortunately, that morning they chose my subway car and gave me the scare of my life.

Although the fear of going to jail was always there, I never regretted carrying a gun on the subway. I felt safe. Thousands of hardworking New Yorkers were being victimized every night. But some days I woke up and felt I didn't want to chance the gun charge, so I'd leave it under the mattress at home. There was one night I'll never forget when I wished to God I had my gun with me. This time it was to help someone else.

It was January or February of 1992, in the dead of winter. I waited on the platform at 238th Street and Broadway, freezing my ass off, for the number 1 train to arrive. I made eye contact with a twentysomething black male, who was with a younger Hispanic male. Something in the deepest part of my gut told me to avoid a confrontation with these two. I always acted a lot tougher than I actually was, but with no gang, no gun, and not even my eight-inch folding knife for protection that day, I decided to drop the eye contact with the black guy. It would pay off almost immediately.

As the train approached the platform, I walked a few feet back and entered the subway car directly behind theirs. I settled into my seat and was reading the newest issue of *The Source*. I often read it on my way to work—both to kill time and stay in touch with what was happening in the world of hip-hop. I wasn't done reading the first article when I heard the door to the next car being slammed open. I nearly fell out of my seat in fear. When I regained my bearings, I noticed five to ten people had run into my subway car screaming bloody murder. When I finally got up the courage to get out of my seat and look through the window of my car into the next one, I couldn't believe what I was seeing.

The two young thugs were beating the subway conductor. Conductors were relatively safe if they could get into their metal compartment, lock the door, and radio for help, but if they were attacked outside it, they would have to defend themselves like any other straphanger. Most people on the subway at night would sit in the car the conductor rode in, which gave the passengers a feeling of relative safety.

I could see that the black guy was covered in blood. Each time his hand came up, blood seemed to gush out of the conductor a little bit more. I realized they weren't just beating the conductor; both of them were viciously stabbing him over and over again as he pleaded with them to stop. I stood there frozen in fear. It was one of the moments in my life when I discovered I was no hero. I couldn't bring myself to enter the subway car. The force they were using to thrust the blades into the conductor was vicious. They were crazed and so much bigger than me. If I went in they would kill me. So I did nothing.

At the next stop, the doors of the subway car finally opened and people ran out onto the subway platform. No one wanted to remain trapped on the train if the two thugs decided to continue their attack on other passengers. The train never moved and the two thugs ran off, while a few of us ran over to try to comfort the man who was bleeding so profusely. I saw that he was bleeding in the face, neck, head, and body. I felt sick to my stomach, both because of the amount of blood and because I had been a coward. By the grace of God, the police and paramedics arrived very quickly to the scene after someone alerted the toll booth clerk.

They carried the conductor off the train and out to the ambulance. I remember watching the news and checking the newspaper for three days straight, waiting to hear whether he had lived or died. I hoped he had lived. I hoped it would ease the guilt I had inside for not helping him. I remember hearing some lady say the conductor was trying to stop the two guys from robbing a passenger. The TV news never reported the incident, which made me wonder how many other horrific events went unreported. I guess the MTA and the city prefer not to broadcast the eighteen thousand felonies a year that take place on the transit system. It might keep people from riding the subways at night—that's a lot of profit lost. For whatever reason the story was never covered, but I took solace in *not* hearing that a conductor was killed.

That little voice in my head that told me not to make eye contact and not to get on the same subway car as the two thugs had saved me. Either way, I was grateful to have survived another night in the transit system. Who knows? It could have been me experiencing two knives being viciously plunged into my body, neck, head, and face. Looking up at the horrified facial expressions of the passengers, wishing they could find the courage to help me but understanding why they were too afraid to do so.

Subway Survival 101: Don't make eye contact. Sleep with one eye open, or better yet don't sleep at all, and never get caught without your hand in your pocket, pretending to have a weapon.

Guns carried on the subway.

THE LOST SON OF ELDER AVENUE THE LOST SON OF E
ENUE THE LOST SON OF ELDER AVENUE THE LOST SC
DER AVENUE THE LOST SON OF ELDER AVENUE THE LOST
ELDER AVENUE THE LOST SON OF ELDER AVENUE THE
ON OF ELDER AVENUE THE LOST SON OF ELDER AVENUE
OST SON OF ELDER AVENUE THE LOST SON OF ELDER AV
HE LOST SON OF ELDER AVENUE THE LOST SON OF ELDE
NUE THE LOST SON OF ELDER AVENUE THE LOST SON OF E
ENUE THE LOST SON OF ELDER AVENUE THE LOST SC
DER AVENUE THE LOST SON OF ELDER AVENUE THE LOST
ELDER AVENUE THE LOST SON OF ELDER AVENUE THE
ON OF ELDER AVENUE THE LOST SON OF ELDER AVENU
OST SC   DER AV
HE LOS   OF ELDE
NUE TH   ON OF E

The Lost Son of Elder Avenue

Santeria is a religion practiced by many Caribbean folk. The religion was introduced to the islands of Haiti, Jamaica, Barbados, and the Bahamas via the Yoruba people, who were brought over as slaves from Nigeria. Centuries later, Santeria would have a strong hold over a huge population of Catholic Puerto Ricans living in New York City. Although our parents introduced us to minor forms of Santeria, many would practice the religion in secrecy for fear of being ridiculed or excommunicated from the church.

In many Hispanic neighborhoods in the Bronx, you could stop in a botanica shop to purchase candles, holy water, and herbs that would help you ward off evil spirits or find fortune or love. You could also buy the services of a *santero* (priest or priestess) if you were trying to save a loved one from deathly illness or a curse. In some cases, the *santero* would sacrifice a live rooster or chicken to receive ashes from the *orishas* (saints), thus warding off evil spirits or curing an illness.

My close friend Freddie Martin was given a pillow that had been through a ritual by his grandmother, who gave it to him for protection. Although I never knew what was inside the pillow, the fact remained that it seemed to do its job of protecting Freddie from the violence that befell so many in our neighborhoods. While several members of Freddie's crew were murdered around him, he always seemed to walk away unscathed. And in a neighborhood where shootouts were as common as heroin-addict sightings, surviving another day was an accomplishment not to be overlooked. I don't know the exact number of shootouts Freddie was involved in, but I do know his neighborhood respected him for a reason.

One day, the pillow was destroyed by my cousin Johnny and a few other guys who were messing around. Soon after, the evil spirits would manifest themselves and the violence of the street would destroy many of the people who surrounded Freddie. They would come knocking on Freddie's door in a way none of us could have predicted.

Freddie was raised in the South Bronx, in a very tough neighborhood called Elder Avenue. The guys on Elder were constantly at war with the guys from Watson Avenue, just one block away, and the neighborhood was one of the biggest open-air drug markets in the Bronx. It was one of the craziest places to be at the height of the heroin epidemic that was plaguing New York between the years of 1985 to 1993. You could find a dozen brands of heroin, each stamped with names like THE TERMINATOR, DIE HARD, or some other name that represented violence, on all four corners of Elder Avenue. Many young guys like Freddie were put on those corners to pitch the drugs, making hand-to-hand sales. Freddie began working the corners at the age of eleven or twelve years old.

It was a violent and poverty-stricken neighborhood. The motto was to get money any which way you could and not trust a soul. Only the strong survive in that environment. Freddie was just that—the strongest, most streetwise person I would ever have the pleasure of saying I ran with back in the day.

It was sometime around 1987 or 1988 that Freddie was introduced to the guys on Bailey Avenue through Nina, an attractive young girl he was dating at the time. The only problem was that my cousin Johnny had dated Nina off and on a few years earlier. When Freddie first came to Bailey Avenue, it was to settle a score with Johnny. Not only did Freddie and Johnny not fight that day, they somehow managed to become friends shortly after their first encounter. I'm not sure if mutual respect kept them from fighting, or if it was just fate that the guys on Bailey Avenue and some of Freddie's crew on Elder Avenue would all become family. It was just what the streets of New York needed at the time—another strong alliance.

My partner Manny was one of the first guys to become really close to Freddie. Manny was dating Nina's sister, Jessie. Since they were always with their girls, it was only a matter of time before Manny and Freddie became like brothers. After that, it didn't take long for Freddie to teach Manny the drug game. Soon Manny was out on Elder Avenue with Freddie, pitching heroin to drug friends as fast as they could make their way down the block.

I witnessed Manny out there doing his thing many times, and he was relentless with his shit. "If you motherfuckers don't keep it tight against the wall, I ain't serving you," he'd say to the addicts.

He'd have to deal with heroin addicts all day, trying to cop pleas like, "Yo, little man, if you comp me today I'll pay you double tomorrow. I just need one baggie."

"Ain't this a bitch?" Manny would snap back. "These ain't hamburgers and I ain't Popeye, motherfucker. If you ain't got no dough get the fuck out of here and stop wasting my time."

"You see the shit I gotta deal with, Ive, to make a few bucks?" he'd ask me.

I don't know how they did it, man. I never stopped looking up and down the block, waiting to see the cops roll up, and I wasn't even involved in the game. These guys had brass balls.

The fact that an open-air drug market existed where heroin addicts could line up to cop always took me by surprise. We just didn't get down like that in Kingsbridge. But on Elder and Watson avenues, it seemed like there were no rules.

At five foot three, Manny was a little guy who quickly earned a reputation as a short-tempered soldier ready to take it to the streets with anyone who wanted to test him. To this day Manny reminds me of Pachanga from the movie *Carlito's Way*: "Carlito, you know me, man. I'll take it to the streets with any of these motherfuckers."

Many call it the Napoleon complex, but whatever it was, Manny was quick to jump off the hood of a parked car, raining fists down on the tallest guy trying to test his heart. Manny had the heart of a prize-fighter and that earned him a reputation, street credibility, and the respect he needed to survive on a block like Elder Avenue. I'm sure it didn't hurt that he was rolling with one of the most fearless guys on the block. Knowing Freddie had his back no matter what popped off made them a tough duo to fuck with.

What I recall most about visiting Elder Avenue in the earlier days was observing the guys out there making tons of money. Most of the big bosses in the neighborhood were pushing brand-new Benzes and BMWs that never made it to the dealerships. They had the money to buy cars before the rest of the working public, and they did just that to show off the fruits of their labors in the drug trade. These guys were known all over the city, and I remember them renting out entire night-clubs just to throw parties. There were always flocks of girls, arsenals of guns, drugs, and more money being flashed than I had ever seen on the other side of the Bronx. These guys owned candy stores, coin laundries, and bodegas, but most of their money came from drug profits. Most of the businesses were just fronts for their illegal distribution of narcot-ics, with hidden back rooms in which to conduct business and stash weight, profits, and guns.

It didn't take long for Manny and Freddie to start driving nicer cars, dressing real fly, and rocking bulky jewelry. I always loved being around them because they were ghetto celebrities. They got special attention wherever they went and nobody ever tried to fuck with them. Freddie was also getting close with my cousins Herman and Johnny, something that made my relationship with Freddie possible. When Freddie started introducing me as his cousin, it was a good feeling to know I was on the side of somebody I not only feared but was also beginning to love and respect. Knowing someone as powerful as Freddie was a direct reflection of who I was on the streets. Knowing Freddie was almost as powerful as *being* Freddie. I was automatically backed up by his entire crew, and I walked around the streets knowing I could start shit and back it up with just a phone call.

As Freddie's drug spot grew, it began to get hot and draw the attention of the authorities. I remember being in the house one day when Manny came upstairs and said some guy from Connecticut was downstairs and wanted to buy five thousand dollars' worth of heroin. They discussed whether the guy was a cop, and then Freddie sent Manny downstairs with the drugs to fill the order. I wasn't cut out for that type of game—just being around those types of deals made me nervous as hell. I thought everybody was a cop, so I was a little paranoid motherfucker. I could never have done the job these guys were doing, but it was exciting to see it.

Even if the guy Manny sold to did turn out to be a cop, he wouldn't know it until weeks later, when they would have him in court and the guy would come in to testify that he had bought ten bundles off him four weeks ago. It was a crazy business to be in, but I guess the payoff kept them moving. In their business there was no time to be paranoid or shook. You had to treat every customer as just that, another addict coming to cop.

About three years into the game, Manny had worked his way up to manager of not only Freddie's drug spot but also two other drug spots in the neighborhood. Yes, even in the drug game there are roles and titles, from the lookout to the pitcher to the manager to the big boss who collects all the money at the end of the day.

They were making good money, but in the drug business, the worst is always just around the corner. I've never seen anyone survive the game for more than five years. You have to worry about stick-up kids, snitches, and workers stealing from you—and then there's the undercover cops, the beat cops, and the drug task forces that kick in your door in the middle of the night and arrest anyone in the house, including your *abuela*.

It's a fast and short-lived career. Manny almost got killed over some drugs and money going missing at one of the spots he was managing. After three short years in the game, his time was running out. He must have known that what Freddie and he were doing had to come to an end.

One day I arrived at Freddie's drug spot with him and Johnny. We were going upstairs to change and get ready to hit the club scene. All the lights were off. When Freddie hit the light switch, Manny just about tackled him to the ground and told everybody to hit the floor and turn off the lights. That shit freaked me out. We crawled around on the floor of the dark apartment. Manny was rambling on about how the feds were in the building across the street, on the roof, watching the drug house with binoculars.

All I could think about was what the hell I was doing here. I didn't sell drugs. I didn't want to go to jail for this shit.

When we got to the window, we slowly crept up to the sill to see if we could get a look at whoever he was talking about. My heart was racing. I just knew the NYPD drug task force known as TNT was about to kick in the door and haul all of us to jail. We began to ask one another if we were all seeing the same thing. We were—three black smokestacks on the roof of the adjacent building. There were no feds in sight. With that, Freddie got off the floor and told Manny he had better stop fucking around with all the drugs he was using. I guess Manny was even more paranoid than I was. Soon, his paranoia was vindicated.

Not too long after this incident, TNT did raid Freddie's drug spot. They caught Manny in the house with a large amount of weight, heroin, and cash. The pharmaceutical manager was on his way to jail for a while. The ride on the drug-dealing roller coaster had finally come to a halt. Although Freddie walked away unscathed, he lost an operation that was making five thousand dollars and more every week. He didn't lose only Manny. He lost his drug house, his place to stash cash and weapons, and his base of operation. It wasn't that easy to set up a new spot. You had to find an apartment that wasn't in a building where there was already a spot, in the same area your customers knew you but the TNT didn't see you. Then you had to communicate with everyone about where you had relocated. When Manny got busted, the whole operation tumbled, drug spot and all.

Manny, who was a first-time offender, disappeared for eight months to attend a Shock Incarceration program in the New York State correctional system. Shock was a program for first-time drug offenders in which you ate, slept, and shit in synchronization. One mess-up meant immediate prison time upstate, rotting in jail for your full sentence. In Manny's case, that would have been about three years.

Freddie didn't stay down for long. After a few months of taking it easy, he went back to doing what he did best—getting money on the streets. Freddie also started hanging out with us more on Bailey Avenue while things cooled down in his neck of the Bronx. We quickly began stealing as many cars and music systems as we could get our hands on in one night. We needed the cash coming in. Freddie needed the money to set up shop again, and I just wanted to get money to buy the latest kicks and gear. Freddie, Herman, Johnny, Frankie, my brother, and I began to spend a lot of the time out "shopping," as we called it. This didn't provide the kind of money Freddie was used to, but it was exciting work, and every once in a while there was a decent amount of money to be made in the car-theft racket. No one goes into the car-theft game to make a lot of money, except for chop shops. Stealing a car is an adrenaline rush. I believe it was the reason most of us got into it.

One rainy night we stole a Toyota Corolla on Corlear Avenue, right in front of the house I was living in with my girlfriend, Stormy, and her parents. It took Freddie about three minutes to get the car hot-wired while I kept a lookout. The 50th Police Precinct was only two city blocks away. We didn't steal the Corolla because it had expensive rims or a nice sound system. We stole it because Freddie decided he wanted to go to the movies at the Whitestone theaters across town and we had no way to get there.

Once Freddie got the car running, I hopped inside and we headed off to Bailey Avenue to pick up his friend Lisa. On the way back from the movie theater, Freddie asked me if I wanted to drive so he could sit in the back with her. I never had a problem driving a stolen car, so I got behind the wheel. We had driven a few miles when I noticed a cop car on the other side of the road. It was around 1 A.M. and we were the only other car on the road, so my instincts told me the cops might turn around to see what we were up to. I tried to see if the cop was looking my way and I accidentally made eye contact with him. Now I knew he'd be turning around to pull me over, and I noticed in my rearview mirror that the police car was quickly making a U-turn.

"Freddie, the cops are about to be on our ass, man. What the fuck should I do?" I asked nervously.

Freddie told me to pull the car over immediately.

"Are you sure, man? I'll turn this corner and hit the gas. We might be able to get away."

"Pull the fucking car over right now, Ive!" Freddie replied.

Because I was nervous and because of the conversation I was having with Freddie, I ran the stolen Toyota through a red light. The police car lit up my rearview mirror.

"Stop the fucking car, man!" Freddie screamed. "You just ran a red light, you stupid fuck."

The second I pulled the car over, Freddie jumped out and yanked Lisa out of the car in a very physical manner. The cops pulled up right behind me as Freddie was dragging Lisa by her arm and yelling at her at the top of his lungs.

"What the fuck did I tell you about talking to you ex?" Freddie said.

"I didn't talk to him, he was talking to me," Lisa replied.

Freddie continued to make a scene and I noticed he was walking farther and farther away from the stolen Toyota. I began to understand what Freddie was doing, but I had no idea if it would actually work.

"I swear to you I'm gonna fucking kill you both if I find out you are playing me," he continued.

As the officer approached the staged argument, he went straight to Freddie to ask him what was going on.

"Officer, I don't mean to be out here flipping, but I just caught my bitch cheating again," Freddie said to the cop.

"My man, it's late. You can't be out here acting like this," said the cop. "Take this shit home."

Cops in the Bronx almost always started out their sentences with "my man." I guess they learn that shit in the academy. Maybe they thought it helped them gain our trust or something.

"Officer, can you please tell my brother to drive my girlfriend home? I need to walk a little so I don't kill that bitch. I need to cool off."

"Miss, you should go home with his brother so he can cool off," said the officer.

With that, the officer escorted Lisa back to the stolen car, and as soon as Lisa got in, she told me to take off. I watched in my rearview mirror as the officer stood on the sidewalk trying to console a broken-hearted Freddie.

I'm not sure if Freddie just wanted out of the car so he could have a chance to run or if he knew he could act his way out of all of us going to jail. Freddie saved us that night. It was an example of his undeniable street smarts and instinct for working his way out of the toughest spots. Knowing Freddie the way I knew him, he probably would have taken the whole rap anyway and told the cops Lisa and I had nothing to do with the stolen car, even though I was driving.

About a year after that incident, Freddie and I went into the gun-running business with my brother. With some connections, we would sell guns to the powerful drug dealers Freddie was associated with. We once went to see this woman called La Madrina (the Godmother) in the South Bronx. I wondered how a woman in her fifties could be standing on the stoop of a building wearing more jewels than Mr. T. This woman had some major jewelry on, and she was just chilling in one of the worst neighborhoods in the South Bronx without a care in the world. I later found out that she was responsible for a million-dollar-a-year drug operation and ruled the streets, along with her sons, by intimidation, violence, and murder. Rumor had it that when her son got into a war with some other drug dealers across town, she told them that if anything happened to him she would kill three of their people. When her son was murdered, she was true to her word. Not only did she kill three people, she even had one of her son's associates killed, because he was supposed to be protecting her child. This woman was no joke.

When she looked me in the eye and told me she wanted one dozen TEC-9 submachine guns, all I could do was say, "Absolutely, we'll have them to you soon."

I was connected through Freddie and it was a very powerful feeling.

I had no way of knowing the ATF had already tapped my mother's phone in Virginia Beach and heard the phone conversations between my brother Freddie and me. After Bill was arrested in Virginia, my mother called me and told me in Spanish not to say a word. I guess she didn't think the ATF could decipher her Spanglish way of speaking.

"Ivan, they are coming to arrest you tomorrow. *No le digo nada,*" she said. Don't say anything.

My brother's gut instinct had manifested itself and I was the one who told him to get the fuck on the bus. Now we were apparently all going down for running guns.

Early the next morning, I was arrested by two ATF agents and taken to the federal lockup, just two blocks from where I worked in the World Trade Center.

Ain't this a bitch?

Just like on television, they started the good-cop bad-cop routine on me. I was scared but their routine was laughable. I held it in, though, because I didn't want to be laughing in the face of two ATF agents.

The good cop said, "Son, we know you don't have much to do with this. I know you have a kid on the way, so all you have to do is tell us everything and we'll let you go home tonight."

"I don't know what you're talking about," I said.

"So you're going to tell me you weren't selling guns with your brother and Freddie."

"I haven't seen my brother since he moved to Virginia with my mom," was my reply, with a straight face.

Here comes the bad cop.

As he kicked the chair from under me, he yelled, "Listen to me, you little motherfucker. If you don't sign a statement and tell us everything you know, you are going to jail for a very long time. And after you do twenty years in New York we are going to send you to Virginia so you can do twenty years over there, and they are going to send you to Maryland and then Delaware. You transported guns across all those state lines, and they're going to take turns prosecuting you."

In my head I was thinking, *Fuck, this isn't good,* but I couldn't let them see how scared I was.

"Sir, I'm sorry, I don't know what to tell you but I wasn't involved in this. I don't know what's going on," I said. "I already told you I haven't seen my brother in a year or so."

Even after the bad-cop agent called Stormy to tell her I wouldn't see my child until it was twenty years old, I did what my mother told me to do. I stayed the hell quiet.

I had seen enough movies, and I knew that the best thing for me to do was to keep quiet and seek legal counsel. I was surprised to find out they had wiretaps, and even more surprised when the ATF agent came in the room and said, "Give us Freddie and we'll let you go."

All I could say was, "I want a lawyer."

When the court-appointed attorney came into the room, he said, "Listen, all they want is your cousin Freddie. They already have your brother and he confessed, so he's going down. They know you aren't the ringleader, so if you give up Freddie they'll let you go."

"Aren't you supposed to be helping me?" I asked. "What happened to innocent until proven guilty?"

"You know what, I can't stand your kind. You come to this country and you bring in your guns and your drugs and you hurt innocent people. You are a disgrace to mankind and you are going to rot in jail," said the attorney.

What the fuck is going on here? I thought to myself. *This guy is supposed to be helping me get off and he just threw me to the wolves.*

A few days after I was arrested, I found myself standing in front of a judge. At my first court appearance the judge determined that there was insufficient evidence to hold me, so I was released and the case was postponed for three months. He told the ATF to get their evidence together and be ready when they brought me in front of him again.

I went to see my cousin Johnny to let him know that my brother and I had been arrested. I asked him to send word back to Freddie that he should cut all communications with me until things died down. I also informed him about the wiretaps. And I told him to let Freddie know that the feds had a real hard-on for him. They were trying everything in their power to convince me to give him up in order to have the case against me dropped. One of the agents even said, "Just call us when he's holding and we'll come arrest him. He'll never know you gave him up."

I can only assume they knew of Freddie through the wiretaps. They must have known that he was the one with all the powerful connections and that I was just a delivery boy. They wanted him, and the agent in charge of my case made no secret of it. I knew the code of the streets. Ratting on someone I considered my cousin was just not going to happen. My brother would end up taking the rap for all of us and spending time in a federal penitentiary in Florida after being charged by the ATF.

The worst I got out of the case was being kicked out of my chair after telling the arresting ATF agent that I had nothing to say. I remember sitting in one of the interrogation rooms and hearing how the ATF agents had gotten a gunrunner to come downtown by paging his beeper and telling him he won a television set. They thought it was the funniest thing that ever happened, and to tell you the truth I thought the shit was funny too.

The day I arrived back in front of the judge, the ATF still hadn't collected sufficient evidence against me in the gun-running operation. Nor were they able to convince my cousin to testify against me, so I was about to walk out of court a free man. I clearly heard the judge say the case would remain open for seven years. He said that if any of the guns I was accused of bringing into New York ever turned up on the streets, I would be charged with transporting illegal firearms across state lines. I would be held accountable to the fullest extent of the law, so I better hope none of those guns ever sees the light of day. I stayed silent, but inside I was a complete wreck. I'd helped bring in so many guns. How could one of them not eventually make its way into the hands of the authorities? But it felt good to be free, and I'll never forget what my brother did by taking the rap so I could stay out of jail.

Although I was only in jail a few days, I stayed away from Freddie when I got out. He was smart enough to know that even if I was saying I wouldn't give him up, there was always a possibility I would to save my own ass. That's just the way it was where we came from. You couldn't trust anyone when he was facing time locked in a cage away from his family. People did anything to keep their freedom and Freddie knew that.

I missed him, but I missed the street education he was always giving me more.

"Don't ever park in a spot where you can't get out quick. What are you—stupid?"

"Don't ever have your back to a crowd in a restaurant, in a party, or anywhere."

The more time I spent with him, the less likely I was to get myself killed.

Everyone who knew him loved him. Besides being one of the toughest guys I ever met, he was also one of the most comical. He could make any situation funny. He was fun to be around, and losing that at a time when we were becoming so close was very hard for me. I recall one night we were at a house party full of thugs and there was Freddie dancing like a character. When a young black guy decided to get in his face and show he was the better dancer, Freddie just kept dancing, and when he was done he turned around and pulled his pants down and showed his ass. There were a few tense moments when I thought a fight would break out, but everyone just laughed. I never met anyone in my life like him, and I'm sure I never will.

By the time Manny got back from jail, Freddie had begun hanging out with a character named He-Man. He-Man was one of those guys who somehow manages to make a lot of money selling drugs but has no heart at all; we referred to these types of guys as "butt." It's the type who would stab his own mother in the back for a buck, spineless and heartless, a pure shyster. He-Man was all of these things and he would eventually lead to Freddie's downfall in the drug game. It wasn't because Freddie ever fell asleep on the streets. The only fault Freddie had was that if he loved somebody, he loved them wholeheartedly and trusted them—even those he had no business trusting.

Freddie began working for He-Man as an enforcer. The guy seemed to get into trouble a lot when his "soldiers" were around. I'm sure the guy was real quiet when he was alone, but when he had Freddie around, he used Freddie's heart and respect to make himself more powerful. Apparently, the guy had a beef with some guys from Crotona Avenue, and he sent Freddie to the block to settle a score he wasn't man enough to settle for himself.

Freddie arrived in the rival neighborhood, jumped out of his car, and started shooting at a guy named Buck Four. After just a few shots, the TEC-9 submachine gun that Freddie had been given by He-Man jammed up. Freddie was standing in the middle of the street trying to unjam the gun. By the time he jumped back in his car, a few of the guys on Crotona had gotten a really good look at his face. Freddie had just become the owner of He-Man's beef, and he inherited a rivalry with a crew of cold-blooded murderers. These guys were no different from some of the guys Freddie grew up with on Elder Avenue.

One week after this shooting took place, Buck Four was murdered in a garage—after being tortured. To this day, Manny and I don't believe that the Freddie we knew could have ever been involved in torturing someone, but only God really knows what happened to Buck Four and whether or not Freddie was involved in his murder.

Buck Four's brother, Flex, believed that Freddie was responsible for his brother's death, and for that a contract was placed on Freddie's head. Freddie's time was running out. His wife, Nina, and closest friend, Manny, believe he knew the clock was about to stop ticking for him because of the way he behaved right before his own murder.

The night before the hit, the guys went to a small neighborhood club called Just-Us to drink and have a good time. I was still keeping my distance from Freddie and the block while things cooled down on me. But that night He-Man started a beef with some cats in the club and Manny, Freddie, Herman, and Johnny got into a brawl with the guys and ended up beating up a few of them pretty severely.

Normally, after a big fight like this the guys would get really rowdy, full of adrenaline as they talked shit about the beating they'd just placed on the sorry fools. This night was different. Freddie was sitting calmly on a car, and when Manny went over to ask him what was up, Freddie simply stated that he was cool. Manny said that it was almost as if Freddie knew something was going to happen to him very soon, like he knew all the bad shit he'd done in his life was going to catch up.

On May 4, 1991, Freddie left his apartment in the morning and did something he'd never done before—he told his wife, Nina, not to open the door for anyone. Nina remembers that Freddie looked worried.

Late that afternoon, Freddie was at the garage on the corner of Kingsbridge Road and Kingsbridge Terrace, where we used to hang out and work on cars with the guys from Bailey Avenue. The garage sat on top of Suicide Hill, and we had spent countless hours, weeks, months, and years there just chilling. On this day, He-Man stopped by the garage and told Freddie he'd just been shot at and needed Freddie's gun, because he didn't have his strap with him. Freddie gave He-Man his only gun and He-Man took off in a hurry.

Around the same time, a friend of ours named Wanda received a frantic call from her friend Michelle. Michelle was from the Crotona area. She was dating one of the guys from Flex's crew. Michelle told Wanda that not only had a hit been put out on Freddie but that they were actually on their way to the garage to kill him. She wanted Wanda to find Freddie and warn him to get out of there. As Wanda ran up the hill from her house, she heard the shots. The call had come moments too late.

Freddie was standing at the garage talking to Julie and Gracie. They were the little sisters of older girls from the neighborhood, and at just fourteen years old they didn't really hang out with us much. We treated them like little sisters when they did. The gunman realized the girls were blocking his target, so he shouted Freddie's name. When they all turned around, the gunman started shooting, striking Julie in the face and Gracie in the upper back. He figured he would just get them out of the way—he didn't care about murdering innocent teenage girls in cold blood. I wonder how much money you have to pay someone to pull off a hit like that. In the Bronx, life was cheap, and that day it was worthless.

I heard from many people who witnessed the shooting, including Gracie herself, that Freddie had the opportunity to seek cover behind a parked car, or to run. But that wasn't Freddie. Freddie was a man of the streets. He understood the game. He had heart and he knew he'd have to answer for what he had done.

He charged the gunman and shouted, "You motherfucker, why did you shoot the girls?"

With each step closer to the shooter, Freddie took another bullet to the body. Freddie would be shot multiple times before finally reaching the gunman and trying to grab at one of the two guns, screaming.

The gunman pushed Freddie to the ground. I've heard that the gunman said, "I know you wear a vest, motherfucker!" before pumping two shots into Freddie's head.

Julie and Gracie were in the hospital for a while. When I visited them, their mothers asked us to tell the girls that Freddie was alive. We needed to keep their spirits up.

The bullet that hit Julie passed right through her cheek and out of her mouth. She was going to be all right. Gracie had been shot in the back and was in critical condition.

The first thing they each asked was how Freddie was doing.

Even after taking bullets for being with him, they—like all of us—loved him with all their hearts.

Freddie made it to the hospital and survived overnight, a true testament to the fighter he was. Though multiple bullets had hit him, including at least one shot to the head, he was still alive and fighting the toughest battle of his life. On May 4, 1991, as the medical personnel in the hospital wheeled him into the elevator to take him for a CT scan, Freddie had a heart attack and died before the elevator doors opened on the next floor.

Freddie was a product of his environment, yet he never let that turn his heart cold to the people he loved. He loved us all with every-thing he had.

The last time I saw Freddie was at the garage where he died. It was a few months before his death and the chemistry had changed between us. I still had a lot of love for him and he still showed me love, but I felt like he was worried that I would rat on him in the gun case. He wanted us to keep our distance, which was understandable, and I respected his wishes and went on my way after a very brief exchange. To this day, I regret that this is my final memory of Freddie. I had no idea he wouldn't be around for much longer.

"What up, Fred? Long time no see, kid, how you been?" I asked.

"I'm chilling, how you, son?" Fred shot back.

"You know, just waiting to see how shit's gonna play out with this court case," I said. "I'm sorry about . . ." But before I could finish the sentence I noticed that Freddie was shaking his head, as if to tell me he didn't want to talk about it.

I got the message and quickly changed the subject.

"You putting a new system in the ride?" I asked.

"Nah, just cleaning it up. Making the shit sound crisp so they can hear me coming."

"All right, baby, I'll catch up with you soon," I said as I gave Freddie half a hug and began to break out.

"Be safe out here, little man," said Fred. It was the last thing he'd ever say to me.

His murder put us all on edge and we wouldn't leave our houses with-out our guns, a bullet in the chamber ready to shoot at the slightest sign of danger. I remember walking down Broadway and looking at every single car that was passing by. Suddenly, everyone seemed like the enemy. We knew Crotona was just getting started and we all fig-ured Herman, Johnny, Manny, and anyone else around was on the list.

The night of the wake, we were all strapped at the funeral home and everyone was on high alert. When we went outside, we noticed there were a few motorcycles driving by slowly, checking things out. This sent everyone into their coats, and the guns were cocked and ready. To make matters worse, Buck Four's wake was being held at another funeral home up the block, so we thought for sure the boys from Crotona would shoot up Freddie's wake. In the span of a week, Freddie and Buck Four had both been murdered, and most of us didn't know the real reason behind it.

Years later, Freddie's murderer was killed in jail. It goes to show just how connected the guys he ran with on Elder Avenue truly were. Freddie knew a lot of people in New York. He was well respected, well loved, and he had people willing to avenge his death. He-Man, whom we believe set Freddie up by taking his gun moments before he was murdered, disappeared. Chances are he is buried under some construction in New York. He would have to pay for his role in Buck Four's and Freddie's murders. Most likely someone collected on that debt, we just never heard about it.

No one really knows if Freddie killed Buck Four, but he definitely lived his life by the gun and he died by it. Freddie became the lost son of Elder Avenue when the older guys first introduced him to the street life in his neighborhood. He became another statistic of a very violent time in New York City, which saw over two thousand sons and daughters leave this earth far too early in 1991.

I can't and won't excuse the things Freddie did, but the streets influenced the choices he made. Had Freddie been raised in Westchester County and attended private schools, he would have grown up to be a doctor, a lawyer, or an investment banker. He knew how to make money. He was special, and I'm a better man for knowing him. He allowed me to learn through his mistakes. When he died, many of us saw that the life we were living was taking us straight to an early grave.

In the end, the evil spirits of the streets got to Freddie, and there was no way his grandmother's blessed pillow could protect him. All that was left for us to do was light a candle, pray to the Virgin de la Candelaria, the guardian of the cemetery, and ask her to watch over our lost brother's spirit.

"Blessed are they that mourn for they shall be comforted."   St. Matt V.4

May Jesus have mercy on the soul of

Freddie Martin
May 4 1991

GENTLEST HEART of Jesus, ever present in the Blessed Sacrament, ever consumed with burning love for the poor captive souls in Purgatory, have mercy on the soul of Thy departed servant. Be not severe in Thy judgment but let some drops of Thy Precious Blood fall upon the devouring flames, and do Thou, O merciful Savior, send Thy angels to conduct Thy departed servant to a place of refreshment, light and peace. Amen.

May the souls of all the faithful departed, through the mercy of God, rest in peace. Amen.

R.G. ORTIZ FUNERAL HOME, Inc.

Freddie's funeral booklet.

AILEY AVENUE LAST NIGHT ON BAILEY AVENUE LAST NIGHT
EY AVENUE LAST NIGHT ON BAILEY AVENUE LAST NIGHT OI
VENUE LAST NIGHT ON BAILEY AVENUE LAST NIGHT ON BA
NUE LAST NIGHT ON BAILEY AVENUE LAST NIGHT ON BAIL
UE LAST NIGHT ON BAILEY AVENUE LAST NIGHT ON BAILEY
AST NIGHT ON BAILEY AVENUE LAST NIGHT ON BAILEY AVEN
IGHT ON BAILEY AVENUE LAST NIGHT ON BAILEY AVENUE LAS
N BAILEY AVENUE LAST NIGHT ON BAILEY AVENUE LAST N
AILEY AVENUE LAST NIGHT ON BAILEY AVENUE LAST NIGHT
EY AVENUE LAST NIGHT ON BAILEY AVENUE LAST NIGHT OI
VENUE LAST NIGHT ON BAILEY AVENUE LAST NIGHT ON BA
NUE LAST NIGHT ON BAILEY AVENUE LAST NIGHT ON BA
NUE LA   ON BAIL
UE LAS   BAILEY
AST NI   BAILEY

Last Night on Bailey Avenue

The crew I ran with on Bailey Avenue in 1993 were some of the most loyal, toughest, streetwise characters to ever roam the streets of the Bronx. I would liken our bond to that of brothers, so if someone had told me that CYC's ultimate demise would come in one night, I would have said they were fucking crazy. But that is exactly what happened one cold March night in 1993. The band of brothers would turn into a band of enemies.

I guess God had had enough, although some might argue that only the devil himself could have scripted that night of pain, suffering, and destruction of lives.

March 6 was like any other Saturday night. I was gearing up to go out to a party with the guys from the neighborhood. It was customary to look good, and I had just purchased a Cross Colours jean suit. It was blue with yellow faux-leather pockets, which I wore with matching yellow-and-white Nike Air Force 1s to bring the outfit together. It would be ten years until Nelly made a rap song about wearing Air Force 1s, but in the Bronx we were always starting fashion trends. All that shit started in the inner cities in the Bronx, Harlem, Brooklyn, and Money-Making Manhattan and the trends would spread out to the world from there. I was looking like a ghetto celebrity that night, and I was ready to go out with the boys and see where the night would take us.

My cousin Herman was calling to tell me we were going to a birth-day party for our boy Little Angel. His girl was throwing him a bash up in my old stomping grounds around Marion Avenue, which was a block from where I went to elementary school. I told Herman that as soon as I hung up I would call a cab and meet them on the block in ten minutes.

Before I could hang up the phone Herman said, "Yo, cuz, no guns tonight."

"What the fuck you talking about, no guns?" I said.

Herman told me that Angel's girl was serious about nobody bring-ing guns into her apartment and that if we showed up with guns we wouldn't be allowed into the party.

I remember having a funny feeling in the pit of my stomach. Some-thing just didn't feel right about this situation. But I said, "All right, cuz, I'll see you in a few minutes."

Then I called a cab to pick me up at the house Stormy and I were sharing with her parents on Corlear Avenue—one block up from the 50th precinct, which I knew intimately. It was a quiet neighborhood for the most part, but that quiet life only kept me content for about a year. After that, I was right back on the block, getting into all kinds of shit I had no business being involved with anymore. Riding around in stolen cars, going with the fellas to re-up on their drug supplies, and getting involved in everyday scuffles that came with the territory.

I was waiting for the cab when Stormy started yelling. She always did that when I was getting geared up for a party. But for some reason I could sense something different that night. Tears flowed down her face. She had this look that will forever leave me convinced she had sensed something about that night I had yet to find out. She was begging me to stay, as if it was a matter of life or death that I stay home with her that night and spend some time with our one-year-old daughter, Heaven.

But I was looking damn good that night and I had already called the cab to take me to Bailey Avenue.

I was contemplating my next move when the phone rang again.

"Yo, cuz, where the fuck you at? You said you was on your way fifteen minutes ago," asked Herman.

"Stormy is acting up, cuz. I'm trying to get the fuck out of here. I already called a cab," I said.

"We ain't waiting too much longer. We ready to be out."

"And what the fuck is up with the 'no guns' bullshit, cuz? Since when the fuck do we go out without our joints?" I asked.

"What the fuck you scared, son?" said Herman.

"I'm just saying, what if some beef breaks out? What are we going to do with no guns?"

The last thing I remember my cousin saying to me was, "Catch the cab up to Marion Avenue and meet us at the party. We're breaking out right now."

"Be safe, and I'll catch up with you guys in a few."

Three things saved my life that night: the look on Stormy's face, the cabdriver being late, and my cousin deciding to leave without me. Although I could easily have caught up with them at the party, these three things made me do something I had never done in my life—change my mind about hanging out. I took my clothes off and spent a quiet night with Stormy and Heaven. I didn't know my boys would be put through the biggest test of their lives and that no one and nothing would ever be the same again.

At barely five o'clock in the morning, the phone rang. No one wants to be jerked out of bed at that time. There is never good news at five o'clock in the morning. On the other end of the phone was Manny, one of my best friends, more like a brother, and I could hear in his voice that I was about to get some really bad news.

One million thoughts raced through my head in the few seconds it took Manny to tell me I should sit down. No one had ever told me to sit down before. That shit only happened in the movies, so I knew it was going to be more serious than the average "This guy's in jail" phone call. As I fell into my chair in the darkened living room, Manny began a tale that seemed to be scripted in Hollywood.

I must be having a nightmare.

The fellas from the neighborhood jumped in a few cars and headed over to the party on Marion Avenue, expecting to have a good time and meet a few girls. I'd done this a million times with the guys: smoke a few blunts, listen to some music, and drive over to a party to see who could pick up the baddest bitch at the party.

When the guys from Bailey Avenue arrived at the party that Saturday night, they were greeted with a setup the likes of which had never been seen. Angel, Nitty, and Dumbo were the first to walk into the apartment. The instant the third guy was inside, the door was quickly forced shut, locked, and bolted. My cousin Herman, Rico, Two, Hitman, Keds, Manny, and the rest of the guys could hear a lot of commotion going on inside, but there was nothing they could do besides try to kick in the door.

Inside the apartment, Angel, Nitty, and Dumbo were being sliced up by about twenty guys with box cutters and knives. When the door of the apartment finally opened, my crew tried to push their way in and were met with guns pointed at their heads. Since they had left all their straps on the block, they couldn't retaliate. Angel, Dumbo, and Nitty were shoved out the door and into their arms, completely covered in blood. Manny told me he had never seen so much blood. Considering that he'd seen a lot of blood in his days as a drug dealer on Elder Avenue in the South Bronx, there must have been a lot of fucking blood. The injured guys were rushed into cars and raced to the hospital.

Two ran every red light and Keds followed close behind, both trying to make it to the hospital while the blood of our brothers was pouring. In all the commotion that had taken place, one of our closest brothers had been left behind. Rico would somehow have to find his way to safety.

Once the guys made it to the hospital, the initial planning phase of retaliation began to be laid down in the hospital corridors. I can only imagine the type of adrenaline pumping through the crew. There was no way this was going to go unpunished.

Angel received close to four hundred stitches to close the wounds on his head, face, and neck. Dumbo also received a number of stitches, but Nitty didn't need any. Legend has it that Nitty was catching wreck in that apartment and somehow managing to hold his own against the attack. Since Angel was the primary target, Nitty was able to throw as many knockout blows as possible, keeping his damage to a minimum.

It was almost midnight when the guys were back on Bailey Avenue, getting more and more hyped. The anger was at a boiling point; the guns were being loaded and cocked, the ski masks and gloves were being readied, and the plans for revenge were being finalized.

According to Manny, the guys were saying things like: "We're going to shoot everybody on that fucking block."

And: "Don't leave any of those motherfuckers alive."

Between the anger, the agitators, and the one real murderer in the crew, Hitman, the boys from Marion Avenue were about to be laid to rest. As the guys prepared to load up the two cars and the minivan, they were greeted by Rico's brother, Mike.

"Rico's in the hospital. Somebody beat the living shit out of him."

With everyone's blood boiling, they hadn't noticed that they left Rico behind. Everyone thought he was in the other car. Rico had been found unconscious by Van Cortlandt Park. The boys from Marion Avenue caught up to Rico, threw him in their car, took him for a ten-mile drive, and beat him half to death with fists and baseball bats. Eventually one of the blows knocked him unconscious, and he was found by a passing motorist—his swollen and bloodied body left by the side of the road to die.

They loaded up the cars with a new destination in mind, the hospital on 223rd Street and Broadway. It didn't take long for them to realize how badly Rico had been beaten.

He had nothing to say to anyone from the block except, "You fucking left me to be killed."

With that said, the crew went down to Twin Donuts, an all-night diner we frequented after clubs, parties, and late nights out on the grind, to plan the retaliation on Marion Avenue. Twin Donuts was a good spot, and the employees always put up with all of our bullshit. I can't imagine what it must be like to work in an all-night diner in a tough section of the Bronx and have twenty thugs with guns walk in there demanding all kinds of stupid shit. The Mexican cooks always seemed to hold their own, and they treated us well for the most part, so we treated them with respect in return. They were just trying to make a living and we were just trying to get something to eat, so it was a mutually beneficial relationship.

When the guys reached the diner, they ran into my cousin Tony. Tony had received the news about Rico and was making his way to the hospital to pay him a visit. Tony was a little bit older than the rest of us, about two to five years depending on whom you compared him to at the time. Tony wasn't on the block anymore. He had pretty much disassociated himself with the streets of Bailey Avenue and would only walk by to go get something to eat on Broadway or go out shopping or to see his girl. He had stopped hanging out with us at least six months prior to that night. He didn't want to be a part of what we were doing. Most of the guys had begun dealing large amounts of drugs, and we all carried guns. What used to be fistfights and baseball-bat fights had turned into stabbings and shootings. Tony just wasn't into all that, so he had slowly disassociated himself from the guys on the block.

Tony and I weren't related by blood, but if anyone had told me he wasn't really my cousin, I would have punched them in the mouth. He grew up with Herman and Johnny, my blood cousins, on Bailey Avenue. I met Tony when I was about seven or eight years old; he was in Titi Vilma's house so much that he called her "Mom." Herman and Johnny were like his brothers, and that is how Tony became known as my cousin for as far back as I can remember.

Manny would later tell me that the guys got really out of control in the diner.

The cook got scared and asked the guys to leave; he said he didn't want any trouble, but he just couldn't serve them if they were going to act like that. Manny said a chaotic situation then began to unfold and the guys did some damage to the place, ripping stools out and throwing them at the walls, ripping the countertops off and smashing anything in sight, as well as snatching donuts and food on the way out of the diner. After the free-for-all, the guys walked up the block to the hospital, laughing about what they'd just done to the diner.

Tony had been eating at Twin Donuts for years, just like the rest of us, and he knew most of the guys in the diner on a first-name basis. He started to walk back to the hospital with the guys, but something made him turn around and go back to the diner by himself. When he got to the front of the diner he was greeted by the cook's cousins. Just like all of us, the cook usually called his cousins when he got into trouble or felt threatened. The cook's cousin thrust a small knife into Tony's chest and hit him very close to the heart. I'm sure he never even saw it coming. At about six foot three and two hundred fifty pounds, Tony was a very big guy and a great fighter. Had he seen the guy coming with a knife, he easily could have blocked the blow and beat the shit out of him.

Tony actually stumbled to the hospital by himself.

Manny told me he was the first to see Tony when he walked through the emergency doors of the hospital. He said Tony had a glazed look in his eyes and he was holding his chest.

"They got me, son," Tony said.

With that, they ripped Tony's coat off to unveil a small drop of blood on his shirt. Manny told Tony he'd be all right; it was a small wound, no big deal.

To this day, Manny tells me he thought it was nothing—there was no blood and Tony was walking normally. On the outside of his body, things looked promising, but Tony was bleeding internally. My cousin was dying in the hospital, and I was having a peaceful night's sleep in a warm bed with my girlfriend and child.

The guys stormed the diner and began to destroy everything and anything they could get their hands on. The windows were smashed, the tables flipped and tossed, and the equipment destroyed. Nothing would be left of this place when they were done. Then it wasn't enough for the guys to destroy the place; soon enough the guns came out. My cousin Herman said Hitman—the only real murderer in the neighborhood— began to spray the place with bullets. Hitman killed the cook while Herman and Johnny fought over a second gun one of the guys in the crew had. After Herman got it from his brother, he shot up the place. Hitman then turned to the two cabdrivers sitting on stools in the corner—innocent bystanders but witnesses nonetheless—and gave them a few seconds to look away, to duck under a table, to react in some way. When the cabdrivers failed to react or turn away, Hitman shot them both at very close range. There was no turning back now. They needed to make a clean getaway.

When they left the diner, Herman took off his black hoodie and exposed his face to a cabdriver and a bus full of people—more witnesses. The guys jumped into three getaway cars and raced back to the projects, where they could disappear into the endless holes, apartments, and rooftops. With the sirens getting louder, Keds and Two chose to go straight back to the Marble Hill houses. Fat Ant decided the safer route was to head to Manhattan to lay low. Bad idea: By the time his vehicle reached the bridge, the NYPD had set up a roadblock.

In all the years I lived in New York, I had never even seen a roadblock. Here was another movie moment—a roadblock in the middle of the bridge on Broadway that connected the Bronx to Manhattan.

There was nowhere to go, and the guys in the minivan—Fat Ant, Herman, Johnny, and Jolo—had to surrender peacefully. This would be the beginning of the end of the loyalty, the brotherhood, and the crew from Bailey Avenue.

The next day, I went to Jimmy Jazz's studio to lay down some tracks. I had been working with Jazz and Manny on some new music and I figured the best thing to do was lay the story down on tape while it was fresh in my mind.

I knew it would be a few days before things at the jail were sorted out, and on the bus ride to Jazz's house I wrote a song called "Bailey Blues." I laid the song down and Jazz couldn't believe I had written the entire three verses, forty-eight bars, on the ten-minute bus ride over. While we were laying the vocals, Manny had called to say he'd be over. We planned on going to see Rico and Tony in the hospital. I was still under the impression that Tony had only suffered a small flesh wound and that he'd be coming home that day. This would turn out to be another time in my life when I wished I were not so wrong.

By the time we left the studio, the cops had arrested Manny. As soon as I heard Manny had been taken, I knew someone in the crew was talking. There was no more loyalty, and it wouldn't be long before the rest of the guys' capture would follow. There's supposed to be no snitching on the streets, but the fact of the matter is no one is going to take a murder rap for anyone else. I went to Dumbo's house, where the guys had begun to round up after a very long, rough night. Dumbo lived in the building next to my aunt's, and my next stop was to see how my aunt was holding up with her two sons being held for murder. I stepped in front of the building on Bailey Avenue and I hadn't been there more than fifteen minutes when ten cop cars rolled up and started asking for IDs. I noticed they were handcuffing all the guys who had been at Twin Donuts the night before. When one of the cops checked my World Trade Center ID, he told me to get the fuck out of there. I walked a few steps and leaned against a parked car in shock as they hauled off everyone who had been involved in the previous night's events. That day seemed to take turn after turn for the worse, with no end in sight.

I decided to go upstairs to my aunt's. Titi Vilma seemed to be holding up well under the circumstances and she questioned me about how much I knew. I told her what I'd heard on the phone that morning and then I told her not to worry.

"Herman and Johnny didn't shoot anyone, Titi, they'll be okay," I said.

Not long after I arrived upstairs, the phone rang. It was a collect call from Herman.

"Yo, cuz, where the fuck were you last night?" he asked.

Before I could answer, he told me that Jolo was ratting. He wanted everyone to know that Jolo was talking to the police about what went on in the diner. Herman said that if I saw Jolo I should take care of the situation. I was heated about Jolo being a rat. I had never liked that motherfucker anyway for dating one of my ex-girlfriends, Yanira. It would be my pleasure to take a baseball bat to his head, and I intended to do just that when I caught up to him.

"Don't worry, cuz, we gonna take care of that fucking rat."

It was time for me to step up to the plate and decide just how far I would go for the neighborhood, for the crew, and for my family.

It was probably around four o'clock Sunday afternoon when I found out that Tony's condition had become critical. Up to that point, I believed Tony would leave the hospital alive. But he was on life support, and they were saying he was brain-dead. "Get the fuck out of here," I said when I heard. Manny said Tony was fine. "What the fuck happened?" My aunt explained to me that Tony had suffered a lot of internal bleeding. It didn't look like he would survive the stabbing after all.

My heart was beginning to grow weak. With two cousins in jail facing murder raps and another cousin on his deathbed, my life was quickly starting to seem like a bad nightmare come to life.

I kept asking myself, *How this could happen? Why wasn't I there? Could I've put a stop to any of this shit, or would I be in jail facing a murder rap with my two cousins or lying in the hospital bed beside Tony?*

These were all the questions that raced through my mind on the way to the hospital. They had moved Tony to a hospital by the George Washington Bridge.

I had never seen anyone on life support, and I thought Tony was already gone the second I saw him. It broke my heart to see him lying in the hospital bed all swollen; when I kissed his hand it felt so damn cold. I had kissed cold hands and foreheads before—always friends who had gone before. His entire body was swollen and his arms, hands, and head all looked huge. This wasn't Tony. My heart sunk deep when I realized I would have to say goodbye to someone I loved again. Another young brother lost to the streets for no good reason. It was senseless, and along with the sadness I felt angry that it was Tony lying in that hospital bed. At that moment I was mad at the world. Tony didn't deserve to go out like this. He had left the streets. He walked away from the life and was supposed to go on and do good things. All that was left for me to do was to kiss his shell of a body and say goodbye. His spirit had moved on, and I was going to miss him more than my words could ever express.

To this day, when I think about Tony I can still hear his boisterous laughter and his melodious singing on the corner of Bailey Avenue and Kingsbridge Road. One of the toughest guys in the neighborhood—one of the guys who helped establish the Crazy Young Criminals' tough reputation—would belt out slow songs by Boyz II Men and Jodeci. I will always remember him with his big smile and his love of life. Tony was a distant cousin, but in my heart he was my brother.

I will never forget the last time I saw him. It was two or three in the morning, and I was getting ready to leave the block after a night of hanging out with the boys. Tony was walking to Twin Donuts to get a late-night snack, and I was waiting for a cab to take me home to Stormy and Heaven. He told me to be careful on the streets. I recall smiling and flashing the black. 380 semiautomatic pistol I used to pack like an American Express card—never leave home without it. Showing him the gun was my way of letting him know that I was good.

He said something like, "You young boys are wild, man. You young boys are real wild."

He said it with that same boisterous laugh I can still hear in my head.

Tony had already learned what I now know: The streets are a dead end. It was never clearer to me than when I watched his mother get ready to take him off the machine that was keeping her only son's heart beating. A mother should never have to bury her child. As Tony's mother prepared to take her son off life support, another mother was preparing to do the same thing in the neighboring room. One of the cabdrivers Hitman shot was in the room next door to Tony. He was only being kept alive long enough for his family to say their goodbyes. I thank God that his family members didn't know our crew was responsible for the death of their son. Tony and the two cabdrivers had no business dying on Sunday, March 7, 1993. They were innocent, just trying to get something to eat. But the streets don't pay attention to details like that.

With everyone else in jail, it was only Victor, Fat David, and me at the hospital. My boys Two and Hitman were the last to be arrested. Most of the other guys had gotten out of jail already, including my cousin Johnny. The tension on the block was like nothing I had ever experienced before. As we prepared to bury Tony, we couldn't keep the block together, because half the guys were ratting while the other half were keeping their mouths shut. No one really knew who was doing the talking, but when only Herman and Hitman were left in the box it became clear that enough people had talked about who had done the shooting and who had stood by and watched.

Later on, I saw Jolo walking down the block. I couldn't believe the guy had the balls to show his face in our neighborhood after talking to the police. We didn't have a lot of information, but Jolo came out a few hours after the shooting, so we all knew he had been talking. As I walked toward him, I was looking at Rico and Manny like, "I'm about to pounce on this kid, so get ready to help me beat him into the ground."

When I got close enough to hit Jolo, I shouted, "You motherfucking rat!"

As I started throwing the first punches, Johnny grabbed my arm and slapped me in the head at the same time. Jolo was one of his best friends on the block, but Herman was his brother, so I was confused as hell.

"Yo, Johnny . . . Herman told me that Jolo is the rat. We need to hurt this kid."

"If you want to get to him, you'll have to come through me," Johnny told me.

I'll never understand what took place that day and why Johnny was protecting Jolo when he knew damned well that he was a rat. I do know that Jolo would leave the block that night and never show his face again. Rumor has it that he went to Puerto Rico and has been hiding out there ever since. Fat Ant, the guy who drove the minivan in the wrong direction that night, would also turn state's evidence and rat on my cousin Herman. It seems Jolo as well as Ant named Herman as the primary shooter in the diner that night.

Although Herman didn't actually kill the two cabdrivers and the cook in that diner that night, he ended up taking a plea deal for eight and a half to fifteen years in prison. If he had gone to trial and lost the case, he would have been automatically sentenced to twenty-five years to life. Since we were poor, we couldn't hire Johnnie Cochran, and since they had a few rats and a bunch of witnesses on the city bus who saw Herman exit the diner, they had all they needed to send Herman away for a long time.

I didn't lose just one cousin that night. I lost all my cousins that night. With Tony dead, Herman shipped off to jail for a long time, and Johnny lost to alcohol and drug abuse, I had no family left on that block except for Rico, Will, and Manny. Nothing on Bailey Avenue would ever be the same. There was no going back after that night; there was no more Bailey Avenue for me to return to, at least not the way it had been.

I still carry the guilt deep in my soul for not being there that night. I still wonder if I could have stopped what happened.

But maybe I would have been a shooter on Marion Avenue instead and I'd be writing this story from a cell block in Clinton Correctional Facility, right alongside my cousin Herman.

It turned out that Angel's girlfriend was pissed that he'd cheated on her, so she had set him up. A bitter sixteen-year-old girl's vengeance started a chain reaction that ended with four grown men killed and another in jail for eight and a half to fifteen years.

Everyone knew Herman didn't kill those people that night and it became the guilt of Bailey Avenue. A guilt the neighborhood carries with it as long as the last surviving person in the neighborhood walks this earth. We all walked around with heavy hearts because Herman had to pay that price. But that is what we are built to do in our neighborhoods. Some pay while others drop dime, unable and unwilling to do the time for someone else's crime. However, no one argues that in some way everyone there that night was partially responsible for the crime committed. Someone had to carry the burden on their shoulders. That someone was Herman. It wasn't about wrong or right. But then again, it very rarely is.

Herman left behind six kids when he went to jail. A good father and a good-hearted man. The battle scars and the emotion of seeing all the bloodshed that took place, starting with Angel, Dumbo, and Nitty, and ending with Rico and Tony, drove Herman's actions that night. Herman reacted to pure emotion and it ended up costing him fourteen years of his life. I'm not saying he shouldn't have paid some price for being involved that night, but I *am* saying fourteen years is too costly a price—the price paid when a justice system rushes to declare someone guilty and move on to the next case. It is especially sad when you compare it to the sentence of the actual triggerman that night.

Hitman spent a year in jail for gun possession. With no witnesses placing him in or outside the diner and no one man enough to testify against the only real murderer on the block, Hitman walked out of jail just one year later. He made out just as well as the Marion Avenue boys, who never had to pay the price for their actions that night.

Manny, who called me with this nightmare of a story, is now a cable guy in Florida. He just named his newborn son after Tony, and he continues to be haunted by the events that took place that night. If he ever calls me again and tells me to sit down, I will hang up the phone on him.

Angel and Rico also left the street life and stopped hanging out on Bailey Avenue. Keds would eventually be sentenced to eight and a half years for beating a guy's head in with a baseball bat for looking at him the wrong way at a stoplight, another victim of the *What you looking at?* virus that continues to plague the inner city. Nitty went to trial for a payroll heist that happened in 2004 and was sentenced to eight years. I read about the robbery in the *New York Post* a few weeks after hanging out with him on the block. Just as Nitty held his own with the guys in that apartment, he would beat up an officer and take his gun during the payroll heist.

Hitman is living in an undisclosed location and calls to say what's up occasionally. Hitman and I remain close friends and I still have as much love for him today as I did before that night. I've never been the type to judge. I don't judge him for who he is; he'll be judged one day, but it won't be by me. Maybe if I had to spend fourteen years in prison for his crime I'd feel differently, but that's simply not the case.

Will, or Two, as he's called on the streets, is now referred to as the Last Mo-Rican, the last Puerto Rican on Bailey Avenue making money and doing dirt. He carries on the violent legacy Crazy Young Criminals left behind. My cousin Johnny is still short-tempered and struggles with alcohol and substance abuse. I don't think his life will begin again until after his brother is released from prison. He has the biggest heart of anyone I've ever met in my life and I believe he is the most tortured by that night's events.

I not only left Bailey Avenue shortly after the events that took place that night, I left New York altogether. I could no longer call Creston Avenue, Bailey Avenue, or Kingsbridge Road—or even New York— home. I had a daughter to raise and there was no way I was going to expose her to those streets and that way of life.

In 1993, there were more than two thousand murders in New York City. I can only imagine how many lives were altered by the other murders that took place that year.

ANTONIO "TONY" TORRES . . .
REST IN PEACE, MY BROTHER.

MAY·HE SUPPORT·US ALL·THE·DAY LONG, TILL·THE·SHADES LENGTHEN·&·THE·EVENING COMES, AND·THE·BUSY WORLD·IS·HUSHED·&·THE FEVER·OF·LIFE·IS·OVER·& OUR·WORK·IS·DONE, THEN·IN·HIS·MERCY· MAY·HE·GIVE·US·A·SAFE LODGING·&·A·HOLY·REST AND·PEACE·AT·THE·LAST.
CARDINAL NEWMAN

In Loving Memory

of

Antonio M. Torres

March 7, 1993

—

WILLIAMS FUNERAL HOME, Inc.
(212) 548-1100

Tony's funeral booklet.

EPILOGUE EPILOGUE EPILOGUE EPILOGUE EPILOGUE EP
GUE EPILOGUE EPILOGUE EPILOGUE EPILOGUE EPILOGU
ILOGUE EPILOGUE EPILOGUE EPILOGUE EPILOGUE EP
GUE EPILOGUE EPILOGUE EPILOGUE EPILOGUE EPILOGU
ILOGUE EPILOGUE EPILOGUE EPILOGUE EPILOGUE EP
GUE EPILOGUE EPILOGUE EPILOGUE EPILOGUE EPILOGU
ILOGUE EPILOGUE EPILOGUE EPILOGUE EPILOGUE EP
GUE EPILOGUE EPILOGUE EPILOGUE EPILOGUE EPILOGU
ILOGUE EPILOGUE EPILOGUE EPILOGUE EPILOGUE EP
GUE EPILOGUE EPILOGUE EPILOGUE EPILOGUE EPILOGU
ILOGUE EPILOGUE EPILOGUE EPILOGUE EPILOGUE EP
GUE EPILOGUE EPILOGUE EPILOGUE EPILOGUE EPILOGU
ILOGL   GUE EP
GUE I   EPILOGU
ILOGL   GUE EP

Epilogue

Growing up in the Kingsbridge section of the Bronx, I never knew where the next stop was going to take me. Although I appreciated life a little bit more after the first murder of a close friend, Zen, that never stopped me from praying for death at different times. I always fantasized about my death and my graffiti memorial going up right next to the ones honoring Zen, Binky, Mine 2, Tony, Hefty, or Brolick, just to name a few.

IVE 196 . . . REST IN PEACE.

I could envision my boys standing around the memorial, pouring liquor out onto the sidewalk to honor my life and death. Better yet, they would blow marijuana smoke into the air in the hope that it would somehow reach my spirit and connect us again.

There were days after my mother left the Bronx when I was hungry and couldn't fathom where my next meal was going to come from, so I prayed for God to take me. I just didn't want to be hungry anymore. But I was also happy my mother had left. Her leaving allowed me to run around acting like the little criminal I wanted to be without the neighbors telling her how bad her son had become. I lost respect for adults I had respect my whole life once my mother left. I used to smoke weed in the building right in front of Ray's mom. I no longer cared that she had known me since I was seven or eight years old. My mom leaving gave me the freedom to be the man I thought I was. I didn't feel like she abandoned me. I felt like she freed me.

But there were days when I was overcome with guilt for some of the things I had done in the streets. Again I would ask God to take me. There were days when I was high on cocaine and felt as if I had turned into my biological father, a man I didn't want to be anything like for fear of failing my daughter, and I prayed yet again for God to take me. I was the living definition of a man with a death wish, and most days I really didn't care if I lived or died. Growing up on those streets, everything was a contradiction. One minute we were beating up someone who tried to rob an old woman in our neighborhood and the next minute we were victimizing someone in another neighborhood. Therefore, while I appreciated life at times, I called for death at other times, sometimes in the same day.

I wonder if Binky was praying for death when he danced with the wrong girl at a house party one night and ended up being shot to death by her jealous boyfriend after stepping outside for what was supposed to be a fistfight. He was one of the guys from a rival crew on Morris Avenue, but I became close friends with him after we started taking GED classes together at Walton High School. I only knew him for a short time before he was murdered, and most people from my block didn't know we had struck up a close friendship. I liked Binky a lot and I was sad when he died, but I didn't go to the funeral because I wasn't cool with his crew on Morris Avenue.

Binky's father became a neighborhood legend when he shot the guy who murdered his son. He shot him in the ass on the steps of the courthouse. When the district attorney's office tried to make an example out of Binky's father, Geraldo Rivera came to his rescue and shined the light of positive media on the case—saving Binky's father from spending years in jail for shooting the man who had murdered his son in a very unfair fight. My cousin Herman would become friends with Binky's murderer while they both served out their time upstate. Even crazier, Jolo, who ratted on Herman, was also Binky's brother. It's a small world on the streets, and an even smaller world in the penitentiary system.

I wonder if Sergio was praying for death when he decided to snap on a Dominican kid in the neighborhood one too many times, until finally the kid had had enough and decided to come back with a gun and shoot Sergio to death on the steps of an elementary school. Sergio's murderer would have his five minutes of fame on the television show *America's Most Wanted*. He spent some time on the run but turned himself in after the show aired, bringing an end to another senseless Kingsbridge murder.

I also wonder if Milky was praying for death when he tried to run across the Major Deegan Expressway, only to be struck by several cars and going to meet his maker at the tender young age of thirteen. Milky was one of the youngest guys in the neighborhood. Too young to hang out with us, just one of the little neighborhood kids we'd send to the store to buy shit for us. No one knows why he was trying to run across the highway. Just being a kid, we guessed. Maybe a dare. Who knows? At Milky's wake, a wind actually blew into the funeral home and knocked a huge flower arrangement to the ground, yet there was no wind outside that day. I guess Milky wanted to say goodbye.

In our neighborhood, you just never knew when your time would be up or for what reason. You had to be prepared to welcome death on the streets or risk living life like a paranoid schizophrenic, always on edge and always fearful. Leaving the neighborhood five minutes early or arriving five minutes late on the block often meant the difference between life or death, freedom or the penitentiary. There really was no equation for what happened on the streets; it was always a crapshoot.

For the majority of youths in these poverty-stricken, crime-plagued, violent neighborhoods, it's kill or be killed, steal or starve, and victimize or be victimized. Why else would we choose to live so carelessly? We don't all live by the gun. I always dealt with my own internal good-versus-evil conflicts, not wanting to have anything stolen from me yet stealing from others.

I prayed for death so much and did so many terrible things that I don't know how I am alive today. Maybe God was busy. Maybe it wasn't my time to die. I keep thinking God had other plans for me. Either way, my next stop never turned out to be an early grave in Saint Raymond's Cemetery, where I always believed I would end up. My next stop led me to become a father, a husband, a mediator to my family, a professional in the corporate world, and a productive citizen. More important, my next stop led me to write this book. In doing so, I wanted to document what the streets were like in the late eighties and early nineties for my friends and me. I don't want to glorify our actions. My purpose was to honestly portray what we witnessed and experienced. I wanted to educate the next generation of young street toughs so that they can learn firsthand that the price for this type of behavior truly is the penitentiary or the cemetery. And though we might pray for death and hold on to the no-snitching rule, no one wants to die or rot in a cell.

A great number of the guys I grew up with will be reading this book from a jail cell, some having been sentenced to twenty or thirty years or life in prison. Some have said that the lucky ones were the guys in my crew who took the bullets or the knives in their bodies and went on to that other place, wherever that other place might be. At least they are no longer here to deal with the pain. If I had to choose between life in prison and death, I would choose death without question.

Cages are for animals, and with the exception of a few, we were not animals. We were the products of the environment we were placed in. Products of the streets where single mothers became crack addicts and most fathers left before their children could even say "da-da." I was lucky to have a strong mother, the strongest woman I've ever met. She made sure we understood the pitfalls of the lives we were leading. She always spoke to us honestly about the price we'd end up paying if we continued to lead the lives we were leading. She wanted better for us, but we never listened. She constantly talked to us about education and how we could do anything we wanted to do with our lives if we worked hard for it. We just didn't hear the message until we had children of our own.

I was lucky to have a mother who played the role of both mother and father. My mother struggled to give us a Catholic school education for as long as we wanted it. When I felt I had taken my education as far as I needed to, the tenth grade, I got myself kicked out and hit the streets to further my education. Yet the morals, values, and lessons I learned in Catholic school allowed me to delve only so deep into the streets, where a conscience is seen as a major weakness. I always understood the consequences of my actions, and I paid for all of the mistakes I made along the way. I will forever be grateful to my mother for the sacrifices she made for my brother, Will; my sister, Tanya; and me. When my mother feels like she somehow failed her children, I have to remind her that we are the minority—the lucky few—who made it out alive.

I am grateful that my mother does not have to endure the eight-hour ride up to Coxsackie, Clinton, or Greene—three of the state's correctional facilities—on a bus loaded with mothers, fathers, sons, and daughters en route to visit their loved ones. Family members with all hope lost for their sons and daughters, who must spend decades caged like animals with no hope of ever contributing to society—at least not in the prime of their lives.

No one can tell me where my final stop will be, but I know I have already beaten the odds I was given when I first rolled the dice of life. Born to a drug-addicted, alcoholic, abusive father who would leave my mother to live in an abandoned building, with my brother and I who mirrored him in every way. I was destined to assume his role, to follow his example, and to walk the same path. I was destined to go from one stop to the next as a menace to society, because who besides my mother would have expected any different from me? I had every excuse in the book to throw at the judge, or even my final judge. I could have copped the same pleas and made the same excuses for why I had robbed, beaten, or even murdered. Only then I would have been nothing more than another statistic.

Not me, baby! I wasn't born to be anyone's statistic. I made it out and chose to share my story without the fear of being judged for my past indiscretions. I'm the only one left who can bring the story of Kingsbridge Road during that time to life. I feel like it was my destiny to share the memories of friends who are no longer here to tell their stories. It's my proudest moment. And wherever life leads me, I'm up for the challenge of my *next stop*.

Buildings on Kingsbridge Road.

NE LAST STORY ONE LAST STORY ONE LAST STORY ON
ORY ONE LAST STORY ONE LAST STORY ONE LAST STO
AST STORY ONE LAST STORY ONE LAST STORY ONE LAST
NE LAST STORY ONE LAST STORY ONE LAST STORY ON
ORY ONE LAST STORY ONE LAST STORY ONE LAST STO
AST STORY ONE LAST STORY ONE LAST STORY ONE LAST
NE LAST STORY ONE LAST STORY ONE LAST STORY ON
ORY ONE LAST STORY ONE LAST STORY ONE LAST STO
AST STORY ONE LAST STORY ONE LAST STORY ONE LAST
NE LAST STORY ONE LAST STORY ONE LAST STORY ON
ORY ONE LAST STORY ONE LAST STORY ONE LAST STO
AST STORY ONE LAST STORY ONE LAST STORY ONE LAST
NE LAS   ORY ON
ORY (AST STO
AST ST   NE LAST

One Last Story

Bombing and robbing were integral parts of any successful graffiti crew's activities in the early eighties. *Bombing* meant spending a night out tagging your name and the name of your crew on as many trains, train stations, buildings, and metal gates as you could possibly get up on in one night. Bombing the streets of New York became our hobby, and the more we bombed the more respected we were. A respectable graffiti crew stole all the spray paint they could get their hands on: Krylon, Red Devil, and Rust-Oleum were the brands of choice. We collected and stocked up on these paints with frequent trips to Westchester County and other outlying areas that had not yet caught on to the graffiti phenomenon going on in the inner-city neighborhoods. The more paint you robbed the more bombing you could do. It was a cycle that allowed us to experience never-ending excitement growing up on the streets of the Bronx.

The Bombing and Robbing Crew, or B.A.R. Crew, as we were known, was founded by a Puerto Rican kid named Staz. Although the crew began its life of crime as a gang of young street vandals, some members of the crew would eventually go on to gross millions of dollars in drug profits, commit high-stakes robberies, and be involved in a string of murders. Our introduction to criminal activities started as innocent as stealing spray paint and eventually led us to a path of crime that some never returned from. However, it wasn't always like this. In the beginning, it was just a bunch of kids running around with spray paint trying to become ghetto celebrities.

Graffiti was born out of a need for kids to find fame on the streets. With a spray can and a knack for evading law enforcement under the cover of darkness, a graffiti writer could become famous virtually overnight. My first introduction to graffiti was a book called *Subway Art* by Martha Cooper and Henry Chalfant. I saw the book in a store one day and, even though I didn't have the fifteen dollars to buy it, I took it home with me and I still own a copy to this day. Over the next couple of months, I spent all my spare time tracing the graffiti masterpieces in the book by artists with such names as Seen, P-Jay, Tracy 168, Mad, and Zephyr. Tracy 168 was known in the Fordham Road section of the Bronx for the shop murals he would get paid to do on the gates of stores around the neighborhood. For a thirteen-year-old with no positive role models to look up to, Tracy 168 became the man I wanted to emulate. Tracy 168 was the founder of one of the most recognized graffiti crews in the world: Wild Style. I would eventually become a card-carrying member of the Wild Style crew, and I still carry the card around with me as a reminder of where I've been.

My first introduction to real graffiti writing came after I met the new kid on the block named Eric. The day Eric moved into the building, I was sitting on the stoop looking at my *Subway Art* book when a moving van pulled up out front. When Eric walked past me with his second load, I looked up and he said, "Hey, what's up, man, what you got there?"

I showed him the book and he told me he had one of his own. I asked him if he needed help and he said sure, so I began to help him and his mother unload the van. Once we had finished, I told Eric I'd see him another day. It was getting late and my mom kept a tight leash on me, so I had to head home. Eric told me to come back the next day so that he could unpack his graffiti book and show it to me.

The next day when I showed up at Eric's house, he pulled out a black book that was covered with silver marker on the front and back covers. The book not only had tags from some of the more popular graffiti writers in the Bronx, like Cope 2, Trim, Med, Crime, and Tracy 168, but it also had full-blown "burners" and "throw-ups" inside, which were beautifully colored with a remarkable eye for detail. A burner is a graffiti piece that takes a lot of time to paint, while a throw-up is just as the name suggests, a quick tag usually thrown onto a wall, a train, or a book. The fact that Eric was in possession of this book meant that he really ran with these guys. The fact that I now knew Eric meant that I might one day get to write with these street legends. Over the next few weeks, I hung out with Eric as much as possible in order to try to learn from him. I eventually learned that his graffiti tag name was Zerk, which I recalled seeing all over Kingsbridge, Fordham Road, and the Grand Concourse. What fascinated me even more than his graffiti skills was that his mom not only knew he was a graffiti writer but openly accepted him and all of his graffiti-writing friends, including the toys like me. "Toys" back then was slang for a graffiti writer who really sucked. To this day I might still be considered a toy on a wall, but give me some markers and a black book and I'll create a colorful burner.

I was determined to shake the label of a toy as soon as possible, so I asked Zerk if I could go out tagging with him the next time he hit the lay-ups (train yards where all the trains were parked). Eric told me I needed a graffiti name first and that I'd have to practice my craft a little more before I got to roll with the big boys. I assigned myself the graffiti name *Zinc*, but that name was short-lived, as a writer who already used Zinc decided to approach me and tell me that if he heard about me writing Zinc he would come back to beat my ass. I wasn't the type of guy who enjoyed an ass-kicking, so I had to find a new tag name.

One day while I was practicing my graffiti in Zerk's house, Staz, his graffiti partner, arrived. Staz looked at my work and said I was a good writer for a shorty (a young guy in the crew). At thirteen I was two to three years younger than most of the guys I hung out with. Staz asked me if I wanted to be his son. If it meant he got to sleep with my mom I didn't want any part of that shit. . . . But he quickly explained to me that being the son of a graffiti writer meant you carried an abbreviated *little* in front of the writer's name.

So when Staz asked me, "You want to write *Li'l Staz*, shorty?" my reply was a definite yes. Staz went on to explain to me that I would be known as the "son of Staz" on the streets. I quickly realized that carrying the name of a neighborhood graffiti writer would mean automatic street credibility for me. I told him that it would be fresh to write Li'l Staz. For those of you not familiar with the term *fresh*, it basically meant cool back when I was growing up.

By writing graffiti and running with Zerk and Staz, eventually I became more visible in the neighborhood. Before that, I had been a noname to most of the guys on Creston Avenue. Now it seemed like every day I met more guys from the neighborhood and started to feel like I was part of a family. I think my mother liked it too, because even though she knew some of those guys were bad seeds, she understood that you needed to have the protection of those guys walking around in our neighborhoods. You could not stand alone, and it now felt safer for her to walk around in the neighborhoods as my crew greeted her when she walked up the block. The same guys she used to avoid making eye contact with now said, "Hello, Ms. Sanchez." To which she would smile and reply, "Hello, boys," even though her last name wasn't Sanchez.

At her full height of four foot eleven, my mother was the butt of many jokes, but I took it all with a grain of salt. "Your mother is so short, she hops on my shoelace and rides my sneaker to the train station," one of the guys teased. "Your mother's so short, she can lick my balls standing up," another guy said. "Your mother is so short, she has to carry a little stepladder to get up the steps into the building," somebody else kidded. It was never-ending but it was what we did to kill time as we stood on the stoop, telling story after story of past late-night crusades and conquests.

I took it all in as pure humor. Most of the jokes were pretty damn hilarious and I managed to get a few barbs in on each of their mothers when the opportunity presented itself. We spent a lot of time together. Jokes were how we bonded with each other. If you couldn't take a joke then you had no business hanging with us.

Eventually, I started representing the B.A.R. Crew every time I threw a tag up on a wall, store gate, or train station. By the time I really started writing, the Buff System had already been introduced to the Bronx, so I never got to experience the train yards for myself. The Buff System entailed trains from Japan being placed in service that were run through a sort of car wash for trains that virtually buffed both sides of the train every morning, restoring them to all their silver glory. Gone were the old days of graffiti burners running on train lines for days, weeks, months, and years. If you wrote on a train the night before, your work of art would never be seen by the world the next morning. It was the end of the rolling graffiti canvas and the beginning of the street graffiti. Sure, we were vandalizing the community, but we damn sure didn't think that way. We saw it as bringing real credibility to the crew's name, and we were becoming famous for doing it. We were actually becoming a little too famous for our own good.

Sometime in the mideighties, Mayor Ed Koch decided to start a vandal squad to shut down graffiti crews like ours. The city had simply had enough of the vandalism, determined to take down all graffiti crews. It was only a matter of time before I would meet the vandal squad one night on a subway platform in the South Bronx.

My boy Size asked me to go with him to the South Bronx to go over some toys who had been going over his graffiti in his own neighborhood. In the graffiti world, going over someone's piece meant you were showing them the ultimate sign of disrespect; doing it in their neighborhood meant you were truly shitting on them, their neighborhood, and their crew. Retaliation in some form was mandatory. We hopped on the train along with one of his partners and a friend of mine, Tommy, and headed toward the South Bronx.

We arrived at Brook Avenue, prepared to go over any of Size's enemies' tags that we could find. As this was their neighborhood, we immediately found their tags on the walls of the train station. Just as you couldn't go past Fordham Road without seeing a B.A.R. Crew tag, you couldn't walk around this part of town without spotting their tags. The second the subway car door popped open, we hopped off, unzipped the book bags, and began to shake the cans of spray paint we had brought with us. A lot of the pieces looked very clean, as if they had just recently been painted, so going over their shit felt great. Not only did we have to look out for the vandal squad, the Transit Authority police, and the regular beat cops, we had to be very careful not to run into any members of their graffiti crew. If they were alerted to our presence, we could catch the beatings of our lives, if not get murdered right there on the spot. We were in their neighborhood, showing them the ultimate sign of disrespect by crossing out and going over all their graffiti, so we had to make sure we were careful, to say the least. If we were caught slipping, it could mean the difference between going home and going to the hospital, jail, or morgue.

As we worked our way through the train station, going over everything their crew had up and replacing it with B.A.R. Crew throw-ups, we made good time and destroyed shit with the spray paint Size and his boy had racked earlier in the day. Just as we were preparing to finish up, we spotted a beat cop. He stood on the platform across from us and just stared. We had become so immersed in what we were doing that we never saw the other cop pop out onto our side of the platform. Sirens could be heard in the distance as we began to make a run for it. The sirens were getting close fast and I needed to figure out how I was going to get the fuck out of there.

I followed the boys and ran down the stairs, hoping to escape onto the streets. When I exited the subway, two police cars pulled up to the subway exit stairs on each side of the street. I made a dash back into the subway, hopped the turnstile, and ran to the very back of the platform.

When I got to the platform, I decided to take the tracks and try to make it on foot to the Cypress Avenue station, which I hoped would be my path to freedom. Running on elevated tracks, I quickly discovered that a lot of the wooden crossbeams up there were missing. Not only was it dark as hell, but I was twenty-five feet above the street. I jumped every time I saw a dark spot, because I couldn't really tell if there was a missing beam ahead or it was just dirty. As I ran, I could see two cop cars directly beneath me, racing to the next station. My escape options were dwindling by the second. I knew the Five-O would be waiting for me at the next station, but I continued to run and jump as fast as I could. When I reached the Cypress Avenue station platform, I hid behind a huge garbage bin. The smell was gut-wrenching, but if it kept me out of jail I'd lay beside the shit all night. Hell, I would have laid *in* it if I thought it would mean freedom.

Oh shit, I hope they didn't see me. Oh fuck, I can't get arrested. . . . My mom will kill me. Shit, I hope they can't hear me breathing this hard. Disjointed thoughts raced through my mind as I heard footsteps getting closer. I huddled into the smallest ball I could and tried to hide myself in the shadow of the garbage can. The two cops walked right by me and didn't see me—at least not until they turned around to go back the other way.

"Get the fuck up, you little motherfucker," one of the cops shouted. "Get the fuck up!"

When I looked up and saw a cop in jeans and a T-shirt, I knew I was done. The casual dress meant these cops were on the vandal squad. These motherfuckers didn't play around with little vandals like me.

How the fuck did the vandal squad make it here so fast? I thought as the cop backhanded me across the face, knocking the brand-new Yankees hat off my head as I stumbled from the hit. My face instantly went numb and the thought skittered through my mind: *Damn, that cop has a big-ass hand.* I didn't want to get slapped again with that big-ass hand, so I just put both my hands up. "Yo, you got me, man, what the fuck?"

The cops threw me onto the pavement face-first and slapped the cuffs tight around my wrists. I looked over at my Yankees hat and wondered if the cop would pick it up and put it back on my head. As they lifted me off the ground I said, "Yo, Officer, can I have my hat?"

"Didn't I tell you to shut the fuck up? You want to get bitch-slapped again?" he replied. "Where's the fucking spray paint, you little piece of shit?"

Was he stupid enough to think I hadn't thrown the paint onto the tracks, where it had fallen to the street below? "I don't know what you're talking about, Mr. Officer," was my smart-ass reply.

This time I was greeted with a punch in the back of the head. "Damn, man, stop abusing me! When we get to the precinct, I'm reporting you for police brutality."

"Who the fuck said we're taking you to the precinct, you little piece of shit?" the officer retorted.

That was enough to shut me up. I guess he thought I was going to keep talking, so he gave me a nice hard kick in the ass, sending me to the ground once again face-first.

When we got to the police precinct, I started to realize this was no joke. This was my first arrest and I started to get a little scared. *How the hell am I going to tell my mom I got arrested? Sixteen years old and sitting in a jail cell with no belt and no shoelaces. Damn, this is fucked up.*

As I was escorted past the front desk, I screamed at the top of my lungs, "Sergeant, I would like to press charges on the arresting officer for police brutality."

I didn't know for sure if the guy was a sergeant, but his badge had a lot more shit on it than the other badges, so I went with what I had seen in the movies. The sergeant took one look at my swollen face and asked the officer what happened.

"He slipped getting into the squad car and banged his face on the doorjamb," the officers replied smoothly.

I tried to persuade the sergeant to hear my side of the story. "Sergeant, you should still be able to see the officer's four fingerprints on my face. Unless doorjambs have hands, this officer assaulted me."

"We'll have someone interview you about it," the sergeant casually replied.

Officer Mahoney walked in a few minutes later. "Hello, son. Can you tell me what happened when Officer O'Grady apprehended you?"

"Yeah, he slapped the living shit out of me for no reason," I answered.

"Did you try to resist arrest?"

"Yeah, when I ran a marathon on the elevated tracks to escape you guys."

"But you didn't physically try to get away from Officer O'Grady, did you?" he persisted.

"Hell no, no fucking way. I don't hit cops," was my emotion-filled response.

Officer Mahoney said quietly, "Okay, kid, I'll tell you what. I'm going to leave you to fill out this form. If you fill it out and tell me what Officer O'Grady did to you, we'll get you on the next bus to Rikers Island. There's a bus leaving in a few minutes. If you decide you don't want to fill out the official complaint report, we'll write you a court appearance ticket for vandalism and you can be on your way home after we process you."

My choices consisted of (1) a trip to Rikers Island with a bunch of killers, rapists, and hardened criminals, or (2) my warm bed in which to sleep off this nightmare that had come to life. With the thought of my friend Tommy with me in the cell crying his fucking eyes out, I decided to take the punk way out.

"Officer, I tripped and hit my face on the doorjamb. Can I go home now?" I said softly.

After my *titi* came to the precinct to pick me up, I went straight home and finally hit the bed around 5 A.M. My mother was fast asleep and Titi Vilma had promised to cover up the news of my first arrest. She said there was no reason to give my mother cause for concern. She also told me to be a little faster next time I decided to run from the cops. I nodded and promised her I would work on my speed. "I love you, Titi. Thanks for breaking me out of the slammer."

When I appeared in front of the judge many months later, I was told that if I ever showed my face in his courtroom again he would give me a one-year mandatory sentence for vandalism. He also asked me why I was standing in court alone. Since I was sixteen years old at the time, he wondered where my mother was. I basically told him the truth, that my mother was not supportive of my actions on the streets and that she wouldn't come to court to embarrass herself. The judge told me to take my mother's advice and leave the graffiti alone. I decided I wasn't tough enough to go to jail for graffiti crimes, so I hung my spray paint up and never looked back.

Although graffiti led me to commit other crimes, it also taught me the power of having a creative voice. Tracy 168's graffiti art has been displayed all over the world and his paintings are commissioned and sold for upward of twenty thousand dollars. Seen One has also gone on to notoriety with his paintings and graffiti-theme collectibles such as Spraycan Monsters, Planet 6, and Phony-Baloney, a toy line of misfit cops caught in uncomfortable situations. Was it payback for all the years the vandal squad fucked with us on the streets? You decide.

As of this writing, I haven't seen Staz in over fifteen years. The last I heard he was still selling drugs and robbing anything that wasn't nailed down.

Wild Style member card.

ACKNOWLEDGMENTS ACKNOWLEDGMENTS ACKNOWLEDGMENTS ACKNO
IGMENTS ACKNOWLEDGMENTS ACKNOWLEDGMENTS
NOWLEDGMENTS ACKNOWLEDGMENTS ACKNOWLEDGME
CKNOWLEDGMENTS ACKNOWLEDGMENTS ACKNOWLE
ENTS ACKNOWLEDGMENTS ACKNOWLEDGMENTS ACKNC
IGMENTS ACKNOWLEDGMENTS ACKNOWLEDGMENTS
NOWLEDGMENTS ACKNOWLEDGMENTS ACKNOWLEDGME
CKNOWLEDGMENTS ACKNOWLEDGMENTS ACKNOWLE
ENTS ACKNOWLEDGMENTS ACKNOWLEDGMENTS ACKNC
IGMENTS ACKNOWLEDGMENTS ACKNOWLEDGMENTS
NOWLEDGMENTS ACKNOWLEDGMENTS ACKNOWLEDGME
CKNOWLEDGMENTS ACKNOWLEDGMENTS ACKNOWLE
ENTS ACKNC
IGMEN MENTS
NOWLE EDGME

Acknowledgments

In my lifetime I have had several close friends refer to me as "self-made." I can honestly tell you that there is nothing self-made about me. I have been privileged and fortunate enough to have family and friends who have been a guiding light in my darkness and a voice of reason in my temporary (permanent) moments of insanity. You all own a piece of my heart. My gratitude to all those listed below and to those who came into my life whose names I forgot to mention in this book, forgive me for the years of inhaling secondhand marijuana smoke. I knew not what I was doing to my memory, nor do I recall. . . .

To my mother: There are not enough words in the dictionary to express my love and gratitude for all you've done for me. You are the embodiment of strength and the definition of courage and conviction. I love you with all my heart. . . . Jesse James Boone, for showing me what a father looked like and sharing those lessons with me. You unknowingly led the march out of the Bronx and our future generations owe you and Mom a debt of gratitude for that. . . . Willie Sanchez, I harbor no hate in my heart for you. Thank you for donating your sperm to my mother in 1972 and creating a dashingly good-looking son—I've been told I'm quite the looker. I hope you beat your demons one day. . . . Nelson, for being there to take care of my mother in the present.

Stormy, you saved my life on more than one occasion and introduced me to unconditional love. I will always love you more than any written word can express for standing by me through thick and thin when most told you to run like hell. You are one of the strongest women I've ever met, only second to my own mother. You are the rock and the foundation for which we've built this family. No one can ever replace the spot reserved for only you in my heart.

Heaven, my firstborn: I never knew the true meaning of love until I laid my eyes on you. . . . Starr, my second born, my mini me: Please use your comedy for good rather than evil. I love you unconditionally. . . . My littlest angel, Anesa, you were born to do special things in your lifetime.

Will, my big brother, for teaching me how to take a punch or twenty and always being there to block when it wasn't you doing the punching . . . Krissy, Meghan, Alezia, Jesi, and Nico . . . Tanya, my baby sister: I'm sorry I tortured you all those years; I was trying to be like Bill. I love you with all my heart; you and I are twins. . . . Jorge, we will always be brave-heart brothers from the Creston Posse days. . . . Jordan, Jayanna, and Zoë . . . Billie Sanchez, you are just like me. If you are going to dream, make sure you chase those dreams. . . . Sean Boone, you will always be my little brother. . . . the Ramos family . . . Tina, for my firstborn niece.

Sulay Hernandez: my super editor, who believed in placing me in the big leagues and providing me with a voice and an outlet to introduce a piece of Latino history to the world. I adore you and I hope to work with you on many more books in the future. Shawna Lietzke, for your tireless effort in producing this book.

Jenoyne Adams: Thank you for discovering me while I was out there on MySpace trying to find my place in this world of literary madness. Thank you for believing in *Next Stop* enough to help move me to the majors. You are going to have your hands full with me over the next twenty years—I have a lot to say!

Titi Vilma and Uncle Herman, for treating me like a son and giving me the strength to fail knowing I always had a home with you . . . Herman, my brother: There isn't a day that goes by that I don't miss you. I can't wait for you to come home. . . . Johnny, my other brother and protector, I love you. . . . Valerie, Richie, Michelle, and all the kids: I miss you all.

Titi Maria and Uncle Cisco, for introducing me to Connecticut and allowing me to escape from New York for a little while . . . Lulu, Jessie, and your families . . . Helen, for showing me that our bloodline could write professionally and with meaning and purpose. I never miss an article. . . . Mike, glad to have you in the family.

Uncle Jorge, Titi Iris Febo, Elizabeth, and Titi Iris Figueroa, and the rest of my family: My arms and my heart are always open to all of you. . . . Marco and Carmen Olivera, for giving me a home so many years ago when I had no place to go . . . Aaron, Ann Marie, Tyler, Seth, and Jason: You are all my family and I have a lot of love for you all. . . . Aida, Cash, and James Riley.

Max, there are no words to express how grateful I am that this book landed in your hands. For believing these stories *needed* to be told, you became my friend. For having the belief to release the book, you became my brother. Much love and respect to you, Nomad, I expect that we will be partners and friends for many years to come. . . . Wendy, for pushing me to finish the book when I didn't have it in me and editing the first copy of *Next Stop*: I will always love you. Without your push, this book would not exist. . . . Paula Becker, for putting the first, very rough copy of *Next Stop* in Max Nomad's hands. Without that happening there would be a book, but it would still be on my shelf collecting dust. I am forever grateful.

Lori Jean, for loving me when no one else would and for taking care of me when you should have been taking care of yourself. I will cherish our friendship for all my days and I wish you and your soon-to-be husband all the success in the world. . . . Robert and Jean, for treating me like a son when I was nothing more than a little street punk. Your kindness remains embedded in my heart and memory forever. . . . Yanira and the Valentin family: You also treated me like a son, and there were many days I would have starved without your compassion and love. . . . Redd, for waking me up when I was asleep and giving me the gift of a child. I will love our baby girl, Anesa, with all my heart and soul; I will be here for you when you need me. . . . the Redd family, I respect you and appreciate your support with the new baby.

The Sabettis—Dan, Margie, Andy, and Anthony—my fresh-air family, for showing me what the fresh air was like and for introducing me to the power of a stranger's love. You were one of my first introductions to life outside of Kingsbridge Road, and you are my second family, along with Michelle, Shawntay, Baby Ava, and Jordan. I can never thank you enough for what you've done for me and my family.

The Damonds—Richard, Reggie, John, Kristina, and Ian Townsend—for being a second Virginia family to me, introducing me to family dinners, the game of golf, and the joy and pain of rooting for the Yankees in Virginia Beach. I respect and adore you all in so many ways. . . . Gosha Gonzales, Jenn Evans, Billy Goodson, Brenda, and John G.

Wayne Kuykendall, for being a big brother to me when I moved to Virginia Beach and was lost and alone. You always have a brother in me. . . . Guy Wallace, for putting a roof over my head when I was broke and stressed, for telling me there was something special about me, and for believing in me when I didn't believe in myself. . . . Joe Quartararo, my educational mentor and friend: When I need important advice, I still call you. . . . "Big" Melvin Freeman: If I make it big with this book, you'll get your strip club. I just want to interview the girls. . . . Dawn Sinniger (Sinniger family), Crystal Kachuba (Kachuba family), and Mike Hitchcock (Hitchcock family), for being crazy enough to work for me: I have your backs through thick and thin. Demi and Lisa, you are a part of my family always. I think the world of both of you. . . .

David Schwartz, you always have something positive to say to me. Thank you for believing in my talents. I love you like a brother and hope to be in business with you in the future. . . . Carole Cowling, my sister, and Dave Leadbetter, my brother: For all the drinks and all the talks I still managed to screw up, thank you both for keeping me in Virginia when I wanted nothing more than to flee the area and go back home to the Bronx. . . . Steve Meriam, thank you for the mentoring; you are a great man. . . . Craig and Lei England, two wonderful friends to my family and me. . . . Brenda Haegley of Write Outloud Promotions . . . Gary Wilson and New Legend Entertainment.

Manuel Gelpi, my godson, Nico, and your entire family: You were a brother to me in the streets, and you've always believed in me. Thank you for the phone calls that allowed me to reminisce and recall the dates, times, and events I needed for this book. Without you, most of it would seem unreal. I can't wait until we find success together, my brother from so long ago. Small Wonder and MC Hitz forever—Artistic Maniacs live! Mike and John McDonnell.

DJ Disco Wiz and Liz, April Lee Hernandez and José, Patricia "Lady Picasso" Perez, Casper Martinez, Luis Guzman, Luis Antonio Ramos, Gina Rugolo, Jaimie Roberts, Ramon Rodriguez, Rosie Perez, Debbie Medina, Joe Conzo, Lynx Garcia, Karen Torres, La Bruja, Jeff Rivera, Jerry Rodriguez . . . My Sabor Hampton Roads family, My SiTV family . . .

The Crazy Young Criminals (CYC for Life): Cire-Herman, Johnny Dangerously, Manny, Big Rich, Will (#2), Fat David, Hitman, Keds, Joey, Nire, Tain, Rico, Mike, Jimmy Jazz, Black Dre, Gino, Dumbo, Alfie, George, Terrell, Teddy Ted, Frank Nitty, Pink Car Richie, Big Moe, Lil Moe, Chino Caper, Smurf, Prince, Angel, Danny (R.I.P.), Tony (R.I.P.), Freddie (R.I.P.), Sergio (R.I.P.), Milky (R.I.P.), Asthma Steve (R.I.P.), Wanda (R.I.P.). We went through the struggle together. I will never forget any of you. This book is dedicated to the memories we made and the way we played this game called life!

The Creston Posse: J-Loft, Ray Loft, P-Funk, Eric B (Zerk), Muhammad, Sal, Nes, Vince, Zeon, Mario, Mike, Desire, 7-CE, CEE 7, Stac, Judo, Frankie, Ill Will, Randy, Macho, Heavy D, Cockzolio, Phil, Steve,

Angelo, Noel (NYC Breakers), Tracy 168 (Wild Style), Zen (R.I.P.), Zef (R.I.P.), Mine 2 (R.I.P.), Chippy (R.I.P.). I earned my School of Hard Knocks degree on Creston Avenue with all of you. You all exist forever in my memories and in this book.

Binky (More-Us Crew) (R.I.P.), Toothless Rob (R.I.P.), Pec (R.I.P.), Mec (R.I.P.), Matzo (R.I.P.), Porky (R.I.P.), and all the other young men and women who lost their lives during the most violence-plagued years New York has ever seen.

Gerardo and Sheila Abrego, Steve A, and Manuela Abrego, for making me a part of your California Crew . . . Patricia Perez (Lady Picasso), your art is poetry in motion. . . . Isabel Villanueva, a close friend from another life.

Fred Whyte (Whyte family) and Karl Angler (Angler family), thank you for taking an interest in my career advancement, and for providing me with an example of what it means to lead at the top. I hope to see you both at the top one day. Your names should not be associated with this book, but now they are for all eternity. If you ever want a tour of the Bronx, please let me know. . . . Mark and Barb Bartz, two of the most sincere people I've ever met.

My immediate Stihl family—Jan Ashley, Dave Bussey, Bill Nickles, Carol Semenko, Earl Sykes, Rob Hulings, Tina Bernstein, Troy Hedgepeth, Von Logan Brimhall, Walt Yancey, Patrick Worthmann, Dennis Castello, Silja Gabriellini, Vince Benedetto.

The rest of my Stihl family (past and present): Kevin Adamson, Mike Lancke, Laurel Jones, George Hager, John Keeler, Jorge Rosas, Kent Hall, Steve Parmentier, Leslie Weithman, Linda Owen, Doris Doebler, Peter Burton, Stan Redwood, Peter Mueller, Pam McEwen, Patty Johnson, Mark and Sandy Myers, Jim and Susie McGuire, Val Ganucheau, Tom, Cheryl and Daniel Trebi, Olson Padilla, Shawn Drew, Jeremy Mellish, Jim Burris, Tom, John, Dave and Tracy Mitchell, Karen Youngs, Kris Williams, Mary Sanders, Vic, Ray and Little Shawn, Chip Woodring, LaKisha and Moe, Simon Nance, Linda Leitman, Karen Mantel, Dianne

Lyoness, Robin Grosse, Paula Bush, Carter Barrett, Jim Zuidema, Wayne Lemmond, Bob Myers, Kathy Marsh, Guido Feit, Chris Traugh, Jim Funaro, Dale Hines, Bianca Storsberg, Don and Julie Roemer, Scherryl Fairchild, Debbie Jensen, Christian Koestler, Brian Hughes, Walter Bennett, Judi Vieira, John Horbal, Tom Ames, Brian Manke, Nick Tenneriello, Mike O'Grady, Deidre Love, Jane Pickel, Lida Gilley, Linda Rosario, Paul Parker, Michelle Irving, Chris Garman, Ted and Terry Kujawski, Scott Tilley, Jerry Blaine, Lynne Galewski, Lisa Tanner, Effi Vakalou, Nick Virag, Nick Jianis, Cindy Maguire, Jake Brandspigel, Doug Yeates, Nancy Haskins, Mary King, Joanne Black, Stephanie Stefkovich, Murray Bishop, Mark Naas, Pete Homa, Guenther Stohl, Sidney Barrinio and Deborah Lermen, Sally Hamel, Brian Dasher, Steve Therrien, Carleen Evans, Ken Waldron, Roger Phelps, Anita Gambill, Karen Buterbaugh, Jackson D'Armond, Bob Hynick, Robin Stewart, Scott Burdett, Gabriel de la Cruz.

I was recently asked if I exaggerated or fabricated anything for the sake of hyping up this book. Unfortunately, my response was a definitive "I didn't have to— these events really took place." If I made you laugh, made you cry, or made you question anything about life through these writings, I am appreciative. If I can educate anyone and steer them away from the streets, my job will be done. Thank you all for your support.

Heaven and me.

ABOUT THE AUTHOR ABOUT THE AUTHOR ABOUT THE AUTHOR ABOUT THE
ABOUT THE AUTHOR ABOUT THE AUTHOR ABOUT THE AUTHOR
HE AUTHOR ABOUT THE AUTHOR ABOUT THE AUTHOR ABO
UTHOR ABOUT THE AUTHOR ABOUT THE AUTHOR ABOUT
HOR ABOUT THE AUTHOR ABOUT THE AUTHOR ABOUT THE
ABOUT THE AUTHOR ABOUT THE AUTHOR ABOUT THE AUTHOR
HE AUTHOR ABOUT THE AUTHOR ABOUT THE AUTHOR ABO
UTHOR ABOUT THE AUTHOR ABOUT THE AUTHOR ABOUT
HOR ABOUT THE AUTHOR ABOUT THE AUTHOR ABOUT THE
ABOUT THE AUTHOR ABOUT THE AUTHOR ABOUT THE AUTHOR
HE AUTHOR ABOUT THE AUTHOR ABOUT THE AUTHOR ABO
UTHOR ABOUT THE AUTHOR ABOUT THE AUTHOR ABOUT
HOR AB   UT THE
BOUT T   AUTHOR
HE AUT   HOR ABO

About the Author

Ivan Sanchez was born in the Bronx, New York City, in 1972. He left the inner city in 1993 and currently holds a supervisory position with a major manufacturing organization in Virginia Beach, Virginia.

Between 2001 and 2003, he was a frequent contributor to the op-ed section of the *Virginian-Pilot* and became a freelance writer for *Port Folio Weekly,* where he covered the local music scene. In 2004 he was awarded the National Novel honors for his first fiction offering, *The Murder Exchange* (as yet unpublished), about four friends coming of age in the Bronx.

In 2007, he completed his bachelor of science in management from the University of Phoenix. He is also a graduate of the Dale Carnegie program, where he received several awards for his public speaking.

Ivan has recently partnered with actress April Lee Hernández to form a dynamic motivational speaking team. The two speak nationally at schools, Boys & Girls Clubs, youth detention centers, and anywhere else they can draw an audience interested in hearing a message of hope and success.

TOUCHSTONE
READING GROUP GUIDE

Next Stop

Summary

Next Stop is a train ride into the heart of the Bronx during the late eighties
and early nineties, one of the most violent and dangerous periods of New
York City's recent history. From one stop to the next, these memoirs
follow Ivan Sanchez and his crew of friends on their search for identity
and an escape from poverty in a stark world where all-night symphonies
of crime and drug-fueled mayhem are as routine as the number 4 train.
Left alone in his Kingsbridge neighborhood—by choice—at fifteen, Ivan
Sanchez feels free to finally follow his dreams of becoming a ghetto celebrity. But less than a decade later, driven nearly insane by the poverty,
despair, and senseless violence, and desperate to make a better life for his
new family, Ivan leaves it all behind and moves to Virginia with his wife
and daughter. Still haunted by the grotesque images and voices of the
dead, this memoir is his effort to honor their memories while painting
the darkest days of street life in hopes of derailing young and would-be
gangbangers from their fast track to the end of the line.

Discussion Points

1. What do the earliest stories Ivan tells about his older brother, William, tell you about their relationship? How does their behavior throughout the book reinforce your early impressions of them? Does the way that Ivan relates to William ever change?

2. Though his father was absent for most of his life, Ivan still identifies himself as taking after him. In what ways does Ivan resemble his father? How are they different?

3. When you think of a "crew," or "thugs," what comes to mind? How do Ivan and his friends hold up to your stereotypes? How do they defy them?

4. *Next Stop* explores the escalation of violence among poor urban youths living in the Bronx in the late eighties and early nineties, providing a safe window into a terrifyingly dangerous lifestyle. Describe the landscape of New York City, particularly the Bronx, during this period. In what ways is the Kingsbridge crews' world just like that of any American family? In what ways is it different?

5. Ivan states that there weren't any rules in the hood except for one: Don't get caught. How does this maxim affect the development of the boys' moral compass? What other examples are given throughout the memoir of what is morally OK and what isn't?

6. The majority of reported crimes in America, especially in the inner cities, are committed by boys and men. Were you surprised at the role girls and women in this book played in neighborhood rivalries and other acts of violence? Why or why not? Does this knowledge change your perspective on urban crime in any way?

7. Ivan describes his childhood discovery of his father's cocaine habit as a moment of deep resentment and anger. What is it about cocaine that ultimately attracts Ivan, despite the pact he makes with Ray to never use the drug? How often are youths in this memoir influenced negatively by adults? Conversely, identify times when they are inspired by adults to do good.

8. With so little to hold on to, what do these boys feel is worth fighting for? What sort of things can give you a good street reputation? Describe some of the things that Ivan cites as signs of weakness. When is it okay to run away?

9. Guns represent a critical turning point in the way street wars are fought and "beefs" are settled in Kingsbridge during this era. What do the guns symbolize for the residents of the area? What is the significance of the scene on page 16 where P-Funk's mother hands the boys a sawed-off shotgun?

10. In such a tragic life, love is rare and fleeting. How does love transform Ivan? How does it transform the other people in this book? Why do you think this happens?

11. On page 114, Ivan relates how the media referred to the street thugs as "animals." This memoir details many instances of violence or extreme emotional reaction. Identify some of these moments and discuss how

they reveal the private struggles of the people involved. What are some of the very human reasons behind the boys' often animalistic actions? Do you sympathize with them at all? Why or why not?

12. What determines loyalty on the streets of Kingsbridge? Consider moments such as that on page 136, where Ivan returns to the neighborhood after escaping a violent fight and the police to find his cousins playing handball, completely unconcerned about his fate. How do such scenes contradict the concept of a crew "always having your back" and the supposed familylike ties between members? What other forces are at work here?

13. In some ways, *Next Stop* criticizes the media for its haphazard coverage of criminal activity. Discuss some of the instances where Ivan reveals the "other side" of what the media reports (or fails to report). What do you think is responsible for these failures? Do you agree or disagree with Ivan's opinion of the reasons for the skewed news in each case?

14. On page 181, Ivan writes, "I can't and won't excuse the things that Freddie did, but the streets influenced the choices he made. Had Freddie been raised in Westchester County and attended private schools, he would have grown up to be a doctor, a lawyer, or an investment banker." Is this a sufficient explanation for these boys' actions? How much choice do you think people raised in this kind of environment really have?

15. Many authors write memoirs in order to better deal with their painful experiences. In detailing their lives and downfalls, either via jail sentences or death, how has Ivan paid homage to his friends? What clues do you see in *Next Stop* that reveal how the author has or hasn't been able to come to terms with his difficult past?

Enhance Your Book Club Experience

1. Research the history of the Bronx, from Fort Independence's role in colonial America to the "crack wars" of the late eighties and early nineties. You can start with information and photos at www.bronxhistoricalsociety.org and www.bronxmall.com.

2. As a group or individually, watch the movies *Boyz n the Hood*, *Carlito's Way*, or *A Bronx Tale* to get a cinematic view of what street life has been like for different ethnic groups. Discuss the effects of poverty and education, as well as the influence of race and ethnicity, on youths raised in the environments portrayed in these films.

3. Graffiti, though in essence a defacement of public or private property, is also viewed by many as a unique artistic expression born out of the urban landscapes of inner-city America. But did you know that the earliest forms of graffiti date back to ancient Greece? Learn a little bit about the history of graffiti and its influence on the exposure of the urban experience to mainstream America by checking out books like *Subway Art* and websites like www.graffiti.org.

A Conversation with Ivan Sanchez

You grew up in a household where your mother played both parents' roles. You also were raised primarily by your older brother and an assortment of cousins once your mother left you in the Bronx at age fifteen. How have these experiences affected how you relate to other couples in your life? Where have you looked for role models in parenting your daughters and being a good husband to your wife?

I've always seen relationships and couples as very hypocritical. I've observed so many flawed relationships over the years that I have a hard time believing any couple is truly in the relationship for all the right reasons. Usually by the time people find out how imperfect their mate is for them, they are locked into the relationship because of kids or finances. On the rare occasion that I spend time with an actual couple that seems happy, I often wonder if it's a facade or if they are in the small minority of couples who actually are happy.

When I needed to seek advice on parenting I went to the *only* man in my family who, in my eyes, raised three daughters successfully: my Uncle Cisco. I called him in Connecticut and shared my issues with him and he gave me advice I still use to this day. He said, "You are not there to be your kid's best friend. You are there to be their father, provider, and protector. Don't ever get the two confused." I believe some parents get too caught up in trying to be a friend, to be the cool parent, and they forget to teach their kids that there are consequences for their actions. I've been a great husband to my wife in terms of providing for her and protecting her and that came from wanting a better life for my family. I'm afraid I haven't been a great husband emotionally because of the unresolved feelings I had for Lori for so many years. But I do cherish my marriage, and we are trying to find a way to make things work as opposed to throwing away an eighteen-year relationship.

For many, *Next Stop* will be a window into a frightening, sad subculture that still thrives in the inner cities across America. Do you think you and your wife—both from the Bronx—have escaped the stereotypes most people have of "street thugs"? Do you ever feel self-conscious about your background?

I don't know that I'll ever escape the stereotype of street thug. I'm a college-educated professional who is also a youth advocate and motivational speaker, but I still get pulled over by the cops and spoken down to. No matter how intellectual I believe I sound, I know people still hear a thick Bronx accent when they listen to me. I also still look the part when I wear my jeans and Timberland boots, so I still get judged. The best thing that ever happened to me in regard to the book was a middle-aged Caucasian woman reading *Next Stop* and telling me how nonjudgmental she believed she was until she read it. She actually said to me, "I'll never judge people like you again because now I understand your struggle."

Since graduating college I never feel self-conscious anymore. I have a deep understanding that I am on their level now with a college degree. I have no reason to feel like a person has the right to look down on me, and I carry myself accordingly. I demand respect on all levels because I give the same level of respect to the janitor that I do to the president of the company. And I accept nothing less in return.

Reliving these moments of extreme violence and the deaths of your friends must have been very disturbing. How did you deal with the surfacing emotions as you wrote about a time in your life so charged by both love and hate?

Writing *Next Stop* was the best therapy I could have ever given myself. It's hard for me to cry now when I read the stories back, because I cried so many tears when I was writing the book. I feel like I both got it out of my system and finally learned how to move past it. And I also honored the memories of those guys who died so many years ago for nothing. I don't think I could have honored them any better than to share their stories and make sure they wouldn't be forgotten. So as much pain as writing the book caused me, I turned those negative emotions into positives and kept moving in a forward direction, knowing I was doing a good thing. I never doubted that what I was doing was right because I wasn't glorifying their deaths to make a fast buck. I was simply documenting their deaths to make a positive change by educating others about the pitfalls of street life.

The popularity of memoirs has resulted in much scrutiny of the genre, particularly with regard to how unreliable memory is and how much responsibility the author has to the strict relation of events. Did you discuss your writing of this memoir with your family or friends while you worked on it? Were you at all influenced by their versions of the events in this book?

I interviewed many family members and friends about the events that took place. One day I'd be on the phone with my mother and the next with my sister and cousin Johnny. I couldn't have written the book without all of their input. If two people said something happened one way but my memory recalled it a little differently I went with the majority rules, rule of thumb. In one case my brother-in-law Jorge remembered things a little differently, so I called Ray to get his input and his version was closer to mine, so I went with that. I also spent untold hours on the phone with Manny reminiscing and interviewing him about the events that took place on Bailey Avenue and most notably the death of Freddie. I left very little to only my memory because I wanted to be as factual as humanly possible. The danger is in the fact that it's like witnessing a car accident: Two witnesses see the same exact accident but they both see it differently. It's what makes writing a memoir very challenging. You just have to be as true with your memories as possible.

What changes, if any, did you see in yourself and in your friends as your children were born and you found yourselves responsible for lives other than your own? Have those changes persisted? What, exactly, do you think it was that clicked on in your head and made it necessary for you and others to get off at the "next stop"?

I missed my daughter Heaven being born in 1992 because Stormy's mother hated me so much she didn't bother to call me when her daughter went into labor. When I held Heaven in my arms a few hours after she was born, I cried tears of joy and tears of pain. I saw my entire life flash before me and I realized all the pain I'd felt over the years because of not having a father. I never, ever wanted my little girl to know that pain, and at that moment fatherhood clicked in my head and I've never looked back. Everything I do in life is for my daughters. Heaven is sixteen now and I feel the same way I felt the day she was born, I owe her the world and I want to provide her all the opportunities she deserves in life, as well as my other two daughters, Starr and Anesa. My only job in life is to protect them and provide for them. Nothing else matters to me.

I recall telling my boy Will (Two) when his daughter was born how his life was going to change. Much to my surprise, though, he got deeper into the street life after his daughter was born. I guess he wanted to provide for his daughter immediately and the fastest route was the illegal route. He saw only the financial gain and never the price he'd have to pay if caught. I respect him as a friend and as a man and I don't judge him for his decisions. We just took two different approaches to providing for our children.

You write about getting legitimate jobs to "gain an in" for future robberies. What other reasons were there for going straight, either temporarily or permanently? What do you think drove the older members of your crew to give up the thug life and become "suckers" with day jobs? What lured some of them back in?

Getting a paycheck every week is a beautiful thing. Planning heists that may or may not pan out is exhausting and takes a lot of time and effort, usually with very little reward at the end, and sometimes a jail sentence attached. The benefit of going legit is having that stability; that no matter what happens during the week, you'll have a paycheck at the end of the week, or every two weeks. On the streets you can go months without a payday, making every day a struggle and a hustle to survive.

I think maturity and families drove the older members of my crew to go legit. Once you have a wife or steady girl and children it's your responsibility to bring home the bacon and feed your family. The only surefire way to do so is to earn a steady check. What drives many back into lives of crime is that the money doesn't come fast enough. If you work forty or fifty hours a week and only bring home $400, it doesn't always add up, especially when you're used to making $400 a day or even more in some cases. The risk factor sometimes outweighs the need to prosper and drive that nice car, buy the nicest clothes, and provide the same for your family. It's simple mathematics!

What held strongest sway when you were presented with opportunities to help commit a crime—the attraction of making a fast buck, or the loyalty of family and neighborhood ties?

Making a fast buck and loyalty to the crew was interchangeable for me. If I didn't want to commit the crime because I knew the payoff wasn't great, I sometimes went along to protect my family or crew. I remember doing a robbery with my brother and it was the last place on earth I wanted to be that night. But I went to protect him and make sure he came out OK, and if he got caught I wanted to be there to go down with him. If the money was good there was no question I'd go along to make the fast buck, but a lot of times I went as a lookout, especially since I was the young guy in the crew. Honestly, it was the only life I knew at the time. It was just another day in the neighborhood. My entire crew was criminally active, so it was only natural that I'd follow suit.

You write about the hold that Latin *machismo* held over you in your relationship with Lori and in other instances. How did your inability to speak Spanish affect your sense of identity as a young Latino male? Did you generally have a strong sense of membership to this ethnic community while growing up, even without your father's presence?

I was always considered a spic or a Puerto Rican kid from the neighborhood, so that is how I identified with myself. There are a lot of us second- and third-generation Nuyoricans who can't speak a lick of Spanish and have no problem relating to our heritage. But now, as an adult, I often find myself embarrassed when visiting New York and trying to order food in a Spanish restaurant. So it didn't affect me back then but it does affect me now.

I didn't have a father in the household, but I related to uncles and fathers of other guys in the neighborhood and also older guys in the crew. These were the guys whom I emulated and learned that Latin machismo from. What they were teaching me was wrong. They should have been teaching me to respect women; instead, they taught me how to "keep my bitch in check," and it stayed with me until I had a daughter. I treat women the way I want my mother, sister, wife, and daughters to be treated. But it wasn't until I had a girl of my own that I felt this way.

On page 120 you write about taking over your brother's job at a clothing store, an opportunity that saved you from starvation and hopelessness. Many people may find it difficult to understand why a young man in your situation would choose the risk of one quick payday over the low stress and stability of a regular paycheck. Can you describe your thought process at the time?

At the time I was trying to prove myself in the neighborhood. I wanted to be respected by the older guys and set myself apart from the other young bucks in the neighborhood. I knew that anytime these guys went to do heists, they chose the guys around them with experience and the guys they could trust to get the job done. I needed to make a play to get into that inner circle within the crew if I was ever going to see the kind of money these guys were seeing. There were times when I'd go upstairs at 11 P.M. and come out the next day at 11 A.M. to find a few guys in the neighborhood with new cars, new jewelry, new gear, and money bulging out of their pockets. I wanted what they were getting. And planning and pulling off a successful robbery was my only way to prove I should be invited into their criminal jobs. Making $4 or $5 an hour was not what I wanted in life, so I had no regrets when I looked for the in.

Zef, a crew member you looked up to, badly betrayed you during your first inside job robbing the clothing store. And it wasn't the first or last time that you were screwed over by a crew or family member. Why didn't these betrayals affect the love you had for these boys? How did you reconcile the unwritten rules of loyalty with the common practice of "thieves stealing from thieves"?

If I was an older guy I never would have been played like this. It wasn't until years later that I even found out how Zef betrayed me, so I never had the opportunity to address that betrayal with him. But things like this happened all the time; as you say, "thieves stealing from thieves." It was almost an expected practice that went on. If you got caught slipping, someone would take advantage of you, so in reality there was no real loyalty there to begin with. It was a false sense of loyalty and security that kept us together.

Unfortunately that kind of betrayal, if done to the wrong person, would get you beat down and even killed. I wasn't the last person Zef betrayed and he was actually killed after betraying the wrong person. Rumor has it that Zef pulled off the heist of a drug dealer and gave very little cash and jewelry to the drug dealer who set up that heist. When Zef refused to give up the real share of the haul he was shot at point-blank range in the lobby of the building I grew up in. So betraying the wrong person in the streets is a very dangerous game to play, and in Zef's case eventually got him killed.

On page 128, you explain that it would be years before you realized that, contrary to the opinion of your peers, the working man was not a sucker. You said you finally understood how much value was inherent in that kind of daily sacrifice. What led you to this epiphany? Why do you think other boys still entrenched in the gang lifestyle don't get it?

A good friend of mine once said working a nine-to-five job is the equivalent of hanging your soul at the door. I've come to agree with this statement, as the daily grind of corporate America can take a toll on who you are as a person. When you end up working for a boss you don't respect who doesn't respect you, it's the most challenging thing in the world to show up day after day.

The reason guys from the streets have a tough time making the crossover is because everything we are taught on the streets revolves around keeping our respect and dignity. When we are disrespected on the job, our first reaction is to slap the boss in the face. I've had a few friends who made the transition to being a working sucker only to find themselves doing just that. In one case a friend beat up the bosses' son after being disrespected and talked down to. In another case a friend smacked the boss. These guys take the sucker out of working sucker and aren't able to maintain the lifestyle so they go back to the streets where the rules are better suited to them. In the streets, if someone disrespects you, you have the right to take your respect back by assaulting them. Obviously that doesn't hold true in corporate America.

Throughout the memoir, a love of life and a strangling death wish seem inseparable. How do you think these conflicting forces affected the decisions you and your friends made on a daily basis?

Unless we were crying or mourning over the loss of a friend, we were always laughing. I think one of the most false perceptions is that we are a bunch of gangsters running around angry all the time. Yes, we could get serious at the drop of a dime, but we laughed all the damn time. It is a very complicated duality of life that makes us all walk around with split personalities, and it's the reason I can have lunch with a president of a company and dinner with a cold-blooded killer in the same day.

We just adjust to situations in a moment's notice and have no problem doing so. The love of life allowed us to want more, so we broke every law trying to accomplish what we saw as success, the cars, the jewelry, the clothes, and the girls. The death wish allowed us to put ourselves in positions most people would never dare place themselves in. To live this kind of life you have to live a life of complete contradiction. How else can you sell a mother crack and then throw your child in the air and lace them with hundreds of kisses?

Your memoir deals with several difficult subjects: poverty, neglect, drug and emotional abuse, violence, and death. But you also lovingly, warmly portray those close to you, especially your girlfriends and the members of your crew. What do you most hope that readers will come away with after reading *Next Stop*?

I want the readers to understand that there is no clear and concise answer into why we do the things we do. But that there is hope in making a positive change if we educate ourselves as to some of the whys. And that 100 percent of us react to the circumstances placed in front of us. These actions aren't mapped out before we are born; they are reactions to the environments and situations we are born into.

None of us is born wanting to struggle, wanting to sell drugs to feed our kids, wanting to kill or be killed. No one wants to be hungry or watch their mother cry because she can't feed her children. No one wants to see their mother strung out on crack, selling her body for her next high. Or a father coming home drunk and beating their mother and siblings to prove to himself that he is the head of the household and that he is still alive even though he feels no true emotions. We don't ask for these things to happen to us, but they do, and we react to these circumstances of life the best way we see fit.

We do love, we're not the heartless animals educated society and the media makes us out to be. We do feel pain and remorse. I'd estimate that less than 5 percent of the people I grew up with were truly bad people for the sake of being bad. And those 5 percent grew up in unimaginable situations, the likes of which mainstream society can't even imagine. That also means that 95 percent of the people I grew up with love just like you and hurt just like you.

We're not bad people; we just react badly to the conditions due to lack of education, lack of resources, and lack of love and compassion. If there is no structure in the household and no home training, for lack of a better word, we need the school system to step in. If the school system fails we need those who have survived to go back and educate those they left behind that there is hope after growing up in these tumultuous situations. If you've never walked a mile in my shoes, you can't talk to me about what path to take. But if you are in a position of power to lay out a path for me, it is your responsibility to do so. In other words, don't talk to me about how I should walk, just point me in the direction and have the pathway laid out in front of me. Why is it your responsibility? Because we are all one society, and if we don't help one another we all have to deal with the repercussions of a runaway society.

Gangs are out of control. Drug addiction, teenage suicide, teenage pregnancy, STDs killing our teenagers, and a lack of education—just a few of the issues we face—are at an all-time high. And I see so little being done to turn things around. I hope my book will spawn the conversations and pose the questions necessary to spark a change, no matter how small.

Don't judge me, help me. Don't quit on me, fight for me. Don't hate me, love me. . . . Show me your humanity, respect, and compassion, and if you are sincere about it, I'll feel that and I'll know you truly care.